FREEDOM BOUND II

Other books by these authors

Katie Holmes (ed.) *Drawn From Memory: Images of Coburg* Coburg City Council, 1986
Katie Holmes (general editor) *Among the Terraces, vols 1–6* Princes Hill School Park Centre, 1988
Katie Holmes *Spaces in Her Day: Australian Women's Diaries of the 1920s & 1930s* Allen & Unwin, 1995

Marilyn Lake *A divided society: Tasmania during World War I* Melbourne University Press, 1975
Marilyn Lake & Farley Kelly (eds) *Double time: Women in Victoria, 150 years* Penguin, 1985
Marilyn Lake *The limits of hope: Soldier settlement in Victoria 1915–38* Oxford University Press, 1987
Charles Fox & Marilyn Lake (eds) *Australians at work: Commentaries and sources* McPhee Gribble, 1990
Patricia Grimshaw, Marilyn Lake, Ann McGrath & Marian Quartly *Creating a nation* Penguin, 1994

FREEDOM BOUND II

Documents on women in modern Australia

Edited by
Katie Holmes and Marilyn Lake

ALLEN & UNWIN

First published 1995
Allen & Unwin Pty Ltd
9 Atchison Street, St Leonards, NSW 2065 Australia

National Library of Australia
Cataloguing-in-Publication entry:

Freedom bound II, Documents on women in modern Australia

Bibliography.
Includes index.
ISBN 1 86373 736 7.

1. Women—Australia—History—Sources. I. Holmes, Katie. II. Lake, Marilyn. III. Title: Documents on women in modern Australia.

305.420994

Set in 10/12 pt Garamond and Times by DOCUPRO, Sydney
Printed by Kim Hup Lee Printing, Singapore

10 9 8 7 6 5 4 3 2 1

Contents

Introduction

'For the first time in history', declared an article in *The Good Weekend* in March 1994, 'motherhood is an option, not an imperative, for most Australian women'. The authors argued that the ability to control fertility and the development of equal opportunities in education and employment had given women 'real choices and options in their lives'. 'Today's women', the authors concluded, 'are the first generations to have such freedom'.

The documents collected here tell a different story. Decisions about motherhood and employment and marriage and choices between these options have been made by women throughout the century. Indeed, women's determination to control their fertility in the name of personal fulfilment is one of the most consistent themes of women's lives in the twentieth century. It has not, of course, been the same struggle for all. White middle-class women have been the main beneficiaries of knowledge about birth control. Aboriginal women, on the other hand, have had to fight for the right to have children and keep their families together. Too often they suffered the grief and anguish of having children forcibly removed by state authorities. Women's choices and priorities depend on their racial and ethnic identity, their class and their sexuality, as well as on how historical experience has shaped these conditions. We wish to convey the diversity of women's lives, the history of their options, and demonstrate their courage and tenacity in voicing their yearnings and demanding their rights.

Women's historical experience is easily forgotten or erased. The decisions and conflicts faced by young women today are not so new. 'The drawbacks far overrule the so-called joys of motherhood', wrote one young woman in the early 1940s to justify her decision to limit her family to two children. The records collected here chart surprising continuities in women's experience, and at the same time point out changes in the ways women conceptualised improvements in their lives. In the early decades of this century white women harnessed the idea of maternalism to argue for citizenship rights, independence and improved living and working conditions for women. By the 1970s the concept of 'liberation' provided a new framework in which women could press for more revolutionary changes. At different historical moments we hear women demanding equal pay, child-care, sexual freedom, economic independence and protection from male violence.

Women have envisaged their goals differently at different times—as autonomy, self-determination, freedom and equality. They have also manoeuvred, within personal relationships, to assert control over their bodies, their time, their work and their children. The documents collected here also reveal the historical conditions and constraints, institutionalised in legislation and arbitration judgements, for example, that shaped women's lives and the nature of their demands.

The various forms of women's activism and the conditions of their mobilisation are two of the themes explored in this collection. Petitions, songs, charters, manifestoes, all represent the diverse forms through which women voiced their demands, while poetry, letters and diaries reveal a more personal dimension to women's public activism. We wish to establish the link between personal and political experience, for women's experience of subordination provided the emotional dynamic that inspired public critique, which in turn generated a sharper analysis of their own situation and that of other women. As many of these documents suggest, when women entered public life they brought the concerns of their domestic and personal lives into public focus—the humiliations of economic dependence, the stigmatizing of lesbians, the confinements of home, the repugnance of forced sexual relations, the fear of venereal disease.

One theme to emerge from women's more personal writing is their pursuit of love and pleasure. Frequently this is expressed in women's explorations of desire, their experimentation with sexual pleasure and their negotiation of the meanings of sexuality. The boundaries between heterosexual and lesbian sexuality emerge as more fluid and contested than is often assumed, while women's experience of love finds expression through complex interpretations of the importance to women of friendship, sex, passion and intimacy. Often enough, love was experienced as both a source of pleasure and, as Lesbia Harford wrote, a tyrant that enslaved women.

The pursuit of freedom can be traced through women's reproductive struggles. Repeated child-bearing denied women a sense of fulfilment and frequently brought poverty and ill health. Abortion played a crucial role in women's fertility control, at least from the 1920s, enabling them to restrict their family size or avoid childbearing altogether. Despite the reported prevalence of abortion, however, few written sources record women's own experiences or the trauma and risk to life that it incurred. Here we draw on oral testimony to document aspects of women's lives that seldom appear in official records. The costs to women of sexual freedom, a concept central to the emergent meanings of modernity, preoccupied feminists and non-feminists alike. While many heterosexual women were enraptured by the new sexual encounters made possible by contraception, feminists, alert to the prevalence of venereal disease, the burden of large families and women's degradation as 'sex creatures', generally condemned sexual freedom as vice, equating the advancement of women with autonomy, independence and living life on a higher plane. There was a general fear that sexual desire would simply enforce women's thraldom. Not until the 1970s did a new phase of feminism incorporate sexual freedom as a woman's right, a shift that gave lesbians a new space and sense of legitimacy, but not without having to fight for their rights within the women's movement as well as beyond it.

In the course of the nine decades covered by this collection, Australia has moved from being a society that proudly declared itself 'White', denied citizenship rights to Aborigines and rejected 'non-white' immigrants, to a nation that officially prides itself on its multiculturalism and has recently legislated to recognise original Aboriginal title to the land. The change in official policy disguises, however, the persistence of distressing experiences of racism and prejudice among large sections of the people. We have sought to represent a range of voices, although the documents more fully reflect the lives of white English-speaking women than they do those who have been marginalised, silenced and disempowered. The voices of Aboriginal women emerge more forcefully in the late 1960s, but memoirs and petitions suggest the strength and determination of generations of indigenous people in resisting oppression and securing the survival of their communities. More recently Aboriginal women have become vocal activists in the struggle for land rights and human rights, and have played central roles in building communities of resistance. The concerns of white feminists with sexual freedom and equal opportunity in the professions often seem irrelevant to indigenous women living in communities without adequate housing, running water, sanitation and health facilities. In order to meet the specific needs of non-English-speaking women, who often combined stressful paid work with caring for families, ethnic minority women have formed their own organisations and networks, some of whose concerns we document here.

This collection not only challenges the view that women's situation today is unprecedented, but also the common idea that the feminist movement in Australia has consisted of two distinct 'waves' with a trough of inactivity in between. Feminists have been active throughout the century and especially in its middle decades. The benefits now unequally enjoyed by Australian women have culminated from over 100 years of struggle. Women from a range of racial, ethnic and social backgrounds have consistently found innumerable ways to speak about their aspirations to freedom and have made persistent efforts to achieve it. Women have long dreamt of becoming mistresses of themselves, all the while cherishing the attachments that made such a condition elusive. A knowledge of this history enables us to reflect more critically on our own priorities and goals and to recognise the energy, bravery and determination of the women who fought for the rights and freedoms we have come to take for granted.

Acknowledgements

The editors and publisher wish to thank the following for permission to use copyright material: the Australian Government Printing Service, the *Age* newspaper, Barbara Baird, Faith Bandler, Wendy Bowler, Geraldine Briggs, Rachel Buchanan, Narelle Couter, Curtis Brown Australia Pty Limited, Kay Daniels, Ruth Ford, Grosvenor Books, Sevgi Kilic at WICH, Ruby Langford, the La Trobe Library Collection, State Library of Victoria, the Marriage Guidance Council of South Australia, J.D. McGrath, the National Library of Australia, Pat O'Shane, Pan MacMillan, Southdown Press, Anne Summers, the University of Melbourne Archives, the Victorian Government Printer, Mrs A.V. Wallace, Women's Redress Press.

While every care has been taken to trace and acknowledge copyright, the editors and publisher tender their apologies for any accidental infringement where copyright has proved untraceable. They would be happy to come to a suitable arrangement with the rightful owner in each case.

The editors also wish to thank the following for sharing documentary materials with us: Ruth Ford, Sue Langford, Chris Nihill, Fiona Paisley, Tim Rowse, Gaye Wilde. We wish to acknowledge the research assistance provided by Sheridan Clarke, Catriona Elder, Esther Faye, Heather Gunn, Sue Langford and Penny Russell and thank Carol Courtis and Brenda Joyce for their accurate typing and generous support.

Part 1
Maternal citizenship, 1900–1920

The federation of the Australian colonies to form a new nation state had profound consequences for all women. White women were enfranchised for the national parliament in 1902 and their responsibilities were redefined as those of citizen mothers. As mothers—as the producers of the state's 'greatest asset'—women were said to render a national service parallel to that performed by citizen soldiers. Like soldiers, mothers risked death and disability in their service to the state. This was the argument put by Labour Prime Minister Andrew Fisher when he introduced the Maternity Allowance in 1912. Feminists and labour women activists attempted to turn this national investment in motherhood to their advantage, applauding the recognition of mothers' 'maternal rights' and campaigning for the complete economic independence of mothers.

The legislation providing for the Maternity Allowance, like the Franchise Act of 1902, excluded Aboriginal women from these citizen rights. In white Australia Aborigines were considered a 'dying race', while people of mixed descent would, it was hoped, be rendered invisible by intermarriage, the 'breeding out of colour' and cultural assimilation. Aboriginal languages were actively repressed. Aboriginal children were systematically removed from their parents under the guise of 'state protection': it was assumed they would be better off in white homes and institutions. Although deemed ineligible for motherhood, Aboriginal mothers fought hard to retain or reclaim their children.

White women were urged to give themselves fully to their vocation of motherhood, but a growing proportion of all women had to earn their income in the paid workforce. In order to feed and clothe their families, more people had to go out to work. Women active in trade unions asserted a woman's right to a living wage, the same as a man's. Whereas arbitration courts and wages boards discriminated in favour of male workers because of their assumed domestic needs— their 'need' for conjugal and domestic service—women unionists and feminists argued for a wage rate appropriate for the job and not according to gender.

Feminist campaigns were dominated by the image of woman as 'sex slave'. The treatment of women as creatures of sex was assumed responsible for their continuing exploitation and vulnerability. Society, it seemed to feminists, was organized to make women constantly available to men, to satisfy their perverse desires. Political economy and wage structures were designed to meet man's alleged needs: his need for sex, his need to be looked after, his need for someone to look after his children, his need for leisure. Rose Scott considered that the agitation for a larger population was a mere excuse for men's 'unbridled license'. She argued that women's right to control their bodies was essential for a purer patriotism. Vida Goldstein argued that the proposal for the medical management of venereal disease endorsed men's desire to continue using women to satisfy their appetites. It was men's desire that was also held responsible for the white slave traffic—the traffic in women and girls—that preoccupied many feminists in the years leading up to World War I. Opposing men's presumed right of access to women's bodies, feminists asserted that women should be 'mistresses of themselves'; they should be vigilant, economically independent and free. And lest women and girls could not defend themselves, or were tempted into wayward paths, there would be new women police who would perform a special sort of police rescue work.

Not all women were so ready as some feminists were to renounce the pleasures of the passions and the flesh. Many knew the rapturous delights of love-making and sometimes wrote of them, as did the poet Lesbia Harford. Like many women, however, she also anguished over the contradiction between the modern woman's aspirations to freedom and her thraldom in love. And like many women, Lesbia Harford, perhaps, felt more at ease sharing passionate sensual love with a woman, which escaped the connotations of lust and licence associated with heterosexual relations.

When state governments announced the establishment of a women's police force they were rushed by applicants. Wartime opened up many new fields for women—offices, banks and factories— although at the war front they were confined to the traditional selfless role of nursing the sick and wounded. Nurses wrote of the horrors of war and the terrible ordeal of caring for mutilated and dying men.

The new mobility and freedoms brought about by war conditions prompted some commentators to conclude that the wartime experience had generated 'a revolution in the world of women'. *The Age* newspaper feared that women would neglect home life and urged them to reconsider their choices. For most women, however, the reality was less than glamorous. Most adult women were occupied in ceaseless toil: working-class mothers especially were forced to do constant, arduous work merely to feed, clean and clothe their families. Muriel Heagney argued that mothers should at least be spared endless sewing, that the basic wage should at least be sufficient to pay for basic clothing. But more than this, labour women activists began to insist that mothers should receive a state income which would render them independent of their husbands. The position of 'mother of the race' gave women a certain political status and a powerful negotiating position, but it also locked Labor women, especially, into a racist vision of nationalist politics and social reform.

Document 1.1 Women's service to the state
The Maternity Allowance

The inauguration of Australia as a nation state cast motherhood as white women's supreme national service, analogous to men's military service. In White Australia, however, Aboriginal, Pacific and Asian women were deemed ineligible for the rewards that this national service earned and Aboriginal mothers suffered the trauma and grief of having their children taken from their care. Women activists appropriated the politics of motherhood to their own ends. While Labor women applauded Prime Minister Andrew Fisher for introducing this maternal 'right', male church and community leaders deplored the transgression of the 'law of marriage' implied by the extension of the right to single (white) women.

Assented to 10th October, 1912

No. 8 of 1912

An Act to provide for Payment of Maternity Allowances

BE it enacted by the King's Most Excellent Majesty, the Senate, and the House of Representatives of the Commonwealth of Australia, for the purpose of appropriating the grant originated in the House of Representatives as follows:

1. This Act may be cited as the *Maternity Allowance Act* 1912.

2. This Act shall commence on a day to be fixed by proclamation.

3.(1.) There shall be a Commissioner of Maternity Allowances, who shall, subject to the control of the Minister, be charged with the execution of this Act.

(2.) An Assistant Commissioner and Deputy Commissioners may be appointed, who shall have such powers and functions as are assigned to them by the Commissioner or are prescribed by the regulations.

(3.) Every assignment of any power or function by the Commissioner under this section shall be revocable at will, and no such assignment shall prevent the exercise by the Commissioner of any power or function.

4. Subject to this Act, there shall be payable out of the Consolidated Revenue Fund, which is hereby appropriated accordingly, a maternity allowance of Five pounds to every woman who, after the commencement of this Act, gives birth to a child, either in Australia or on board a ship proceeding from one port in the Commonwealth or a Territory of the Commonwealth to another port in the Commonwealth or a Territory of the Commonwealth.

5.(1.) A maternity allowance shall be payable in respect of each occasion on which a birth occurs, and the child is born alive, or is a viable child, but only one allowance shall be payable in cases where more than one child is born at one birth.

(2.) Where the child is not born alive, or dies within twelve hours after birth, a medical certificate must be furnished certifying that the child was a viable child.

(3.) Where the Commissioner is satisfied that no medical practitioner was available to attend the case, and he is satisfied by evidence that the child born was born alive, or was a viable child, he may dispense with any medical certificates required by this section.

6.(1.) The maternity allowance shall be payable only to women who are inhabitants of the Commonwealth or who intend to settle therein.

(2.) Women who are Asiatics, or are aboriginal natives of Australia, Papua, or the islands of the Pacific, shall not be paid a maternity allowance.

7. A maternity allowance shall not be paid in respect of any birth unless a claim for payment of the allowance has been made to the proper officer within three months after the date of the birth.

8.(1.) Notwithstanding anything contained in the *Audit Act* 1901–1909 or any other Act, payment of a maternity allowance may be made by forwarding by post a money order to the person to whom the payment is to be made or to a person appointed by her in writing to receive it, and in either case it shall not be necessary for the claimant or other person to send a receipt for the payment to the Commissioner.

(2.) Where payment of a maternity allowance has been made in the manner provided by sub-section (1.) of this section the Commonwealth shall not be liable to any action claim or demand for any further payment in respect of the allowance.

9. In the case of the death of the mother the Commissioner may pay any sum payable to her by way of maternity allowance to the person who, in his opinion, is best entitled to receive it.

10. Any person who—(a) obtains any maternity allowance which is not payable; (b) obtains payment of any maternity allowance by means of any false or misleading statement; or (c) makes or presents to the Commissioner or to any officer doing duty in relation to this Act or the regulations, any statement or document which is false in any particular, shall be guilty of an offence.
Penalty: One hundred pounds or imprisonment for one year.

11. Any person who aids, abets, counsels, or procures the commission of any offence against this Act, or who, by act or omission, is in any way directly or indirectly knowingly concerned in the commission of any offence against this Act, shall be deemed to have committed that offence and shall be punishable accordingly.

12. The Governor-General may make regulations, not inconsistent with this Act, prescribing all matters which by this Act are required or permitted to be prescribed or are necessary or convenient to be prescribed for carrying out or giving effect to this Act and in particular for prescribing—

(a) the powers and duties of the Commissioner and other officers; and
(b) the procedure to be followed for the purpose of obtaining maternity
allowances.

DEPUTATION TO THE PRIME MINISTER: THE LAW OF MARRIAGE

Rev. Professor Adam opened the case for the objectors, first disclaiming
any intention to discuss the general policy of maternity grants. The
deputation was only concerned with the moral issues and interests involved
in the feature of the proposal of the Government which granted the bonus
to the mothers of illegitimate children. The main question raised was:
Assuming the State thinks it wise to give a maternity allowance in token
of its appreciation and approval of the honorable service rendered by a
mother—and not as a dole—was it right to make no distinction between
honorable mothers who became mothers under the sanction of the law of
marriage approved by the State as the foundation of true national welfare
and those who became mothers in a dishonorable way, and in a way the
State did not and could not approve. They claimed that a distinction should
be made. (Hear, hear). They feared that in practice the granting of the
bonus with respect to illegitimate children would lead to an undesirable
increase in illegitimacy. There were 6721 illegitimate children in 1910. If
they were the subject of a £5 grant each there would be £33,000
involved—a sum which could be much better spent in subsidising useful
voluntary charities dealing with the necessities of unmarried women who
became mothers. (Hear, hear). It announced beforehand to unmarried
women as yet unfallen that if they did fall and had a child they would be
entitled under law to the £5 bonus. A bonus system which made a proper
distinction might act as a stimulus to marriage and a check to illegitimacy,
whereas an indiscriminate bonus might even increase illegitimacy. While
admitting that that kind of woman should receive—

The Prime Minister (sharply): I don't like that expression, 'that kind
of woman'. We don't use such words in Parliament.

Professor Adam substituted 'these unfortunate women', and proceeded
to urge the fear that the bonus would go into the pockets of men who led
girls astray. (Hear hear). Let not Mr. Fisher think this deputation unsym-
pathetic because it submitted the grave dangers it feared for his
consideration. (Hear, hear). The work the churches had done showed how
deeply sympathetic they were and how practical their help to unmarried
mothers. (Hear, hear). They were specially concerned in maintaining the
sanctity of marriage as an institution of supreme importance—(Hear,
hear)—and one on which the true welfare of the nation rested. (Hear,

hear). They were concerned lest that institution be belittled through the Government's proposal.

Rev. T. Adamson spoke from his experience as head of the Mintaro Home, and said that if they could show a girl how she could escape some of the penalties of maternity, they would in many cases remove the last barrier between her and her downfall. (Hear, hear).

The Prime Minister: Do you mean the physical danger or the feeling of the public—the howling her down? Maternity is more dangerous than going to war; more dangerous than the battlefield. (Hear, hear).

Report of Deputation from Council of Churches to Prime Minister
The Age 5 September 1912, p. 11

LABOR WOMEN APPLAUD THE MATERNITY ALLOWANCE
The following resolution was carried at a meeting of the women's organising committee [of the Australian Labor Party, Victorian branch] representing the women workers of Victoria:

That this committee, on behalf of the working class women of Victoria, expresses its utter detestation of and resentment at the foul slanders levelled at our class by the members of the deputation which waited on the Prime Minister on the 4th inst. in regard to the maternity bonus, viz., that the moral nature of poor women is so low that £5 would be an inducement to a girl to sell her honour and even enough to buy a mother's consent to her daughter's shame. We further desire to express our warm appreciation of the noble and wise act of the Prime Minister and his party in conferring this instalment of the mothers' maternal rights, and we hope, when the finances permit, to also have a child pension.

The Age, 6 September 1912, p. 8

WOMEN'S POLITICAL ASSOCIATION PROTESTS AGAINST EXCLUSION OF ASIATICS
The Women's Political Association comments;
Women who are Asiatics or Aboriginal natives are not to receive the allowance. As Aboriginals are State wards, their exclusion may be justified, but we question the exclusion of Asiatic women who are residents of the Commonwealth. This exclusion is supposed to be part of the White Australia policy, but surely it is the White Australia policy gone mad. Maternity is maternity, whatever the race, and the Asiatic woman who gives birth to a child in the Commonwealth is giving birth to a British subject, and is, we think fully entitled to the allowance.

Woman Voter
9 October 1912

MATERNITY ALLOWANCE ELIGIBILITY: MEANING OF 'ASIATICS'

3 January 1913

The Attorney-General Advises the Secretary to the Treasury:
The Secretary to the Treasury asks to be advised whether maternity
allowances may be paid in the following cases:

(1) The mother was born in Spain. Her parents were born in Asia and
were of Asiatic descent.

(2) The mother was born in Australia. Her father was a Chinese and her
mother a European.

Section 6 of the Act provides that 'women who are Asiatics' shall not be
paid a maternity allowance.

In my opinion 'Asiatics' in this section means 'of Asiatic race'. I
therefore think that a woman of wholly Asiatic blood is disqualified,
wherever she may have been born.

In the case of mixed descent, I think that a woman should be
considered as an Asiatic or not, according as the Asiatic descent does or
does not predominate; and that in the case of a woman of the half-blood
(i.e. one of whose parents only was Asiatic) she should, as the Act is a
beneficial one, be considered as *not* being an Asiatic. This is the rule that
has been laid down with regard to section 127 of the Constitution and
section 4 of the *Commonwealth Franchise Act* 1902.

My answers to the specific questions asked are therefore—
(1) No.
(2) Yes.

R.R. Garran
Secretary, Attorney-General's Department
Opinions of the Attorneys-General of the Commonwealth of Australia
vol 1, 1901–1914

Document 1.2   Full control and custody of the child of any Aborigine

*During the twentieth century Aboriginal children were regularly
taken from their parents and placed in white homes and institutions
under 'protective' legislation passed by Australian governments. The
NSW Act of 1909 was amended in 1915 to extend the state's power
over Aboriginal children.*

ABORIGINES PROTECTION ACT NO. 25, 1909.

An Act to provide for the protection and care of aborigines; to repeal the Supply of Liquors to Aborigines Prevention Act; to amend the Vagrancy Act, 1902, and the Police Offences (Amendment) Act, 1908; and for purposes consequent thereon or incidental thereto. (20th December, 1909)

Be it enacted by the King's Most Excellent Majesty, by and with the advice and consent of the Legislative Council and Legislative Assembly of New South Wales in Parliament assembled, and by the authority of the same, as follows:

1. This Act may be cited as the 'Aborigines Protection Act, 1909,' and shall come into force on a date to be fixed by proclamation of the Governor in the Gazette.

2. The Acts specified in the Schedule hereto are, to the extent indicated, repealed.

3. In this Act, unless the context or subject matter otherwise indicates or requires:
'Aborigine' means any full-blooded aboriginal native of Australia, and any person apparently having an admixture of aboriginal blood who applies for or is in receipt of rations or aid from the board or is residing on a reserve.
'Board' means board for protection of aborigines constituted under this Act.
'Liquor' means and includes wine, spirits, beer, porter, stout, ale, cider, perry, or any spirituous or fermented fluid whatever capable of producing intoxication.
'Local Committee' means committee appointed by the board to act in conjunction with the board under this Act.
'Prescribed' means prescribed by this Act or the regulations.
'Reserve' means area of land heretofore or hereafter reserved from sale or lease by the Governor, or given by or acquired from any private person, for the use of aborigines.
'Regulations' means regulations in force under this Act.
'Stations' means stations on reserves.

4.(1) There shall be a board, to be styled 'The Board for Protection of Aborigines', to consist of the Inspector-General of Police, or Acting Inspector-General of Police, who shall, ex officio, be chairman, and not more than ten other members who shall be appointed by the Governor.

(2) The board shall, subject to the direction of the Minister, be the authority for the protection and care of aborigines under this Act.

(3) The board shall annually elect one of its members as vice-chairman.

5. The board may appoint managers of stations and such other officers as may be necessary.

6. The board may appoint local committees consisting of not more than seven nor less than three persons, to act in conjunction with the board, and also officers to be called guardians of aborigines; and may at any time abolish such local committees, or remove any members therefrom, or cancel the appointment of any guardian.

Such committees and guardians shall exercise and perform the powers and duties prescribed by this Act and the regulations.

7. It shall be the duty of the board—

(a) to, with the consent of the Minister, apportion, distribute, and apply as may seem most fitting, any moneys voted by Parliament, and any other funds in its possession or control, for the relief of aborigines;

(b) to distribute blankets, clothing, and relief to aborigines at the discretion of the board;

(c) to provide for the custody, maintenance, and education of the children of aborigines;

(d) to manage and regulate the use of reserves;

(e) to exercise a general supervision and care over all matters affecting the interests and welfare of aborigines, and to protect them against injustice, imposition, and fraud.

8.(1) All reserves shall be vested in the board, and it shall not be lawful for any person other than an aborigine, or an officer under the board, or a person acting under the board's direction, or under the authority of the regulations, to enter or remain upon or be within the limits of a reserve upon which aborigines are residing, for any purpose whatsoever.

(2) The board may remove from a reserve any aborigine who is guilty of any misconduct, or who, in the opinion of the board, should be earning a living away from such reserve.

(3) Any building erected on a reserve shall be vested in and become the property of the board, also all cattle, horses, pigs, sheep, machinery, and property thereon purchased or acquired for the benefit of aborigines.

9. Any person who gives, sells, or supplies, except in case of accident, or on the prescription of a duly qualified medical practitioner, any liquor to

any aborigine, shall be guilty of an offence against this Act. Nothing in this section shall affect the operation of the Liquor (Amendment) Act, 1905.

10. Whosoever, not being an aborigine, or the child of an aborigine, lodges or wanders in company with any aborigine, and does not, on being required by a justice, give to his satisfaction a good account that he has a lawful fixed place of residence in New South Wales and lawful means of support, and that he so lodged or wandered for some temporary and lawful occasion only, and did not continue so to do beyond such occasion, shall be guilty of an offence against this Act.

11.(1) The board may, in accordance with and subject to the provisions of the Apprentices Act, 1901, by indenture bind or cause to be bound the child of any aborigine, or the neglected child of any person apparently having an admixture of aboriginal blood in his veins, to be apprenticed to any master, and may collect and institute proceedings for the recovery of any wages payable under such indenture, and may expend the same as the board may think fit in the interest of the child.

Every child so apprenticed shall be under the supervision of the board, or of such person as may be authorised in that behalf by the regulations. Any such child so apprenticed shall be liable to be proceeded against and punished for absconding, or for other misconduct, in the same way as any child apprenticed by his father with such child's consent.

(2) For the purposes of this section, the words 'neglected child' shall have the same meaning as that assigned to them in the Neglected Children and Juvenile Offenders Act, 1905: Provided that for such purposes a person shall be deemed a child who is above fourteen and under twenty-one years of age.

(3) Nothing in this section shall affect the provisions of the Neglected Children and Juvenile Offenders Act, 1905.

[Clauses 12–20 omitted]

Aborigines Protection Act 1909
Statutes of NSW

ABORIGINES PROTECTION AMENDING ACT

[Assented to 15 February 1915]

Act No. 2, 1915
An Act to amend the Aborigines Protection Act, 1909; and for other purposes.

Be it enacted by the King's Most Excellent Majesty, by and with the advice and consent of the Legislative Council and Legislative Assembly of New South Wales in Parliament assembled, and by the authority of the same, as follows:

1. This Act may be cited as the 'Aborigines Protection Amending Act, 1915,' and shall be read with the Aborigines Protection Act, 1909, hereinafter called the Principal Act.

[Clauses 2 and 3 omitted]

4. The following new section is inserted and shall be read next after section thirteen:

13A. The Board may assume full control and custody of the child of any aborigine, if after due inquiry it is satisfied that such a course is in the interest of the moral or physical welfare of such child.

The Board may thereupon remove such child to such control and care as it thinks best.

The parents of any such child so removed may appeal against any such action on the part of the Board to a Court as defined in the Neglected Children and Juvenile Offenders Act, 1905, in a manner to be prescribed by regulations.

[Clause 5 omitted]

Aborigines Protection Act 1915
Statutes of NSW

Document 1.3 His normal need was for a domestic life: she might merely want money for a dress

Wage decisions in Australia were based on the principle that they should provide for employees' 'needs'. In two influential judgments in 1907 and 1912, Justice H.B. Higgins argued that men's and women's needs differed: whereas most men had to provide for 'a domestic life' , women's only need was for dress. All men were to be paid as if they were married with children; women were to be paid as if they were single unless they were employed in men's jobs. In the following judgment the case of fruit-pickers was considered:

1912

This is the first time that this Court has had to deal directly with the problem of female labour. The Unions here insist on 'equal pay for equal work'. This phrase has an attractive sound, and seems to carry justice on its face; for, obviously, where a woman produces as good results as a man in the same kind of work, she ought not to get less remuneration. But the phrase is really ambiguous. If it means equal pay for those who turn out the same result in quantity, it means piecework—for 100 tins of fruit, so much pay; for 80 or 50 tins of fruit, so much less. As Mr. Cater justly says, equal pay for equal work involves unequal pay for unequal work. Mr. Spence, in his thoughtful speech delivered on behalf of the Australian Workers' Union, expressly repudiated the phrase. It is also inconsistent with the other claim, made expressly by the Rural Workers' Union, and made by implication by the United Labourers' Union, that piece-work be not allowed. If, however, the phrase means that there shall be equal pay given to men and to women for work of the same character, its meaning is consistent with the prescribing of a minimum wage under section 40 of the Act. The employer is not bound to retain a woman in his employ if her work is not up to his standard; but if he do retain her, he practically admits that it is. But Parliament, recognising that an employer, with his tremendous power of giving or refusing bread, can often force an applicant for work to accept less than is just in order to get bread, prescribes—or allows this Court to prescribe—a minimum below which the employer must not go. It still leaves him free to dispense with the services of any worker who does not come up to his standard, and to give higher wages to exceptionally good workers whose services he desires to secure. Now, in fixing the minimum wage for a man, I have been forced to fix it by considerations other than those of mere earning power. I have based it, in the first instance—so far as regards the living or basic wage—on 'the normal needs of the average employee regarded as a human being living in a civilized community'. No one has since urged that this is not a correct basis; some employers have expressly admitted that it is. I fixed the minimum in 1907 at 7s. per day by finding the sum which would meet the normal needs of an average employee, one of his normal needs being the need for domestic life. If he has a wife and children, he is under an obligation—even a legal obligation—to maintain them. How is such a minimum applicable to the case of a woman picker? She is not, unless perhaps in very exceptional circumstances, under any such obligation. The minimum cannot be based on exceptional cases. The employer cannot be told to pay a particular employee more because she happens to have parents and brothers and sisters dependent on her; nor can he be allowed to pay her less, because she has a legacy from her grandparents, or because she boards and lodges free with her parents, and merely wants some money for dress. The State cannot ask that an employer shall, in addition to all his other anxieties, make himself familiar with the domestic necessities of every employee; nor can it afford to let a girl with a comfortable home pull down the standard of wages to be paid to less fortunate girls who have to maintain themselves. Nothing is clearer than that the 'minimum rate' referred to in section 40 means the minimum rate for a class of workers, those who do work of a certain character. If blacksmiths are the class of worker, the minimum rate must be such as recognises that blacksmiths are usually men. If fruit-pickers are the class of workers, the minimum rate must be such as recognises that up to the present at least most of the pickers are men although women have been usually paid less, and that men and women are fairly in competitition as to that class of work. If milliners are the class of workers, the minimum rate must, I think, be such as recognises that all or nearly all milliners are women, and that men are not usually in competition with them. There has been observed for a long time a tendency to substitute women for men in industries, even in occupations which are more suited for men: and in such occupations it is often the result of women being paid lower wages than men. Fortunately for society, however, the greater number of bread winners still are men. The women are not all dragged from the homes to work while the men loaf at home; and in this case the majority even of the fruit-pickers are men. As a result, I come to the conclusion that in the case of the pickers, men and women being on a substantial level, should be paid on the same level of wages; and the employer will then be at liberty freely to employ whichever sex and whichever person he prefers for the work.

Rural Workers' Union Case 1912
Commonwealth Arbitration Reports, 72

Document 1.4 Women should receive just as great a living wage as a man

In direct response to judgments such as those by Justice Higgins in the Rural Workers' Case that explicitly discriminated against women workers, trade union women and other feminist activists argued for equal pay—that is, a rate appropriate for the job and not the worker's sex. Victorian unionist Sarah Lewis argued at the Women's Industrial Convention in 1913 that women needed the same living wage as men.

Miss Lewis said she had much pleasure in moving—'That in the opinion of this Convention a Bill providing that women shall receive equal rates of pay as men when engaged in work of the same character should be

introduced in the State Parliament House and that the elimination of the
word "sex" from the existing Factories Act be asked for'.

She claimed that when Wages Boards or the Arbitration Court were
fixing wages they should not take into consideration the sex of the workers.
In the Factories Act at the present time it was not laid down that Wages
Boards should take into consideration the sex of the workers. It was put
that they 'may take into consideration the age, sex and experience of the
workers'. The word 'sex' in the act was an open invitation to the employers
to make capital out of it and to bring down the wages. They considered
that a woman should receive just as great a living wage as a man and for
that reason they advanced arguments to show that women had as many
responsibilities as men. The Federal Labor Government had placed a Bill
providing for equal pay for equal work on the Federal Statute Book, but
a Bill should be introduced into the State Parliament House. Victoria was
the most backward of all the Australian States in the matter of payment
of women. A greater number of women worked for a small wage in
Victoria than in any other part of Australia. The women of Victoria should
therefore make a very strong effort indeed to get the principle of equal
pay for equal work established. They must bring the matter before everybody and gain sympathy for the cause. The Federal Clerks' Union was
instrumental in getting the same rates for men and women clerks, but the
employers have brought the matter to the Appeal Court, and Mr Justice
Cussen, as they all knew, made a distinction between the rates. Mr Justice
Higgins made a distinction in the living wage between men and women.
In one case where there was no danger of the women undercutting men
because it was essentially women's work they were only paid 9d an hour,
whereas the men were paid 1/-. In looking at the matter from all points
of view they would be quite in order in dealing with Mr Carter's proposals.
One question 'should women work the same number of hours as men'
was a very big one. They, as Unionists, both men and women, considered
that the workers nowadays were working too many hours altogether. They
wanted to reduce the number of hours for both men and women. In an
industry or section of industry where men were not employed at the same
work as women they considered that whatever was fixed as a decent living
wage for a man should be paid to a woman. As a rule there were very
few women representatives on Wages Boards to represent women workers.
Even in trades where the proportion of women to men was as four to one
they found that men represented women in the proportion of four to one.
They knew that employers viewed with alarm any action on the part of
women to get the same rates as men. They knew therefore that was a very
strong point against the employers, and, consequently, a very strong point

for Unionists to uphold. Both men and women must fight for the principle she was advocating.

Minutes of Proceedings
Women's Industrial Convention, Trades Hall, Melbourne
23 and 24 September 1913

Document 1.5 Mistresses of themselves: Arming women against the white slave traffic

The growing freedom that young women in urban Australia enjoyed brought new dangers. Just before World War I feminists were especially concerned with the activities of those they called 'traffickers in white slavery'—men who kidnapped young women and forced them into various forms of prostitution. The Woman's Christian Temperance Union advised girls on how to remain 'mistresses of themselves'.

WARNING TO THE GIRLS OF AUSTRALIA
From the W.C.T.U.

The present day girl, having more freedom than was the custom in her mother's day, has to face more risks than her mother did. We would like to warn you of those risks, and tell you of possible dangers which might assail you.

It will be a surprise to you to hear that there are people who are engaged in what is known as the 'White Slave Traffic', whose object is to decoy young, bright, attractive girls to their ruin and degradation. Many sad cases are known of innocent girls who have been decoyed away by the false pretences of the wicked agents of this 'White Slave Traffic', and they have never been heard of since. In England, America, and on the Continent of Europe this dreadful traffic has grown to such a extent that in England special and stringent laws have recently been passed, in order to suppress this evil.

Prevention is better than cure

It has been asserted in letters in the Press that agents of this traffic are in Australia. Some of those who are interested in the young womanhood of our State wish to warn you in time to prevent such a shocking traffic getting a foothold here—and if it does exist to put you on your guard.

To be forewarned is to be forearmed

The girls from sheltered homes, tenderly guarded from the knowledge of evil, who only read the nicest books, are often the easiest prey. In order to deceive the unwary, the agents of this awful traffic are often *disguised* as nurses, sisters of mercy, clergymen, or well-dressed and kindly spokén ladies and gentlemen.

There is no danger to a girl who is mistress of herself and well-informed. She has only to say she will call a *policeman* if they insist on worrying her, and she will have no further trouble.

We commend the following warnings to you

1. *Never* enter a strange house under any pretext, even if there should be shouts of *Fire!* or *Distress*, as sometimes this method is adopted to entrap. Call a *policeman*, but do not go inside yourself.

2. *Be cautious in conversing with strangers*, whether men or women, either in train, tram, shop, or other place, no matter how they may be dressed, or under what condition they accost you.

3. *Never loiter* in the street, or *stand about alone*. If accosted by a stranger, quickly walk away and seek the protection of the Police. *Do not accept from strangers presents* of any description, such as sweets, fruit, flowers, scents, or anything that may be drugged, *nor buy anything* at the door that might *contain drugs*.

4. *Never take any situation or lodging* (even if it is only for one night) without first applying to some personal friend, or some society, such as the Travellers' Aid Society, Y.W.C.A., Girls' Friendly, or W.C.T.U., who will investigate, and, if possible, find out if the situation or lodging is what it is represented to be in the advertisement, or by the Registry Office.

5. *Never accept* from a stranger an offer to *ride in a motor or vehicle* of any description, *nor enter any house, restaurant, or place of amusement at the invitation of a stranger*; neither go to any address, with even a note, given to you by a stranger.

6. If going to a lonely part, be sure to get full directions before starting, either from friends or directory, which is generally available at all Post Offices.

If you are in need of help or further information in this respect, apply to—

Mrs. M.E. Kirk, General Secretary,
Woman's Christian Temperance Union of Victoria.
'Carlisle House', 96 Exhibition-street (4 doors north of Collins-street), Melbourne.

Woman Voter, 13 May 1913

Document 1.6 The control of their own bodies

Policymakers in the new Commonwealth of Australia usually equated future national greatness with a large (white) population. Thus the NSW Royal Commission into the Birthrate in 1904 condemned women's selfish desire to limit their families. Some feminists believed that this demand for a larger population was only an excuse for men's 'licensed or unlicensed vice' and for the sacrifice of women to their 'hideous desire'. They defended women's 'right to the control of their own bodies' in the name of a eugenic concern for the quality of the population and a 'purer patriotism'.

1913

THE FUTURE OF THE RACE

This momentous question is agitating the minds of all thinking people. The birth-rate is rapidly decreasing, not only in Australia, but also in most of the civilised countries of the world. The increased demand for more room in our hospitals, our asylums, and our charitable institutions is alarming. How many patients, after submitting to a course of drugs for internal complaints, are finally told that an operation is the only cure? The removal of the tonsils of children has largely increased of late years. How was it that in our grandfathers' time operations were scarcely ever heard of, and yet in those days people lived to a good old age and reared large families of robust boys and girls? It is also painfully evident that nine out of ten of such operations do not cure; they only alleviate. Everyone knows that hundreds of our young men were disqualified for active service in South Africa by varicose veins, bad teeth, etc., and there is an ever-increasing number of births of imbeciles, cripples, deaf, dumb, blind, and deformed children.

The late J.A. Froude wrote: 'What is a nation's greatness? Whether a nation be great or little depends entirely on the sort of men and women it is producing. A sound nation is a nation composed of sound human beings, strong in limb, healthy in body, true in word and deed, brave, temperate, chaste, to whom morals are of more importance than wealth or knowledge. The Commonwealth is the common wellness, and no nation can prosper long that attaches to its wealth any other meaning.' That is so true that no one would venture to call it in question. What are we to do? The mothers of the race must learn the supreme lesson—'a healthy mind makes a healthy body' (E.M. Orgill).

The importance of the population question cannot be over-rated, but its true gravity does not appear to be realised by the general public. For a country merely to produce anything in quantity is not in itself necessarily either a good or great thing. Quality is far more needed than quantity. We would not pride ourselves upon the production, in our country, of quantities of wild fruits, or of Bathurst burrs, of thistles, nor yet again of inferior sheep, cattle, or a mongrel breed of dogs. Is the production of vegetables or animals of a country of greater importance than that of its men, women, and children? We know that if we desire good fruits and beautiful flowers we carefully prepare their environment, and that of the plants they will produce.

With regard to animals, much pains and care are taken, for no country prides itself upon any breed of horses, sheep, dogs, cattle, or poultry that is not of good and excellent quality. But when we look at our own race, what do we see? That their boasted freedom has too often in this great question become nothing but unbridled license, and we often find that even the natural instinct, which animals obey, is on a higher plane than the use which man makes of his freedom. There is a profession of a patriotic desire for population, but beneath this is, often, merely a desire for liberty to be freely licentious. The question of noble fatherhood and motherhood is lost sight of. Women and children must be sacrificed to this hideous desire, and women injure their own health, and that of their children, in submitting to or encouraging this subversion of an instinct given only, in the first instance, to *secure* and *protect* the race. Population, as population, can be of no benefit to a country. A population must be one of worth, physically, mentally—and morally. We look round. What do we see? A population, thousands of whom are handicapped by being illegitimates—sick weaklings—the sins of the fathers, and of the mothers also, visited upon the children. We see drunkards, idiots, criminals, and lunatics. We see slums, where neglected children swarm; we see half-castes, prostitutes, and the vast and ever-increasing army of the unemployed. Even wild animals and wild thistles are, as a rule, decent and healthy. What does this mean? It means that licensed or unlicensed vice can only breed evil. It means that all true patriotism must contain the element of purity, of self-control, as well as that of all other great virtues; so only can the race be benefited. The glorious word 'Freedom' brings with it a message, especially to women—freedom to be virtuous, the right to the control of their own bodies as well as souls, so that the children of the future may have a nobler environment, physically, mentally, and morally, before and after their birth.

To inherit the virtues of purity and self-control is to lay the foundation-stone, through her citizens, of a glorious people. What matter if they are fewer? Righteousness alone maketh a nation.

Rose Scott, Sydney, N.S.W.
Woman Voter, 15 July 1913

Document 1.7 Police rescue: The appointment of lady policemen

Australian women were first admitted to the police force during World War I, partly as a response to feminist concern that women moving beyond the protection of the home would fall into men's hands. Women were appointed to discipline and rescue other women. Proponents of the changes likened their work to the 'rescue work' performed by women in the Salvation Army. Some legislators worried, however, that the propensity of the 'frail and beautiful sex' to be distracted by passing fashions rendered them unfit for such demanding work.

POLICE WORK, RESCUE WORK IN VICTORIA

Mr. McLeod (Chief Secretary): In reply to the honorable member for North Melbourne, I may state that I do not intend to appoint policewomen in the strict sense of the term. The women will not be sworn in as policewomen till the system has been given a trial, though they will be given duties to carry out in connexion with the police. I have been in communication with a number of societies—the Salvation Army and others—who have had women engaged in what might be described as police work in different parts of the State, and I have asked them to make recommendations. It will be necessary to employ women who know something about the duties they will be called upon to fulfil, and when the recommendations have been made, I shall go into the qualifications of the women, and appoint those who are best adapted by experience and knowledge to do the work.

Mr. Prendergast: Call for applications.

Mr. McLeod: It would be difficult for a stranger to do the class of work required. We need women who have been doing the same class of work. I shall not necessarily accept any nominations at all. I have communicated with several societies, but all that I want to get from them is a list of women doing police work, rescue work, and so on.

Mr. Prendergast: Get the best women, wherever they come from.

Mr McLeod: Quite so. But those women who have been doing rescue work and similar work would naturally have an advantage over a stranger.

Victorian Parliamentary Debates
Legislative Assembly
1916, vol. 143, p. 869

THE APPOINTMENT OF 'LADY POLICEMEN' IN NEW SOUTH WALES

J.C.L. Fitzpatrick: Now I desire to turn to one or two matters relating to the administration of the Chief Secretary's Department. The Minister has been very industrious, but he has not been dealing with those questions in respect to which he might well have made a name for himself. One of his first acts was to appoint two lady policemen, and he received applications from no less than 400 aspirants to those positions. What a wild scramble there must have been—a regular stampede to the Chief Secretary's Department! I want to know what these lady policemen are going to do? We are told that one of their duties will be to assist in the direction of street traffic. But while they are standing on the tram-lines looking at the latest fashions, wondering where this hat came from or that frock was made, they will probably be bumped off by tram-cars. Where is the sense of making an experiment of this kind with a view to utilising the services of two members of the frail and beautiful sex for the performance of work that could be much more efficiently carried out by mere men. It seems to me that the hon. member has fallen into a pit. I know that a proposition in this direction has been put forward for some considerable time. Other states have adopted it; but why tinker with these little experiments when there is good solid work to be done by the department?

Parliamentary Debates
New South Wales, House of Assembly
22 June 1915

Document 1.8 Venereal disease and the exploitation of woman's body

The prevalence of venereal disease, with its devastating impact on women's health—disease often spread to women by husbands engaging in promiscuous sex—provoked feminist hostility towards free sexual relations. Feminists opposed medical proposals for practical preventives and treatment, demanding instead that men practise restraint and liberate women from their status as creatures of sex.

VENEREAL DISEASE

A woman's question

The subject of the meeting of the W.P.A. of 2nd March was the discussion of the report on venereal diseases at the Medical Congress recently held in Auckland. Miss Goldstein read to the meeting extracts from some of the medical statements there made as to the terrible prevalence of these diseases. The reports showed that in the Dominion, especially in the seaside cities and towns, the statistics bore out those used by Christabel Pankhurst about European and American cities, and which there was some attempt when they were quoted in the *Voter* to deny. Dr. J. W. Barrett's remarks at the Congress were read, in which he gave startling figures of the terrible effects of the disease on the whole human race.

The day for modesty is past

'The day for modesty is past,' said Dr. Barrett (we think he should have said 'mock modesty'). 'Sixty per cent, of the operations on women were rendered necessary directly and indirectly by venereal diseases.' In view of recent matter in the *Voter*, and Miss Pankhurst's articles in the *Suffragette*, this was not altogether news to many present, though it was noticeable that a painful thrill went through all who heard it. 'Surely this is woman's business,' it seemed to say. The members of the W.P.A. have, indeed, for some time realised that the time has come to put aside mock modesty, and to be alive to this, perhaps the most far-reaching of all women's questions. The proposal that the Commission's inquiries should not be made public found no acquiescence in the association, but a strong feeling in the other direction was expressed.

'Let There Be Light.'

It was agreed at Monday's meeting that it was fully time that the hideous state of affairs that is poisoning social life and wrecking the individual should be dragged into the open, and that lay people as well as the medical profession should have the facts. The young must be taught, the surest prevention of all—taught medically, taught spiritually. Prevention of disease following on immoral conduct is a poor suggestion. The self-restraint that comes of a finer sense of duty and of higher ideals is what is wanted.

Congress 'remedies' condemned

Speakers on Monday night felt that there was little of this aspect voiced at the congress, the only alleviation of the trouble recommended being apparently precaution against contagion with infected persons, and early marriages. Neither of these 'remedies' put forward at the congress was regarded as satisfactory. The recommendation regarding early marriages carried with it the suggestion that the economic (indeed, any) independence of women should not be encouraged. Boiled down to bald conclusion it means that women are still to be regarded primarily as sex creatures; they are to be on hand in numbers, indigent, unskilled of hand and brain, to be chosen by men as sex mates, not primarily even as mothers for the race, but as outlets for the sexual impulses and alleged needs of men. In fact, the suggestion is not any advance on the old chattel idea of things; there is no equality, no aspiration from the mere animal about it. Miss Weekes strongly repudiated the idea latent in the proposal that woman's struggles towards independence should be discouraged by the medical profession in seeking a remedy for the vices of the oversexed males of to-day. Already the small degree of economic independence obtained, she declared, had been one of the causes that had forced the whole vital question of the relation of the sexes to the front. A greater degree of independence for women should be striven for; marriage must be placed on a higher plane: men must make themselves more worthy of women of exalted ideals.

Morality the first consideration

Exception was taken to the implied suggestion that there can be separation between medical science and morality in the consideration and treatment of this urgent question. Even if man is to be regarded as an animal alone, ethical considerations must inspire his prudence. It is not himself alone that his acts affect, but the physical well-being of his wife, his children, and of the race. In forcing men to regard that aspect, 'practical' though it be in the—shall we say—political meaning of the word, we are bringing in the ethical. Unfortunately, the tendency of the few men who seem to be partially awakened to the reality of this evil, in their apparent anxiety to be thoroughly 'practical,' will largely defeat the aim of their proposals if they persist in divorcing body from spirit. If we have people physically 'fit' merely, it will not advance things much. There is no way but the creation of a changed outlook, a better knowledge of self, a sublimer consideration of others.

Exploitation of women must cease

The W.P.A. believes that woman's rebellion against the exploitation of her body in and out of marriage, together with the gaining of a greater independence (enabling her, as one speaker said, to insist that she be *won* as well as *chosen*), education, the awakening of a finer sense of human dignity, and a spiritual conception of life are the only cures for this cancer of body and soul that is amongst us. The hour is past for this association at least to stand aside in a false delicacy in this matter. It earnestly intends to do its utmost towards the destruction of the bad old order, and the creation of the new and sweeter order, which will help to bring the kingdom of heaven upon earth.

The following resolution was unanimously agreed to:

That this association condemns the recommendation of the Medical Congress held at Auckland, that girls should be educated primarily for motherhood, as leading to as great a neglect of God-bestowed gifts as would be a recommendation that men should be educated primarily for fatherhood. This association sees in the over-emphasis of sex in women one of the most prolific causes of domestic unhappiness and racial impurity, and holds that the partial economic independence of women already obtained has been a powerful factor in creating the demand for a higher moral standard in the community. This association repudiates the hideous suggestions of Dr. J.W. Barrett that the problem of morality must be separated from the problem of medicine, and that early marriage is the cure for prostitution and venereal disease.

Woman Voter
10 March 1914

Document 1.9 Women at war

Praise for the bravery and mateship of Australian men in their 'baptism of fire' at Gallipoli was seldom extended to the courageous work of Australian nurses in tending the sick and wounded. Over 2000 Australian nurses served overseas during World War I. These diary extracts record the experience of coming face to face with the suffering and horrors of war.

LYDIA KING, ON A HOSPITAL SHIP IN THE DARDANELLES

28 April 1915

There has been heavy and brilliant work done by sea and land and all the reports at home persuade people to believe that it is a very simple affair, this forcing of the Dardanelles; that they will eventually be forced it would be un British to doubt, but it will be at enormous loss of life, limb and ships . . . Am frantically tired; it is weird our ship first quivers with the English guns then with the French . . . There is certainly a tremendous amount of excitement and fascination in the work before those men if fortunate enough to pull through. But one loses sight of all the honour and glory in work such as we are dealing with. We have nought but the horrors, the primary results of the war. Nothing will induce any of our staff to tell of the horrors they have seen and dealt with and no one who has not seen it in its awful reality could imagine a portion of this saddest part of the war. The fighting men push on and leave such sights behind. We took our human cargo of suffering to Alexandria.

May 5, 1915

Shall never forget the awful feeling of hopelessness. On night duty it was dreadful. I had two wards downstairs each over a hundred patients and then I had small wards upstairs and some officers altogether about 250 patients to look after with one orderly (an Australian) and one Indian sweeper. Shall not describe the wounds, they were too awful, had one poor boy who had a fractured (compound) femur developed tetanus and died but I had to keep watching him all the time and every now and then I would hear a groan.

Diary of Lydia King, Australian War Memorial

ALICE KITCHEN, AT THE AUSTRALIAN HOSPITAL IN CAIRO

3 May 1915

Had another turmoil of a day and got off late. Yesterday was the first day we have had leave granted for nearly a week. . . . Everyone has felt the strain of the last week and there is so much personal element in it. If we had been nursing strange troops we may have felt it less, but among our own people the horrors of war are brought home to one more intensely. Almost everyone on the staff has some relation or friend and so you are constantly dreading to hear the latest news, in case it is some one we know or are interested in. God preserve them all, but that seems an impossibility unless [the] war ends suddenly.

5 May 1915

Another horrible day. Everyone working all sorts of hours and scarcely time to think of meals for one's self. So many men have arm and hand injuries: at least among the officers . . . The work seems to get heavier and one's brain feels rather like a mashed potato and fairly buzzing. Have very little time to speak to the men about their experiences. Most of them think the casualties were heavier than anticipated but it is very difficult to really know. Many think 6000 about the number, but one man told me 8000 would be nearer the mark. There will be grief and sorrow in many a home and I'm afraid few of the first AIF will return except as cripples. It is all too dreadful and everyday we hear of some one we know being killed or wounded.

Alice Kitchen Diary, La Trobe State Library of Victoria

Document 1.10 To prolong rapture by turning it into a song: The poetry of Lesbia Harford

Feminist activists condemned sexual desire as dangerous for their sex, yet several women writers explored the pleasures, ambiguity and risks of sensual love, between women as well as between women and men. Lesbia Harford's poetry spoke of the pleasures, addictions and tyrannies of rapture.

My mission in the world
Is to prolong
Rapture by turning it
Into a song.

A song of liberty
Bound by no rule!
No marble meaning's mine
Fixed for a school.

My singing ecstasy
Winged for the flight,
Each will hear differently,
And hear aright.

July 1915

Lie-a-bed
My darling lies down in her soft white bed,
And she laughs at me.
Her laughter has flushed her pale cheeks with red.
Her eyes dance with glee.

My darling lies close in her warm white bed,
And she will not rise.
I will shower kisses down on her sleepy head
Till she closes her eyes.

Gioja's no happier fresh from the South.
But my kisses free
Will straiten the curves of this teasing mouth,
If it laughs at me.

July 1915

The Tyrant
When I was a child,
I felt the fairies' power.
Of a sudden my dry life
Would burst into flower.

The skies were my path,
The sun my comrade fair,
And the night was a dark rose
I wore in my hair.

But thou camest, love,
Who madest me unfree.
I will dig myself a grave
And hide there from thee.

July 1914

[*Untitled*]
I can't feel the sunshine
Or see the stars aright
For thinking of her beauty
And her kisses bright.

She would let me kiss her
Once and not again.
Deeming soul essential,
Sense doth she disdain.

If I should once kiss her,
I would never rest
Till I had lain hour long
Pillowed on her breast.

Lying so, I'd tell her
Many a secret thing
God has whispered to me
When my soul took wing.

Would that I were Sappho,
Greece my land, not this!
There the noblest women,
When they loved, would kiss.

April 1915

Grotesque
My
Man
Says
I weigh about four ounces,
Says I must have hollow legs.
And then say I,
'Yes,
I've hollow legs and a hollow soul and body.
There is nothing left of me.
You've burnt me dry.

You
Have
Run
Through all my veins in fever,
Through my soul in fever for
An endless time.
Why,
This small body is like an empty snail shell,
All the living soul of it
Burnt out in lime.'

February 1918

Document 1.11 This revolution in the world of women

*A vacuum created by the departure of over 300 000 Australian men
for the front between 1914 and 1918 drew women into new fields
of work such as banking, insurance and the public service. These
middle-class women workers attracted the attention of contemporary
commentators who were also influenced by the more vigorous
mobilisation of women's labour in England. Some commentators
regarded women's entry into industry and commerce as the most
threatening social change effected by the war.*

1919

It will be easier for the nations to put off the outward panoply of war—to
beat the sword into a ploughshare—than to rid themselves of the new
factors that have sprung up like mushrooms to add to the complexities of
life. The greatest and perhaps the most threatening social change that has
been worked by the conditions of nearly five years of war has been the

enormous influx of women into industry and commerce. As men laid down their tools for the weapons of war, women took them up and learned to use them. There is hardly one avenue of employment that in pre-war days was regarded as man's sphere alone that women have not invaded. In England they have staffed public and private offices; they have farmed the land; they have worked in the ship yards, in the engineering works, and even in the mines. They have driven buses and acted as bus conductors . . . It is difficult to balance the desirable and undesirable results arising from this revolution in the world of women. The age is long past when women were regarded as the ornamental adjunct to the furnishing of man's home. Long before the war, women were demanding economic and political equality with men. They were entering into the economic sphere by the natural process of showing themselves at least as well suited as men for some forms of economic employment, and often better. But the upheaval caused by the war was not a natural process. Would women in such number have taken to industries demanding hard manual labor had there not been a sudden artificially created demand for their services? Before the war it was arguable that women were not playing as large a part as they might in industrial life. Now it is equally arguable that women are playing a greater part than they should. It might not be desirable, even if it were possible, to persuade women to revert to pre-war conditions. But it may be desirable, if it be possible, to persuade them to see that women's work in the world is done before they start doing man's also.

Women have cause to be flattered by all the praise that has been bestowed upon them for the manner in which they helped the Empire to carry on while so many of the men were in the field. But when that flattery is continued after the war women may do well to become a little suspicious of it. The principle of 'equal pay for equal work' is not in operation, and employers may be looking upon the huge supply of female workers as a fortunate return to the more profitable days of cheap labor. If women in large numbers are prepared to accept low wages in all the industries they have found employment in during the war, they will add enormously to the difficulty of the industrial repatriation of the men from the army. The supply of female labor will be large enough as it is without the influx of any women who seek work more because they are attracted by the freedom and independence than through necessity. Thousands of women have been robbed by the cruel slaughter of war of the chance of homes of their own. These women will have to work for their living. They will have to enter a crowded world on the best terms they can obtain. The possible choice of employment has widened, but the labor market has become overstocked. Yet it is not only those women to whom wage earning is a necessity that are crowding into the labor market. Very many women having the chance of home life are deliberately choosing what they fancy to be the greater freedom and independence offered by business or industrial employment. This tendency, if it is not checked, is bound to have a serious influence on the domestic life of the people. In the early days of the suffragette movement in England, women were surfeited with the argument that their sphere was the home. We are probably experiencing a revulsion from an overdose of that platitude, and it is the truth, not the falsity, of the old argument that now needs to be emphasised. We know that there is a place for women in political, social and industrial life as well as in the home, but the home remains the sphere round which women's work should centre. We have ploughed the fields, worked factories, and run motor buses without women's help, and would doubtless be able to do so again. But we cannot have homes without women to manage them.

John Leech, the great cartoonist of London *Punch* in mid-Victorian days, used to extract a great deal of humor from the picture of a world in which women went out to work and men stayed at home to wash the dishes, to look after the baby, and to gossip with his fellow men over a cup of afternoon tea. Leech would probably be shocked to know how near his quiet fun has come to prophecy. If women are to claim an absolute equality with men in the economic sphere, who is to look after the home? If both are to go out to work in the morning and return from work in the evening, it is obvious that there could be no home, and the great business of bringing up families would fall into disuse. No argument can get over the fact that there are two sexes in the world, and that Nature has best fitted one sex for the life of the home. For the nonce the home as a calling is in disfavor with women, but the sooner it comes into favor again the sooner will the troubled world settle back in the quiet paths of peace and progress. The world of business and industrial struggle is a poor world compared to the world of the home; its duties by comparison are trivial, and its opportunities are paltry. The glamor of wage-earning is tinsel. Let women who are turning their backs on the home in search of a 'wider life' take to heart these words of the genial philosopher Chesterton—'To be Queen Elizabeth within a definite area, deciding sales, banquets, labors and holidays; to be Whiteley within a certain area, providing toys, boots, sheets, cakes and books; to be Aristotle within a certain area, teaching morals, manners, theology and hygiene—I can understand how this might exhaust the mind, but I cannot imagine how it could narrow it. How can it be a large career to tell other people's children about the rule of three, and a small career to tell one's own children about the universe? How can it be broad to be the same thing to everyone, and narrow to be everything to someone? No; a woman's function is laborious, but because it is gigantic, not because it is minute.'

The Age,
5 June 1919

Document 1.13 A step towards the complete emancipation of women

The lives of most ordinary women in the first decades of this century were dominated by endless, arduous labour—cooking, cleaning, washing, child minding and sewing. Labour women activists maintained that overwork was a serious problem, especially for mothers. Muriel Heagney, as a researcher for the trade unions, told the Royal Commission on the Basic Wage in 1920 that the current wage could not provide for 'ordinary decencies'. Moreover, it meant that women were forced to work even longer hours sewing items, such as clothing, that could be purchased with a decent wage. Heagney argued that wages should not be subsidised by women's unpaid work at home. The Commissioners expressed astonishment at her 'theory' that women should not continue to do all the work they had always done—'in all ages and in all countries'.

11633. *By Mr. Harper*: Have you worked out what this claim for clothing alone without household commodities represents? It represents £3 17s. a week?—I know it comes out very high. I have regard to the fact that wages can only be valued by their purchasing power. I disregarded the total altogether, and took each article separately and put down the maximum and the minimum.

11634. *By the Chairman*: Is it quite clear that your committee, in assisting to draw up this list, took into consideration first of all the question of the standard of reasonable comfort only? —Yes, that is all. They did not consider whether it could be provided; they said it should be provided, but they did not take into consideration the possibility of it being provided at this stage, that being the subject of other consideration.

11635. There was no effort at all made to provide an alternative regimen on the assumption that the average woman does something in the way of contributing to the clothing of the children? —No.

11636. It is really put before us on the theory that for the future women would do nothing of the work in the house that they have done in the past very largely. We may say in all ages and in all countries, in the way of assisting in the preparation of the family clothing? —No, that is so.

11637. If that is so, all the sewing classes and technical colleges and schools and so on might just as well be abolished; I only want to know if that is the theory on which this regimen has been framed? —That is the modern woman's idea, whereas the other, the technical schools idea and so on, is the men's idea from all times. It is man's idea to have a technical school. That is actually the fact. There is a definite expression of opinion after consideration that that should be provided for in the wage. We have discussed that point, and no provision was made for an alternative.

11638. *By Mr. Harper*: In other words, you consider this is a step towards the complete emancipation of women? —That is so.

11639. *By Mr. Cheney*: A very modest step I should say? —Yes. We will be asking for the complete State maintenance of the family next.

Document 1.14 One woman, one job: The order of the day

Labour women activists led the way in Australia in campaigning for motherhood endowment, to secure the economic independence of married women and to ease all women's workloads. With their own independent income mothers would not be forced into a double or triple shift. Lilian Locke-Burns, a labour organiser, linked the case for motherhood endowment to nationalistic claims about Australia's proud reputation as a pioneer in social reform, which distinguished it from the barbaric traditions of the Old World.

STATE PROVISION FOR MOTHER AND CHILD

(By Lilian Locke-Burns, President of the N.S.W. Association of Women Workers.)
In no other part of the world, as far as one can ascertain, is so much being done by the State in the way of providing for mothers and children as in the Australian Commonwealth. And yet how far we are still from a proper realisation of the value of a child as an asset of the State, and how little we realise the true position the mothers of the community would ocupy in a properly-organised social system where the economic independence of women was fully recognised and assured!

In Great Britain and some other countries which lay claim to some share in democratic reforms, the mothers are only protected (if protection it may be called) under some form of social insurance. In the American States also very little has been done so far in this direction beyond some attention to delinquent children, and the usual institutional efforts that we find in most countries which have evolved beyond the barbaric stage. Neither in England nor America do we hear of any such humanitarian provision as the Australian maternity allowance, small as it is, and daily rendered less effective on account of the ever-increasing cost of living. At present mothers have to pay at least a percentage of the higher price of the doctor's petrol and the nurse's uniform; consequently, the bonus will not nearly cover the cost of an accouchement even to the woman whose standard of living may be much below the average. However, if the doctor and the nurse swallow up the maternity allowance, and a balance still remains to be made up on time-payment, the Australian mother is still a long way better off than her sister in other lands, and she is thankful for it, to say the least. And after the war a part of the policy of the Labor movement will be to increase this allowance to mothers, along with an increase in old-age and invalid pensions if possible.

Most of the Australian States adopt the one system as regards caring for the needy little ones in the community, though there are slight differences in the methods pursued in the various States. Besides the usual institutions for neglected, uncontrollable, or defective children, they have established a system of boarding children out, either to their own mothers or to foster-mothers, who have been carefully selected, and who are all subject to Governmental inspection.

In New South Wales, under this system, a large number of children have been assisted in recent years, over 7000 under 14 years of age receiving help in 1916–17. Widows and deserted wives are only eligible for assistance from the department, which is called the State Children's Relief Board. Deserted wives are divided into two classes, i.e., wives technically deserted and wives deserted de facto. The term technically deserted applies to women whose husbands may be in gaols, insane asylums, hospitals and sanatoriums. More of this class received assistance in 1917 than did women who were actually deserted, though the latter seem to be steadily increasing.

The relief afforded, though at least only amounting to a few shillings a week, is, no doubt, a tremendous boon to the mothers who are struggling to do the impossible—that is, to rear their children decently and at the same time take their places in the industrial field as the breadwinners. We must, of course, welcome any such system of State relief as a temporary expedient or palliative until we arrive at the stage of world evolution where 'One woman one job' is the order of the day. Then indeed a mother as such will not be expected to combine half a dozen occupations to the serious detriment of herself and of the children she is rearing.

Under a new social regime the mother will be adequately provided for, in order that she may devote herself to the all-important work of rearing and training our future citizens in the best possible manner. However, as we are not, I fear, in sight of such a development as yet, we must be content with such reforms as we can get from time to time, and one for which women should press without delay is an extension of the present system of State relief to cover the cases of mothers in homes where the breadwinners are disabled, though still struggling on through weary years of invalidism, watching perhaps with broken hearts the almost superhuman efforts of their wives to provide the necessaries of life for the family. The invalid pension for the father often is in such cases the only income they can depend on at all, and, in addition to earning the family bread, caring for the children, and multifarious household duties, the unfortunate woman must give a large share of her time and attention to her sick husband, spending perhaps every possible cent of the pension on necessaries for him. The objection has been raised that the man ought to be in a sanatorium; but, apart from the natural desire to be at home when sick, many women placed in circumstances like the above look on the pension as a help to the family income. Several cases of the kind have come under my notice, and there must be thousands in the Commonwealth. In two cases 5/- per week was allowed for two or three children while the father was in a consumptive sanatorium. When he returned home, apparently improved, but, in reality, to die before long, the mother was ever so much worse off, as the State allowance was stopped. She was neither a widow nor a deserted wife, even technically. This should certainly be remedied. To all intents and purposes the breadwinner is not there at all—at least, as far as his capacity to earn is concerned—and the mother's responsibilities have become much greater. In one of these cases the woman attempted the impossible, for, besides nursing the man and caring for children and house, she tried to keep things going by desultory charing, never at ease lest her husband should suddenly be stricken worse, never with sufficient food herself because the children were hearty and hungry and often had not enough despite her efforts. Small wonder is it that she broke down herself. Her nerves threatened to give way entirely, and she had to give up her work. The little help from the State had stopped, and the children had not got as far at school as the leaving certificate. Except for kind neighbors, they could not have lived. And yet these people had always held their heads up previously, and hated to accept charity. The cruel part of it all was that the husband had become a wreck through bad industrial conditions. No single employer could be blamed for the fine dust from the sand paper used in his industry settling in his lungs. I have known cases of painters much the same. The injury could not be traced to any one employer, and no one bothered about any compensation for the wife and helpless mites of children. Father was still alive, so there was no help. In cases of this kind it is time we put up a strong plea—not for a few paltry shillings that will reach nowhere now that commodities are so costly, but that sufficient allowance should be made to feed, clothe and house the mother and children, even if the father prefers to share his pension with them and die at home in preference to a sanatorium, where he can only see them very infrequently. This whole question of mothers and children needs to be looked at from a very different viewpoint than that of the district visitor, who gives a lecture on thrift as she deposits a tract. We have yet to realise the value of a child to the community; we have to consider deeply the potentialities that may be lying dormant in those little neglected atoms of humanity; we have also to recognise that, if a woman desires and chooses motherhood, she should be as economically free, as little dependent upon others as the well-paid woman who has climbed to the top of the ladder in the scholastic, commercial, literary or any other arena of her own choosing.

Labor Call
26 June 1919

Document 1.15 The duties of a citizen mother

The political importance that a new nation accorded motherhood was turned to women's advantage by many feminist activists. But as this article (on the Royal Society for the Welfare of Mothers and Babies and its accompanying cartoon by Percy Lindsay) made clear, the feminist politics of motherhood were intertwined with the racism of national politics.

FIRST AUSTRALIAN BABY WEEK: TO-DAY AND TO-MORROW OUR NATION MUST LOOK TO THE BABIES

(Specially written for *The Lone Hand* by E.S.H.) It will be generally admitted that Australia badly needs population. We are a mere handful of people occupying the fringe of a great continent, and envious eyes are being cast upon our potential and actual wealth from more than one quarter. So far we have decidedly not been pulling our full weight to safeguard our heritage.

Think for a moment! Australia lost fifty thousand killed in the war, and many thousands more maimed and debilitated, whose efficiency value to the country is sadly reduced. These men, remember, were our physical aristocrats; sturdy adventurous youngsters, mostly the pioneer type that supplies a nation with red blood and stamina. To make matters infinitely worse, there were practically the same number of fine babies permitted to die in Australia during the period of the war as there were diggers killed, but without the publicity of casualty lists and honour rolls.

A large percentage of this disastrous infantile mortality was due to causes which could, and should, have been prevented.

An epidemic of Small-pox and Influenza gives rise to alarmist head-lines in the newspapers and the whole State is agitated and panicky. Public opinion insists on immediate and vigorous action on the part of the Health authorities. Yet the number of deaths from these occasional outbreaks is comparatively small to the number of preventable deaths among infants. The following table, showing the condition of things in the Commonwealth at the beginning and end of the war, tells a sorry tale:

Year	Marriages	Births	Deaths under 1 yr
1914	43 311	137 983	9861
1918	33 141	125 739	7364

In 1918 there were actually 12 244 less births than in 1914, but only 2497 less deaths among infants. Nor have matters shown any sign of improvement recently. December, 1919, and January, 1920, have achieved an unenviable reputation by presenting an unusually high death rate among babies, and a correspondingly low birth rate. A continuation of this process of attrition can only lead to one thing—National extinction. We shall be as infrequent as the Dodo or Moa if this goes on unchecked.

Is the race that bred the heroes of Gallipoli and Amiens to decline like ancient Rome? We can not only stop the rot, but by taking thought, add a cubit to our national stature.

What then must we do to be saved?

This is the question that the Royal Society for the Welfare of Mothers and Babies is attempting to solve, and as a means to that end is inaugu-rating Baby Week on March 29th. It aims at upholding mothers' and children's rights in a very broad sense; it fights for raising standards and obtaining better conditions physically, socially and economically. The immediate objects of Baby Week may be summarised thus:

1   To arouse in every citizen a sense of responsibility for the children of the State.

2   To ensure that each individual man and woman realises the wanton wastage of infant life now going on.

3   To drive home the fact that if we only cared enough, at least half the babies who die might live and grow up into robust Australians and that the proper care of maternity and the improvement of conditions surrounding it is a national work of paramount importance.

Such a scheme presupposes energy, organisation, enthusiasm, and last, but not least, money, to be successful. It is essentially propaganda work on a large scale, to awaken the sovereign but slumbering will of the people. After the Week has demonstrated the disease, and prescribed the remedy, it will require perseverance, patriotism and unrelenting effort and more money to get the best results.

If every citizen does their bit we can secure the birthright of health, happiness and efficiency to the children of Australia. We must realise the need, and demand the supply.

Once it is accepted that children are a National Asset, the first bridge is crossed. Apathy and stolid acceptance of bad environment and penalised motherhood give place to prompt action and a healing of discontent. If babies are really worth so much to the nation, then surely the nation should shoulder some of the responsibilities. The three basic duties of a citizen are to contribute to the population, the defence and the finances of his country. Huge departments entailing vast expenditure make sure that the two latter are duly looked after. Nobody will attempt to suggest our own wealth of infant life is conserved as it should be, or that motherhood has received anything like adequate recognition . . .

Lone Hand
2 March 1920

Reinforce him, or he will go under.

Part 2
The modern desire for pleasure and freedom, 1921–1940

When women entered politics in the first decades of this century they invariably assumed that there was a distinctive women's interest and it centred on maternal and infant welfare. Feminists appropriated for their own purposes the nationalist definition of (white) women as mothers of the race, crucial to national wellbeing and future greatness. They argued for special services and an income for what Jean Daley called the 'national work of mothering'. Edith Cowan, the first woman to be elected to parliament in Australia, combined a characteristic interest in motherhood and the status of women. Women had special needs, but they also had equal rights. In parliament and out, Cowan worked tirelessly to secure justice for women, in the professions, in politics and at home.

Edith Cowan's candidacy was initially endorsed by the conservative Nationalist party. When they withdrew their support, she lost her seat. Women independents were often squeezed out of politics by the combined forces of labour and anti-labour. Regardless of party affiliations, however, women activists often shared many goals and platforms. Labour and socialist women argued, like Cowan, for motherhood endowment and an end to the 'slavery of the married woman'. Nelle Rickie, a delegate to the Victorian Trades Hall Council and early member of the Communist party, campaigned for the three interrelated

planks of equal pay, motherhood endowment and childhood endowment, to secure all women's economic independence. She welcomed
industrial developments that drew women into the labour market. That
women had become a 'permanency in industry' was hailed by Rickie
as the most important step along the path to women's emancipation.
Waged work allowed women a measure of independence; women
doing the work of mothering should be provided for by the state.
Labour organiser Jean Daley also campaigned for women's economic
independence, and exhorted all mothers to ensure that their daughters
would become self-supporting. She linked women's poverty and
dependence to the unequal moral standard and women's sexual
exploitation. As one who had suffered the ignominy of bearing an
'illegitimate' child, Jean Daley's concern for the vulnerability of
women, as those who paid the price for 'free love', infused her politics
with a personal passion.

Many women activists, endorsing Jean Daley's views, preserved
their independence and autonomy by remaining single. They enjoyed
the friendship and support of other women at a time when passionate
love between women could still be openly declared, as it was seldom
associated then with sexual desire. During the 1920s and 1930s,
however, this began to change as the ideas of sexologists such as
Havelock Ellis and writers such as Radclyffe Hall became more widely
circulated. Women, alerted to the stigma attached to lesbianism,
became more self-conscious in their friendships. Feminist activism was
nevertheless sustained by loving friendships between women as well
by formal organisational networks. These were extensive. Numerous
Australian feminists attended overseas conferences between the wars
and joined international networks of women.

Feminist commitments to the freedom and empowerment of
women in all nations and cultures, as well as to world peace, led to
international alliances, lobbying at the League of Nations, and a strong
sense of world citizenship. Feminist activism could also challenge
nationalist exclusions and British–Australian assumptions of racial
superiority. Eleanor Hinder, a Bachelor of Science graduate from the
University of Sydney and pioneer 'industrial hygiene' reformer, proceeded from the contacts she made at the Pan-Pacific Conference in
1928 to active involvement with the work of Chinese women, and
became a publicist of Chinese affairs and critic of the racist assumptions underpinning the White Australia policy.

There were other expressions of women's desire for freedom and
independence. 'New Women' often distinguished themselves by their

appearance, their pastimes and their clothes. Some observers regretted this challenge to traditional femininity and sexual difference. Younger women seemed to be aping men, adopting masculine styles of dress and comportment, which suggested to some that a 'third sex' of mannish women was emerging. There were also criticisms of those called 'flappers', who combined boyish figures and haircuts with painted faces and feminine frivolity. The freedom to drink and smoke, to be 'naughty and still be nice' was not, however, a freedom championed by feminists, who joined with the critics in condemning these unashamed pleasure-seekers.

Sexual fulfilment, however, rapidly came to be seen as the right of the modern woman, for whom kissing became a much analysed subject. The passionate kiss, magnified on the big screen by Hollywood cinema in these years, became a diagnostic gauge. From the kiss a woman could tell whether her partner was Mr Right, her true 'soul-mate', and it became part of a ritual by which women learned to tell the right story, the story of the 'real thing', a story that justified sexual relations for the respectable single woman.

Women's imaginations were stirred in these inter-war years by stories of freedom, exploration and mobility. The adventure and excitements of independence beckoned, but women also felt the power of old ties and traditional consolations. Family, love and marriage still had a powerful attraction, but might not domesticity be too stifling in its cosiness? Modern women were self-conscious women, negotiating the contradictions and tensions of twentieth-century femininity. One expression of these negotiations—also a means of resolution—was the widespread resort to abortion in the 1920s and 1930s. Alarmed at the implications of this trend, political and medical authorities enquired into the meaning of women's willingness to risk their lives to avoid child-bearing. Research suggested that poverty was one of women's chief motives for limiting family size, but there was also the 'modern desire for pleasure and freedom'. As feminists had noted, however, the pursuit of freedom and pleasure could be hazardous for women in a man's world.

Aboriginal women were also demanding their freedom in these years—they wanted release from the degrading 'Aborigines Acts' that regulated and controlled their public and private lives. Aboriginal women and those deemed (in the language of the day) 'half-caste' asked for the freedom and the right to raise their own children, to marry when and whom they chose, and to work as they wished. They demanded citizenship and the freedom of their country. Margaret

Tucker, herself taken away from her mother as a child, was one activist who campaigned courageously for Aboriginal rights in the 1930s. Some feminists also worked to support Aboriginal women's claims. Deploring the persistent effects of their dispossession and sexual exploitation, feminist reformers such as Mary Montgomery Bennett campaigned for Aboriginal land rights, citizenship rights, educational opportunities and economic independence. Aboriginal women, in Bennett's view, needed rescuing from masculine licentiousness, especially the white man's perversely primitive lusts. But in rescuing 'native women', white feminists also sought to rescue white Australia whose future, they reasoned, was jeopardised by white men. Feminism endorsed and was shaped by imperialist views of the world, even as it sought to challenge them. Feminists proclaimed the sisterhood of all women, confident in their own authority as civilized enlightened reformers to become the 'protectors' and guides of Aboriginal women, as well as their 'sisters'.

Document 2.1 The work of a woman in parliament

Edith Cowan became the first woman in Australia to take a seat in parliament when she was elected to the Western Australian Legislative Assembly as an endorsed National party candidate. Her friend and feminist colleague Ada Bromham stood in the same election as an independent 'woman's candidate' but was defeated by the combined forces of labour and anti-labour. These notes were prepared in 1931 as part of a campaign to commemorate Cowan's pioneering work with the erection of a public monument.

Some of the Political Work done by Mrs. Cowan, O.B.E., J.P., and M.L.A. during her three years in Parliament in addition to the ordinary work of each Session and other outside avocations and home duties.

In 1921 and 1922 [Mrs Cowan] introduced a deputation to City Council of several mothers from West Perth, asking for improvements to Duke Street Playground Area. The ground has been cleared and fenced and planted with trees, and is being put in good order. This was in Mrs. Cowan's Constituency and is now a real asset to the district.

She spoke in Parliament against the charge of 1/- for a pram ticket on suburban trains—the charge was soon after reduced by half owing to her efforts.

Questions in Parliament from Mrs. Cowan elicited information that room for 575 families existed in the Avon valley—this report had been pigeonholed for two years, and though several men legislators had been unable to get the report—an important one—tabled, she was successful in doing so. This was a matter of Land Settlement.

She moved and obtained concession that Speaker's Gallery be opened to women, in September 1921, thus breaking down a precedent that had existed for many years to the detriment of women, the result being that all galleries were made accessible to both men and women.

When Parliament was in recess in February 1922, attended Hobart Conference of National Council of Women; spoke in favour of Motherhood Endowment and obtained information thereon, and supports it.

In Melbourne interviewed the Commonwealth Director of Industry etc. and brought back to Perth information on Knitting Mills; also obtained first hand information regarding Melbourne Child Clinics—visited Ballarat and its Honour Avenue, 16 miles long, the effort of working women—was given a reception there by the Mayoress, and spoke on the value of art etc. in modern life, by request.

In Melbourne was asked to speak against the continued high price of sugar, at a crowded public meeting, convened by Housewives' League in February 1922. Moved Resolution, and price was reduced just after a Deputation waited, later, on Mr. Stanley Bruce—Prime Minister.

A Baby Health Centre Conference was convened in Perth on 17th June, 1922, by the Children's Protection Society. Mrs Cowan laid before it information obtained.

Exhibition of Soldiers' Work (one-armed needle workers) etc. was held—Mrs. Cowan was head of the Committee—successful work was done to help sick and disabled soldiers.

Obtained Premier's permission to form a Women's Auxiliary Immigration Council in August 1922, and was with Mrs. Manning a Convenor of the first meeting; declined nomination as President, but became its first Senior Vice-President.

7th September 1922, introduced first Parliamentary Bill to give mother equal inheritance rights with father when a child died without a will—formerly the father took everything—Bill was finally passed and assented to.

Compulsory Voting questions were asked by her 10th December 1922—and is still doing her best to bring it about.

On 11th January 1923 spoke against increased tram and train fares on holidays.

25th January 1923—underwent all night and all day sitting—27 hours during Redistribution of Seats Bill, though only just recovered from a serious operation.

30th January 1923 visited Eastern States—Melbourne—Sydney and

Queensland—attended Baby Bonus Federal Conference in Melbourne and voted and spoke in favour of retention of Baby Bonus—also attended deputation in favour of cheaper postage for the Housewives' League—spoke at public meeting in favour of League of Nations—attended another deputation on the sugar question and addressed several societies etc. Was given Mayoral Reception in Brisbane also Reception by N.C.W. and various Men's and Women's Organisations.

Just after Opening of Parliament 1923, obtained leave to introduce a Bill to remove Sex Disqualification in Civil matters; this was ultimately passed and two women have been admitted as barristers, one last year (1930) and one this year (1931)—also a woman architect.

On 28th July 1923, after steady pressure of argument, obtained a grant of £200 from the Premier for subsidy for Children's Clinic, although this had been refused to the Deputation which Mrs. Cowan took at an earlier date to the Premier. There are now about 18 in the State and the subsidy is over £1000 per annum.

On 20th July 1923, introduced and spoke on deputation to stop trams at Emerald Terrace—convenience to residents and safer for school children—this was granted by Mr. Scaddan, the Minister and the trams now stop there; previously it had been for years dangerous in every way and yet no male member had taken it up to remedy.

When speaking to Address-in-reply in August 1923, dealt with the Mental Deficiency Problem; need for reductions in tram and train fares; on infant mortality problem (78.26 in Western Australia against 54.16 in tropical Queensland); thanked the Premier for £200 for Child Clinic—objected to sale of books and pictures of immoral tone—strongly upheld payment of Public Servants increments; spoke on housing shortage and the need for manufacturing water pipes locally.

13th August, took deputation for further Travelling Exhibition to advertise West Australian Goods—this was granted. The original suggestion—to do this work by the Railways—having been made by Mrs. Cowan.

23rd August 1923, took Deputation—regarding Extension of Workers' Homes to the Metropolitan Area—to make houses and rents cheaper—this was favourably received and at later date was done.

25th August 1923, took Deputation to Minister to ask for cheaper tram and train fares to enable people to live in the country more cheaply. Refused on account of financial conditions.

27th August 1923—took Deputation to ask Minister for Education to approve of a University Scholarship for Industrial and Economical Research. Government was unfavourable for financial reasons and postponed action being taken then.

5th September 1923—introduced a Bill in Legislative Assembly to remove sex disqualifications against women in civil matters—permitting them to be lawyers etc. if they wished. *Bill passed December 1923.*

In Parliament asked a round dozen of questions regarding Group Settlers and Women's Hospital needs—obtained a promise of better treatment for them from the Premier (19th September 1923) and their grievances were remedied shortly after.

Bessie Rischbieth papers, NLA MS 2004/4/-

Document 2.2 The economic dependence of woman on man is sex slavery

During the 1920s women in the labour movement formulated a plan for the emancipation of all women—in paid and unpaid work. Their platform consisted of three interrelated planks: motherhood endowment, child endowment and equal pay. Motherhood endowment was necessary to free women from sex slavery; that is, from depending on an individual man for their living. Childhood endowment was necessary to support children, while equal pay or an individual living wage could be justified only if men's 'dependents' were provided for by the state. In this letter to Labor Call, *socialist and trade unionist Nelle Rickie casts capitalism as ultimately progressive in forcing women through the 'gate of freedom'.*

To the Editor, *Labor Call.*
The letters of your correspondents in last *Call* make delightful reading. After thirty years of working class literature being circulated in this country, one asks is it possible that men in our Movement could hold such views?

The restriction of work as between members of the working class is a stupid doctrine. It is a doctrine that suits the employers, who evidently have us at the stage when we are ready to reduce the working class when we have sunk to such a slavish extent that we will do anything, try anything, before we will attempt to overthrow Capitalism. The number of workers who require food, clothing, shelter is not what is causing the trouble, but the fact that the means of life are in the hands of the Capitalists.

This country could support millions if it were not for the fact that the means of life are privately owned. The man or woman who talks restriction of competition as between the members of our class who takes no active part in propaganda to overthrow Capitalism is a traitor to our class. Did restricting the number of apprentices raise wages? Has the secondary, or skilled worker, maintained his margin of skill? Will the people who believe in the restriction of competition among workers for jobs answer? What is the history of the rise of the I.W.W. in America? Was it not the unskilled workers locked out of the skilled trades? Women married or single cannot be locked out. Women are permanently in industry. The economic dependence of woman on man is sex slavery—the only slavery that exists to-day. Woman will be a sex slave until such time as the community, and not the individual father and husband, is responsible for the provision of the necessities of life for the rising generation—until such time as there is Childhood and Motherhood Endowment.

Away back at the dawn of mankind, as soon as a lasting connection was established between man and woman . . . the man, and not the group, was responsible for the care of woman in her periods of occasional helplessness. In order that the race may go on woman was enslaved. Whatever reasons there were for that in primitive times, no such reason exists to-day. With science, machinery, inventions of every kind we have the knowledge and means at hand to supply the inhabitants of the world with food, clothing and shelter on a liberal scale—practically enough medical knowledge to eliminate disease, enough knowledge to allow of freedom for every man, woman, and child, and what stands between— private ownership of the means of life in the hands of a few.

Capitalism stands between woman and her freedom, and as long as woman remains within the four walls of, for the most part the vermin-infected cribs the workers are forced to call home, the longer she will be a slave. Ichabod thinks strong men are to emancipate the workers. The working class will be forced to emancipate themselves . . . the unrestricted entry of woman into industry is the only gate by which woman can travel to her freedom, and Capitalism itself is forcing her through that gate.

Women are now a permanency in industry, and we have generations of prejudice to live down. The division of labor, as between the sexes in primitive times, was on physical lines—men to the heavy work, and women to the light. With the introduction of machinery, naturally men took the heavier and woman the light machines. There was the tendency to look down on woman in purely physical strength days in industry, but with ever-increasing invention, when not brute strength, but patience, dexterity, [and] skill ruled, woman was able to compete, take the same kind of work, and, of course, not fear that [she would] be displaced . . . The preservation of the race is a deep, strong desire in us all, and it is absurd for people just to say, for the sake of argument, that women would be down on the wharf before electric gear for loading is introduced. There are restrictions under the Factories Act, and there are regulations as to weights that are to be lifted by men. Without further legislation, there are enough restriction[s] to protect woman. Furthermore, women would be useless from a purely physical strength basis, so there is no danger of the capitalists employing them on roads or wharf. Why waste time in raising stupid bogies?

The real concern ought to be to gain a uniform basic wage for all adults in industry, irrespective of sex or occupation. Our standard of living is menaced by the fact that women are receiving lower rates of pay than men . . . if we permit the dual standard of wages to continue, we are placed in the position of allowing one-half of the supply of labor to be available to the employers for the same jobs at a lower rate of pay than the other half . . . This being so, we affirm the time-honored principle of Labor, of Unionism, that the level of the lower-paid be risen to the level of the higher paid. Women are in industry, and are a permanency in industry, and are in competition in general with men.

The figures as here supplied will show the increase of female labor into recognised industries since 1886.

Increase in the ratio of females to males since 1886:

NSW	1886	1 to 7
	1891	1 to 5
	1903	1 to 4
	1921	1 to 3
Victoria	1886	1 to 5
	1896	1 to 3
	1921	1 to 2
South Australia	1921	1 to 4
Queensland	1921	1 to 5
Tasmania	1921	1 to 5
West Australia	1921	1 to 6
Ratio for the Commonwealth		1 to 3

Juveniles under 16 years of age in factories. Gains in the past four years.

Females	2 499
Males	2 072
Total males in factories	10 452
Total females in factories	9 128

If the same ratio continues for the next four years there will be 19,124 females and 18,640 males.

There are 18,000 more females in Victoria than males. The marriage rate is very low. The average marrying age for males is 35, and for females 26 years. So, allowing that females start work at 14 (there is no provision for children over 14), that gives (even if all women were to marry and not return to industry, and that is practically an impossibility), women 12 years in industry: and, as the average life of a worker in industry is 20 years, there can be no denial of the fact that women are permanently in industry. The 'meantime' character of employment of women as a factor in the 'decision of wages' for females should be dispensed with.

Women are a permanency in industry, according to the general application of a principle laid down and accepted by Australian Courts and Boards as perfectly legitimate in those special industries in what the Courts were pleased to regard as men's work (because men were largely engaged therein).

A specific case in point was the award in the case of the A.W.U. versus Fruit-growers in 1912, when Mr. Justice Higgins laid down that when women are in competition with men in an occupation that was originally in the hands of men, that they receive the same rate of pay. We ask that this principle should be applied in general; and that as the wage is only a single man's wage, that women require the same standard as men.

The Trades Hall Council adopted a statement prepared by a special committee which lays down that the present basic wage is only the standard of a single man, and that, by allowing the dual standard to operate we will leave the way open for a reduction in our standard of living. On the other hand, the Council of Federated Unions are going into the Court to try and raise the family wage (which we say does not exist). It cannot be forgotten that after the Basic Wage Commission that the Court refused to award the £5/16/6 on the ground that industry could not stand it (that is always their cry). It was pointed out that the average employee did not support a child [and] that the average family was 1.34. Whilst this is perfectly true, the *normal* family consists of three or four children. That is, if we take the total number of children under 14 years of age, we find that nearly half are in families of three and four. But if the Council of Federated Unions were successful in getting the Court to award on the basis of the needs of the normal family, and not on the needs of the average employee, I would still oppose their going to the Court, on the ground that women are a permanency in industry, that immediately thousands of women could be introduced at the lower rates of pay, that if the wages of men were to be raised to provide for the normal family, it would mean the wholesale displacement of men and a lowering of the standard of living. The 35 per cent of the people who are doing the great service of providing the future generation should be rewarded (and liberally), but it can only be done by a uniform basic wage for all adults in industry, irrespective of sex and Motherhood and Childhood Endowment. The community should pay the cost of the rising generation, and it can be done by payments to the mothers out of general revenue. The present basic wage must not be reduced by one penny, as it is only the wage of a single man—the standard the single man in Australia has grown long accustomed to—and the one the single woman hopes to gain soon.

Nelle Rickie
Labor Call, 6 May 1924, p. 9.

Document 2.3 Together we'll do great things for the women of the world

Many women were sustained in their lives, work and politics by the love of other women. In this letter home, Jean Lloyd conveys the excitement of participating in an international women's meeting, and the importance of her own loving friendship with Winifred Tait.

When I got here last night, dearest, Will [husband] had my Aust. mail waiting for me. You might have seen me about midnight sitting up in bed & reading your dear letter—now it is 7 a.m. & I am sitting up in bed writing. Last night I stayed with Will's cousin—Alice de Jough & Will & Bill remained at the hotel where they had been. Today Bill goes to Brussels & then on to Paris on his way to Switzerland. Will & I are going to a pension near here & will stay in Holland for a fortnight—the three of us meet in London about Aug 14 & one fortnight later sail. It will be very lovely to be at home & have you all together again . . . [responses to letter follow this]. I am longing to know all about Dora—I perfectly understand how you felt. Of course it was far easier for Ella Winifred's sister. She is quite wrong about the Fed^n not admitting Germany. The only difficulty is that G. has not been able to form its own Fed^n which is the necessary preliminary to entering the International Fed^n but the key people there are very hopeful that by July next year they will be able to apply for admiss^n & of course there is no question at all of their being accepted.

My dear I have had absolutely the most thrilling five days of my life—you will get the full account of details in the general letter but I want to tell you [about] some of the inner thrills—Can't you imagine what it meant to be sitting in the square at Bruges—the belfry before me—& the life of the city entering there as it had done for centuries! (Just out of the window I see the milk-man—a hand cart with what looks like three big brass kettles, shining, & besides them bottles of milk—) clean as one expects Holland to be.

But the Council meeting!—the whole thing was thrilling beyond words—I am just longing to talk to you—it is so slow to have to write & any minute Alice will be here—(By the way she is such a nice woman—Kind & good & happy & with a dear Dutch husband who can't speak Eng, but we all beam at him & he at us)—Imagine the Council table—Dean Gildersleeve in the chair—Dr Cullis & Dr Gleditsch (Norway) beside her—Switzerland—Italy—Canada—Checko-slovakia—Austria—Ireland (Fed[n] N. & S.)—Belgium—New Zealand—Finland—S. Africa—France—Holland—Bulgaria—Australia. All gathered together to do what they could to promote peace & friendship & understanding. I felt sorry we could not have the Lord's Prayer—because the Spirit of it was certainly there. It was a tense moment when Bulgaria entered. She was a woman about fifty I should think with a strong, rather Mongolian type of face & you would know she had been through much suffering—She could not speak English—but I still have the feeling of the strong, warm clasp of the hand with which we were able to speak to each other.

Then my idea of having an Aus[n] party at the Lyceum, because it is quite impossible that we could ever give them Hospit[y] in having a Conference . . . [it] was really an inspiration! It was no trouble—the director for the Club did everything perfectly—as a *dinner* it was exquisite. I did wish you could have been with me in body as you were in spirit to see Prof Spurgern (1) me (2) Dean Gildersleeve (3) Belgium (4) looking down at the twenty one other countries, all so happy & jolly. Dr Cullis & America insisting on France smoking & Finland who had been quiet & rather shy convulsed with laughter—all so gay & happy together & they all loved the thought that Australia gave it. Dr Gleditsch (Norway—1st Vice Pres of the Fed[n])—slipped her arm into mine as we were walking round to continue our Council meeting after dinner & said—giving my arm a squeeze—'We feel Australia is always *giving us* things'—Rather sweet for Aust wasn't it? Because I had the boldness to give the party of course everyone knew me & quite a number thanked me for my *kindness*—which is absurd. But all the same, dear, I felt that you would have been very happy with it all. And with all these wonderful and famous women I realised that the spirit of love and understanding is even more important than intellectual prowess.

Together we'll do great things for the women of the world—for the world altogether—& our own friendship makes it possible to believe in friendship & on that foundation to build up more & greater things—I don't want to stop but I must. My heart is very full. Good-bye, dear one—

Lovingly Jean Lloyd

Jean Lloyd to Winifred Tait,
31 July 1925
(Written from The Hague, possibly at the Women's
International League for Peace and Freedom)

Document 2.4 Every mother should strive to make her daughter self-supporting

*As independence was the primary goal of feminists between the wars,
so the dependence of the wife became a major preoccupation. The
emphasis on independence enabled activists to avoid the conceptual
trap of choosing between equal rights and special conditions, between
sameness and difference. Jean Daley, a labour movement organiser,
assumed that women and men were the same and different, but also
assumed that this was not the main issue.*

WOMAN TO WOMAN
by *Jean Daley*

Independence

A number of men, and even women, declare that the woman with
independent means wrecks married happiness. But when that is so it is
generally the man's fault. So many husbands—even nowadays—demand
absolute subservience from their wives, and it is the fear of losing their
dictatorship that makes them resent independent women . . . The economic
dependence of women is responsible for the double standard of morality
that now obtains in our society, and this attitude of men has been at the
root of most women's troubles in the past, and every mother should strive
to make her daughter self-supporting.

The truly equal and happy marriage is often the one in which both
husband and wife are wage-earners and share the household expenses in
proportion to their income. When children come, however, they complicate
the situation, and until the great task that is peculiarly women's, i.e.
mothering the races, is regarded as national work and paid for as such,
some period of dependence is inevitable for the working-class woman.
However, the man of today is beginning to realise the injustice of this
dependence, and largely is feeling that this state of affairs is not quite fair
to his wife. He knows that the slavery of the married woman can be as
soul destroying as the old forms of chattel slavery, against which mankind
has long since rebelled.

Woman's Clarion vol. 4, no. 40, February 1925

Document 2.5 Quasi-men or a third sex?

The new look of modern femininity conveyed to many alarmed observers only an aping of men. Smoking, drinking, slicked-down hair, slender bodies—whether the figure be the mannish woman or frivolous flapper—all were disturbing challenges to the old-fashioned certainties of sexual difference. Readers of the New Idea *were moved to offer advice.*

GIRLS, DARE TO BE OLD-FASHIONED!

Dear Editor, I wonder if we really are evolving a third sex, a sort of semi-woman, who craves masculinity, and succeeds in being neither one thing nor the other. At all events, for those unfortunate enough to cherish any ideals of beautiful womanhood, there are aspects of our modern life that offer many a jar. The desire to be considered broadminded, up-to-date, and tolerant, etc., has apparently led many worthy folk to smile indulgently at the pathetic and revolting spectacle of women climbing down to man's level to prove their equality with him. The girl who thinks that she has to be masculine to be 'sporting,' evidently believes that it is impossible to lead a free, unshackled existence without turning herself into a quasi-man. The result is the deadly monotony of standardisation and the dearth of individuality.

All is imitation. The smoking and drinking habits among women are (to my mind) just a foolish and rather cheap aping of man's unloveliest habits. It may be flattering to the male; it is anything but flattering to the flatterers. It is all so futile and undignified. Nothing is gained, and something very precious is lost; for nothing hurts like disillusionment.

'Oh, there is no harm in it,' say the would-be tolerants. But, I ask, sisters, where is the good in it? These habits cannot be anything but coarsening and marring. I am quite convinced that a woman of true refinement, with any instincts toward clean, wholesome living, is instinctively revolted by them. She has the intelligence to see that they are absolutely not worth while and she knows, moreover, that the drinking, smoking type is not in harmony with a true man's ideal of womanhood. Foolish ideal, you say. Not at all. Idealism is indispensable and is a much needed quality to-day. If you would be different, girls, dare to be old- fashioned!

'Old-Fashioned'

ADVICE TO FLAPPERS—BY ONE OF THEM

Dear Editor, Recently, on reading a par in the 'Hot from Readers' Pens' corner of your delightful magazine, I came across an article criticising the

modern flapper. On reading this, I decided to write a poem for the especial
benefit of that person who wrote it, 'for what is sweeter', they say, 'than
the language of the poets?' Wishing your magazine every success, and
may it live to see more of my poems published therein. I am, yours
sincerely, 'A Flapper' (age 16).

> Why do they mumble,
> And grouch, and grumble,
> And try to repress,
> And criticise the dress
> Of the poor little flapper?
> Why do they groan,
> And grizzle, and moan,
> With many grimaces,
> At their bedaubed faces
> And cigarette cases?
> For moral's sake they ought
> To air the views our grandmas taught,
> And, by my aunt that's sainted,
> Not judge a thing by how it's painted.
> So, flappers, don't care;
> Slick down your hair,
> Slouch your hats and have no hips;
> Black your eyebrows, paint your lips.
> You can be naughty and still be nice,
> You can be good, yet taste life's spice;
> So be snappy and happy and have your day,
> For all these old fogies will talk anyway.

New Idea, 14 February 1930, p. 42

Document 2.6 We have a national religion . . . the 'White Australia' policy

*Often frustrated in their aspirations to full citizenship in Australia,
many feminists between the wars concentrated on their responsibilities
as 'world citizens', actively involving themselves in the numerous
international organisations that were formed to strengthen bonds
between women of different countries and cultures and to promote
women's rights and status. Especially important to Australian women
was the Pan-Pacific Women's Conference which first met in Honolulu
in 1928. The networks and friendships formed with women of the*

Asian and Pacific regions prompted some to question their country's policy of racial exclusion. Eleanor Hinder, a Bachelor of Science graduate from the University of Sydney and a pioneer social worker in 'industrial hygiene', was one such feminist.

LETTER FROM MISS ELEANOR HINDER

8 Young Allen Court,
Shanghai China
February 12: 1930

My dear friends in many continents:

Some ten months ago I remember writing just that address at the top of a letter which may have reached some of you who may get this: that letter was written in Hobart, Tasmania at Easter time in 1929, amid the loveliest scenery—something far different from Shanghai in winter! But I fear that that letter was the last word which went from me to many good friends with whom I would like to keep closely in touch. So I take the liberty of writing thus generally again.

It always seems as if I have to explain my being where I am when I write. I went home to Australia at the end of 1928, after having spent several months in Honolulu in connection with the first Pan-Pacific Women's Conference of which I was the programme secretary. During 1929, I found ample opportunity for international education work in Australia. First, I gave a good deal of time to trying to set up machinery for the participation by Australia in a further Conference of Pacific women which is due to take place in Honolulu in July or August of this year. I had a real conviction about the necessity of linking the women's organisations in Australia to any effort of this kind. We are, as you know, very isolated, with a population 98% British in origin: we have a national religion—the 'White Australia' policy: every organisation looks in affiliation to international groupings which centre in Europe. For the majority of the women of Australia, the women of Oriental countries simply do not exist as a concrete factor. I had the joy of seeing the delegation of twenty women from Australia, and twenty from New Zealand, the majority of them on their first journey out of their own country, measure themselves up in achievement against some of the women from Japan and China at the first Conference. I knew it to be a wholsesome educative process, and for this reason among others, I was ready to put a good deal of time into planning for Australia's participation in succeeding Conferences. I had other reasons, too: I knew the movement as a whole in Pacific countries could only succeed if every national grouping made serious efforts to plan, and I knew enough about the situation in which the women of Japan and China find themselves legally, socially and politically to believe in a continuing women's conference. I believe I could do as much for the future of the conference by working out feasible plans in Australia, as by any other means.

So, I agreed to help Dr. Georgina Sweet, who assumed the Chairmanship of the Australian Committee. Either alone or in company with her, I was in every capital city during the year, speaking about the past conference, and telling of plans for participation in the next. This meant much travelling—to go to Perth across the continent by train is not only to travel three thousand miles, but to undergo an endurance contest. There are six changes of gauge in the journey . . . I do not further expose the weaknesses of modern methods of travel in my country.

In addition to the many opportunities that came to me as a result of this journeying, for speaking, for conferences, I had some still more valuable opportunities. The University of Melbourne asked me to give a series of lectures on 'The China of this Decade'. It was ambitious of me, of course, to attempt them, but I worked night and day for six weeks in the preparation of the material from all the sources which were at my disposal. They met with a very interested reception on all sides. Whereupon the University of Sydney asked [me] to come across and give the series twice in the State of New South Wales—once in Sydney, and once in the industrial city of Newcastle, one hundred miles North of Sydney. So it came about that I journeyed to this city every week for two months. Otherwise I was able to spend that time in Sydney, which is my real home, though the bulk of my time was spent during the year in Melbourne.

Meantime, also, I was getting opportunity for newspaper work along the same line. One of the Melbourne papers gave me chance to comment upon cables received. When cables concerning China came in, the office got me by phone, and asked for explanatory statements. It was because of this new opportunity, whose importance I realised a good deal, that I decided to accept the invitation of the Australian Council of the Institute of Pacific Relations to join the Australian group coming to the Kyoto Conference of that organisation in November 1929. I know that if I could add to my own experiences in the Orient that additional education which the Conference would give, that it would enlarge my possibility of usefulness in international education. I purposely refrained from accepting any of the offers which came to me for work which would have tied me up so that I could not get away, and strained every nerve to find the means to get to Kyoto. Hence I sailed from Australia on September 18, [en] route for Japan.

Some two months before I set out, I had had a cable from China asking me to return for working upon a project which was another international one. During the time I was in Shanghai, I had moved a good deal among all kinds of people, and as a result, knew a great many, of many nationalities. I was, as some of you will remember, previously attached to the YWCA to help to make a policy for work in relation to the standards of industrial women. The Association had received a gift of money from John D. Rockefeller himself for this purpose. But the Association had no adequate modern premises: there was a small Chinese Association, and a small Foreign Association: the former had taken significant lead in the matter of drawing public attention to the conditions of child labour in the International settlement and had done other valuable work of a non-institutional form. But in the sense of having a service building for women in the modern sense, neither of them had taken any steps. They had decided that they needed to do so, and cabled to me to come and help.

There was one particularly interesting feature about the proposal—it was that the effort was to be made to obtain a building whose use would be open to women of all nationalities. Just what a revolutionary step this is can scarcely be realised, except by those who live in this city. This, however, did intrigue me, and so, when I came to Shanghai before going across to Kyoto to the Conference, I promised to come back and work for a period of three months at first, in a survey to find out what people in general thought of this idea, and to discover what were the needs of the women of the city generally from a housing, recreation, and service point of view . . .

Bessie Rischbieth papers, NLA, MS 2004/6/17

Document 2.7 'They found our mother still moaning and crying'

As Aboriginal Protection Boards throughout Australia proceeded to take Aboriginal children into white custody, families everywhere were torn apart and plunged into inconsolable grief. Margaret Tucker, a determined fighter for her people's dignity and freedom, recalls how she and her sister were taken away and the terrible effect on their mother.

One day when we were at school I was thrilled because an older boy and I were the only ones to get the answer to a difficult sum. Mrs Hill praised us and as I am not brainy it really meant a lot to me. Between morning school and the lunch break, we heard the unmistakable sound of a motor car. Out where we were motor cars were very rare at that time, and although we were seething with curiosity, we did not dare to move from our desks. One or two ventured to ask if they could leave the room, but were not allowed. Our schoolmistress was called outside. She cautioned us not to move until she returned. Some of the boys got on the desks and took a peep through the window. They relayed to us what was going on outside. A policeman and a young man and Mr Hill were talking together. Mrs Hill came in for a minute, but did not take any notice of the few boys who she must surely have seen jumping down from the window. She seemed very upset. She called Eric Briggs and Osley McGee and spoke quietly to them. They left the school through the back door. I cannot remember everything that went on, but the next thing I do remember was that the policeman and Mr Hill came into the school. Mrs Hill seemed to be in a heated argument with her husband. She was very distressed.

The children were all standing (we always stood up when visitors came and the police were no exception). My sister May and another little girl, an orphan, started to cry. Then others. They may have heard the conversation. I was puzzled to know what they were crying for, until Mr Hill told all the children to leave the school, except myself and May and Myrtle Taylor, who was the same age as May (eleven years). Myrtle was an orphan reared by Mrs Maggie Briggs. She was very fair-skinned and pretty.

I had forgotten about Brungle and the gang of men representing the Aborigines Protection Board who had visited when we were staying there. But then it came to me in a rush! But I didn't believe for a moment that my mother would let us go. She would put a stop to it! All the children who had been dismissed must have run home and told their parents what was happening at school. When I looked out that schoolroom door, every Moonahculla Aboriginal mother—some with babies in arms—and a sprinkling of elderly men were standing in groups. Most of the younger men were away working on homesteads and sheep stations or farms. Then I started to cry. There were forty or fifty of our people standing silently grieving for us. They knew something treacherous was going on, something to break our way of life. They could not see ahead to the white man's world. We simply accepted the whites as a superior race. Around that particular part of Australia, I feel we were fortunate in having a kindly lot of white station owners.

Then suddenly that little group were all talking at once, some in the language, some in English, but all with a hopelessness, knowing they would not have the last say. Some looked very angry, others had tears running down their cheeks. Then Mr Hill demanded that we three girls leave immediately with the police. The Aboriginal women were very angry.

Mr Hill was in a situation he had never experienced before. He did not take into account that Aboriginal hearts could break down with despair and helplessness, the same as any other human hearts. Mrs Hill, the tears running down her cheeks, made a valiant attempt to prolong our stay. I did not realise she had sent our two radicals Eric and Osley to race the mile and a half to get our mother. I will never forget her for that. She stood her ground, against her husband, the police and the driver of the car. 'Well, they can't go without something to eat, and it is lunch time,' she said, in a determined way.

'No thank you Teacher, we are not hungry,' we said.

'All the same, you children are not going that long journey (first to Deniliquin, then many more miles to Finley, where we would catch the train to Cootamundra) without food,' she insisted.

She went out to her house at the side of the school, taking as long as she dared to prepare something to eat. Her husband, his face going purple, was looking at his watch every few minutes. At last she came in with a tray with glasses of milk and the kind of food we only got at Christmas time. We said we couldn't eat it—we were not hungry—but she coaxed us to drink the milk and eat something. Mr Hill couldn't stand it any longer and said a lot of time was being wasted, and that the police and the driver wanted to leave.

We started to cry again and most of our school mates and the mothers too, when our mother, like an angel, came through the schoolroom door. Little Myrtle's auntie rushed in too. I thought: 'Everything will be right now. Mum won't let us go.'

Myrtle was grabbed up by her auntie. We had our arms round our mother, and refused to let go. She still had her apron on, and must have run the whole one and a half miles. She arrived just in time, due to the kindness of Mrs Hill. As we hung onto our mother she said fiercely, 'They are my children and they are not going away with you.'

The policeman, who no doubt was doing his duty, patted his handcuffs, which were in a leather case on his belt, and which May and I thought was a revolver. 'Mrs Clements,' he said, 'I'll have to use this if you do not let us take these children now.' Thinking that policeman would shoot Mother, because she was trying to stop him, we screamed, 'We'll go with him Mum, we'll go.' I cannot forget any detail of that moment, it stands out as though it were yesterday. I cannot even see kittens taken from their mother cat without remembering that scene. It is just on sixty years go.

However, the policeman must have had a heart, because he allowed my mother to come in the car with us as far as Deniliquin. She had no money, and took nothing with her, only the clothes she had on. Then the policeman sprang another shock. He said he had to go to the hospital to pick up Geraldine, who was to be taken as well. The horror on my mother's face and her heart-broken cry! I tried to reason why all this was happening to us, and tried not to think. All my mother could say was, 'Oh, no, not my Baby, please let me have her. I will look after her.'

As that policeman walked up the hospital path to get my little sister, May and Myrtle and I sobbed quietly. Mother got out of the car and stood waiting with a hopeless look. Her tears had run dry I guess. I thought to myself, I will gladly go, if they will only leave Geraldine with Mother.

'Mrs Clements, you can have your little girl. She left the hospital this morning,' said the policeman. Mother simply took that policeman's hand and kissed it and said, 'Thank you, thank you.'

Then we were taken to the police station, where the policeman no doubt had to report. Mother followed him, thinking she could beg once more for us, only to rush out when she heard the car start up. My last memory of her for many years was her waving pathetically, as we waved back and called out goodbye to her, but we were too far away for her to hear us.

I heard years later how after watching us go out of her life, she wandered away from the police station three miles along the road leading out of the town to Moonahculla. She was worn out, with no food or money, her apron still on. She wandered off the road to rest in the long grass under a tree. That is where old Uncle and Aunt found her the next day. They had arrived back with Geraldine from the Deniliquin hospital and they were at once surrounded by our people at Moonahculla, who told them the whole story. Someone immediately offered the loan of a fresh horse to go back and find Mother. They found our mother still moaning and crying. They heard the sounds and thought it was an animal in pain. Uncle stopped the horse and got out of the buggy to investigate. Auntie heard him talking in the language. She got down and rushed to old Uncle's side. Mother was half demented and ill. They gave her water and tried to feed her, but she couldn't eat. She was not interested in anything for weeks, and wouldn't let Geraldine out of her sight. She slowly got better, but I believe for months after, at the sight of a policeman's white helmet coming round the bend of the river, she would grab her little girl and escape into the bush, as did all the Aboriginal people who had children.

Margaret Tucker, *If Everyone Cared*
Grosvenor, Melbourne 1977, pp. 90–3

Document 2.8 An Australian woman's work for native women

In the late 1920s and early 1930s Australian feminist groups campaigned at home and abroad on behalf of Aboriginal women and girls. Foremost among the activists was Mary Bennett, who worked for a time as a teacher on Pastor Schenk's mission at Morgans in Western Australia and who formed close links with Edith Jones and Bessie Rischbieth of the Australian Federation of Women Voters. In her writings and speeches Bennett lobbied for land rights and federal jurisdiction over Aboriginal affairs. Her protests against the sexual exploitation of Aboriginal women also highlight the ways in which feminist solidarity was informed by a powerful imperialist and missionary impulse. Although Bennett was moved by genuine humanitarian concern for the conditions of Aboriginal women and girls, she also feared that white men's perversely primitive lusts would jeopardise white supremacy in the Pacific.

MARY BENNETT TO MRS RISCHBIETH, MORGANS, WESTERN AUSTRALIA, APRIL 1932

Ever since I have been here I have been longing for you to see this place, and the department of the work which particularly appeals to me—an Australian woman's work for native women. It is grand, beautiful! an inspiration! And since you cannot be here and see it for yourself, I am sending you a little raffia brooch made by a girl here, and another for Mrs King, and I feel that for the girls' sakes and Schenk's self-devotion, you will wear them sometimes . . . She taught them to do this beautiful work, so they had the joy of creating, and every morning she paid them for that morning's work, and paid them by piecework. Of course it meant endless calculation to find out what was a fair morning's work, and what she could sell their work for, so that this way of earning a living honestly could go on and not end in bankruptcy. The money thus earned all goes back to the workers. It is enough that the women and girls can be self-supporting, and are self-supporting. Economic dependence is the root of all evil.

The half-caste problem also results very largely from the same cause—their dependence. The evils of the patriarchal system and polygamy have been intensified by having become *commercialised*, the unfortunate women having acquired value as merchandise from white settlement. This is the cause of most of the half-castes and entails more suffering and degradation for the women. And so, though all the hunting grounds have been taken up as sheep stations, and the native culture has been completely destroyed, there has been an extraordinary recrudescence of polygamy for prostitution. *Because* the old men can barter their surplus wives (as they also barter the unpaid labour of the young men). But the women intrinsically are fine, and ready for a position of respect and independence. This is why I have asked that they shall be permitted to invoke and obtain the protection of the law of the land, and not be bartered like a bale of goods, or taken by a claimant.

The girl who made your brooch is a half-caste girl of about twenty, called Linda; she is such a fine capable girl, with an instinctive passion for purity. The natives all tell one that she never visited the white men's camps. She was betrothed in infancy to an old man, a witch doctor, and a dirty old man at that. She loathes him but some years back he took her, and there is no escape for her . . .

The girl who made Mrs King's brooch is also about twenty . . . This girl, Theresa, was also betrothed from babyhood to an old native man whom she loathed, but she only escaped from him to fall into the hands of an aged white prospector called Graham, who kidnapped her . . .

This will give you an idea of the loving protection needed by these girls and women, native and half-caste, in the state of transition from native culture to white civilisation, and the shielding from the terrible crop of evils that have sprung up in this borderland of transition . . .

Rischbieth Papers, NLA, MS 2004/12/23.

THE ABORIGINAL MOTHER IN WESTERN AUSTRALIA IN 1933
by M.M. Bennett

A Paper read at the British Commonwealth League Conference, London, June, 1933.
The study of the Aboriginal mother falls into two parts:

(1) Dealing with the Aboriginal mother living the wild life uncontaminated by whites; and
(2) Dealing with the Aboriginal mother living in touch with civilisation.

The chief characteristics of Aboriginal women are affectionate responsiveness, and a great persistence in their work, whether it be the age-old quest for food, or the new industries introduced by the missions, like weaving. The primitive culture of the Aborigines is built up on the duty of every one to his and her kin; kin and duties are specified arbitrarily by the older men of the tribe. All power is vested in these older men, and their rule, as with all primitive cultures, is hard on the women. An example of their estimate of women, and of the fear of arriving at womanhood, is the use of the term 'woman' by girls in their quarrels; I frequently see girls crumple up and cry because someone has exclaimed at them: 'Woman!' The women are, first and last, just 'property' at patriarchal disposal.

Aboriginal girls are bespoken and apportioned in their infancy—and sometimes even before their birth—by the older men, who take them for their wives from the age of ten; the older men usually have other wives already; I know a man who has six wives. Thus the 'property status' causes women and children to suffer also the evils of infant betrothal, child marriage, polygamy, and *wife-lending*. Polygamy causes most of the fights and vendettas of an otherwise singularly peaceful and unresentful people. Polygamy is encouraged by the white settlers and protected by the administration; one official takes credit to himself for ordering native girls who had escaped to return to the old men who had appropriated them.

The girls, like the young men, have to submit to degrading rites of mutilation, which are typical of primitive cultures. *And here is a very particular work to be done for women by women's societies: the work of preventing the exploitation of witchcraft and mutilation by students of anthropology in their hunt for copy* . . .

To sum up, the Aboriginal mother living in wild conditions suffers the evils of the 'property status' and of mutilations and other cruel practices—but we free women are responsible for the continuance of these evils, because we are not sharing our light with our Aboriginal fellow women . . .

Examination of the circumstances of Aboriginal mothers living in touch with civilisation discloses that their condition has become very much worse, and concerns us much more nearly than the condition of the wild Aborigines, because the terrible plight of the 'civilised' Aborigines is the logical conclusion of our own dealings with them. With Aboriginal mothers are included half-caste mothers, who, in Australia, are deemed to be Aborigines. Two outstanding facts confront us:

(1) Slow starvation of the natives through our depriving them of all land to live on, and, arising from dispossession and starvation,
(2) Wholesale prostitution of the women; originally 'property,' they have now become 'merchandise.'

'Prostitution,' wrote Mr. Love, 'is the gravest evil that civilisation has brought to the Aborigine. The Aborigine has quickly learned to appreciate flour and tobacco. Too often the only way in which he can procure these luxuries (perhaps they have become necessities) is by the prostitution of his women. Having travelled across Australia from south to north, and from north-west to north-east, I came to the matured opinion that nearly every black woman in a bush or cattle station camp is at the disposal of any passer-by for the price of a stick of tobacco.' A letter from an educated half-caste man from the North-West Division last year states: 'Poor womenfolk don't get any protection up this way. We went through twelve stations, and on every place you see about half-a-dozen half-caste kiddies running with dark mothers. It's a disgrace to the stations. And half-caste women living with white men on out-camps.'

. . .

The remedy for the starvation and prostitution of the Australian natives is to set apart *in every division adequate territories where the natives can live in communities of their own, unmolested by whites, and learn to grow their own food.*

Further, it is a particular responsibility of women to require that the present iniquitous practice of placing native and half-caste girls and women at the disposal of police officers should be made to cease at once. Some police officers are upright men, but many are corrupt. I know a missionary who reports every white man who keeps a native woman in his camp, and the police always provide an *alibi* for white offenders—*but there are the native women with half-caste babies* . . .

There is another aspect of the position of the Aboriginal mother of half-caste children which demands the attention of Women's Societies: the effect of the mothers' circumstances on the children. I know Aboriginal mothers who were hunted by the police to take their half-caste children from them to the remote Government settlement. These women suffered an agony of fear, and the effects may still be seen in their children. I refer particularly to one of my pupils, a nervy boy with a look of shock. Another half-caste child is nervy and lacking in concentration, and yet another is stunted and timid.

But Aboriginal mothers are inarticulate, so they endure all the untold sufferings of serfdom, because we have deprived them of land to live on, and refuse them education with all the other rights that are founded on education—medical services, wages when they earn them, and a political standing by which they might obtain other rights due to them.

I ask women of goodwill to press for definite reforms:

(1) Adequate native territories in each Division, and
(2) Schools for thousands of our fellow-subjects, intelligent native and half-caste children, who, as the Government report admits, are growing up without any training whatever. Schools are fundamental to all other rights.

At least *fifty native territories are needed, spaced equitably throughout the state for the twenty to thirty thousand native inhabitants.*

Rischbieth Papers, NLA, MS 2006/12/218

LETTER FROM MARY BENNETT TO BESSIE RISCHBIETH, MORGANS,
WESTERN AUSTRALIA, 16 NOVEMBER, 1934

[She refuses an invitation to be nominated for the international meeting in Turkey, because she is busy working on] 'the almost universal traffic in our unfortunate native women and children'.

Mrs Rischbieth! I appeal to you: *What madness 'prius dementat'* our fellow whites in Australia, I cannot see how white supremacy in the Pacific can last out this decade even. We, I mean, white supremacy, is in the most imminent danger, and everybody is blind. In my view, our only chance of survival is to put our 'spiritual' house in order, and do it mighty quick . . . It is such a privilege and source of consolation to me to know that I am doing even the smallest bit to lift [native women] up and set them on their feet, and help them to be what all are potentially, the most magnificent citizens that any country could desire.

Rischbieth papers, NLA, MS 2004/12/64.

Document 2.9 Make us happy subjects of this our country

For Aboriginal people 'protection' was a tyranny that denied them freedom and self-determination. In this petition to the Western Australian Royal Commission in 1934, women calling themselves the 'Halfcastes of Broome' ask to be treated no longer as 'natives', and to be given their freedom to become 'wives or citizens'. They describe how the Western Australian legislation affects their daily lives at work, their chances of marriage and the custody of their children. They denounce the police and ask for the appointment of a 'paid Lady Protector': this might have been at the behest of feminist activists in Western Australia such as Bessie Rischbieth and Mary Bennett, who encouraged Aboriginal women to give evidence to the Royal Commission.

To the President and Members of the Royal Commission at Broome

Honorable Gentlemen,

With humble respect, we, the Halfcastes of Broome, heartily pray you will very seriously consider this our petition.

It is very difficult to explain fully to you the unhappy conditions in which we have to live, through the unfair and unjust treatment meted out to us. For one thing, most of us do not wish to live with natives and should not be classed as natives, because most of us work for white people for a living, and by so doing get used to their kind of living. And by being on the Aborigine Act, after we are 14 years of age are still classed as natives, and some of us are over 40 years old. It is called the Aborigine Act, and is therefore native, with no distinction between the half-caste and native. We have all been educated and resent this way of treatment.

Re Employment: Our intended employers have to seek the permission of the police to obtain a permit to work us. Many of us refuse to work on that account. We also wish to be able to get references from our employers, so that if our last employer leaves the town and a new employer comes along, we can show the new employer that we can work satisfactorily.

Also, if the opportunity [occurs] to do daily work for different people in one week (known as charing), we cannot do it because of this permit. This permit to an employer is issued for 12 months, and that one girl is that *employer's servant* for that time, and we older women can, who have a family, earn more to keep us respectable by the day labour than by weekly wages, let alone the neglect to our homes by the tying down by the permit system. Also that permit costs our employer 5/- just as if they employed a native, whereas our work is much different to a native's work.

Marriage: Sometimes we have the chance to marry a man of our choice who may be in better circumstances than ourselves. A white man, or an educated Asiatic, but we are again rejected, because that man does not wish to ask the Chief Protector's consent. We are worse than aboriginal, they can marry amongst themselves and no questions asked.

Therefore we ask for our freedom, so that when the chance comes along we can rule our lives and make ourselves true and good citizens. Instead of that the Department would and could call us immoral girls. Also it would save our children this disgraceful position.

At present under this system when we get to a marriageable age and we are useful to our employers, and our intending marriage is made public, what is there to protect us against that employer sending word along to say we cannot be spared, whereas otherwise the Chief Protector might have given his consent to us. Whereas the result of such marriage being refused gives some of us fatherless children. Although some of us have fatherless children, we have supported them by our own earnings, and they have not cost the Department anything. So again we ask, why should they ever be under the control of the Aboriginal Department and be classed as a native. Most of these children are three-quarter caste, and by the Act, Octoroons are not on the Act, yet a mother half-caste on the Act, is treated as a native and her Octoroon children too. This is another reason we ask for our freedom.

Marriage Contract: Marriage between natives and half-castes is a very serious mistake, and should not be allowed. It is the missions that force those young people into such contracts, with the result that often happens and has done quite recently, to the half-caste wife an early death. The half-caste wife cannot live the life of a full blood native. The exposure is too great, and the food insufficient or unwholesome. Also the native is looked down upon by his tribe, and the half-caste wife cast aside because of her broken spirit, by having to walk behind her husband obediently and humble herself to him. Life by such a marriage is not worth living, and should not be allowed.

Private Life: We ask for freedom so that we shall not have to suffer anymore of the indignities that we have done in the past. Also so that from the same thing, some of us have fatherless children supported by ourselves, that have been brought into the world through no fault of our own, but through fear, and should we disclose who were the fathers truthfully, through being on the Act we might not be believed, because the officers have not to take the word of the mother alone. And these men who are the fathers of some of the children know this. And take good care that the girl they want is alone. And in a place and at a time when no witness for the woman is or can be there.

So we pray you to grant us our freedom so that as we said before we can and would play the game. And could be good people we can and will assure you should you grant us our favour which is our freedom. We promise you no complaints will be necessary, because we mean to do right.

We ask for a paid lady Protector so that we can be in a position even should our freedom be gained, we could be councilled and guided until we older ones have properly gained the knowledge of the white man's law, which as regards right and wrong have been kept from us unless it was to the convenience of those we came in contact with.

We also beg that you will take the protection out of the hands of the police, who in previous years have more often been our prosecutionists than our protectors. We know there are changes every three years. But what do they learn of our ways in three years. It is not to-day we are looking at. It is the days gone by, and what may if things are left in this condition be to come with new changes.

Surely if we can support our children and no husband like some of us are doing, and which we might not have had if the Act had not held us back, do you not think we are quite capable of being able to make either sensible wives or citizens if given our freedom.

Any one of us older women are willing to come up and give evidence if asked, and given a promise that we shall not have to suffer any injustice from the officers after the Commission leaves.

We also ask for better shelter at the ration camp for our old and infirm natives. Most of our mothers have passed on. We ought to say are not known to us, because we educated half castes who have been sent to the missions have been taken from either our fathers or our mothers when we were children, by the advice of the Department. And by so doing that has been the end of father or mother to us.

Do you not realise the cruelty of this? Would you white people like to think when you send your children to school that you would never see them again? That is one more reason why we want our freedom.

Again to the better shelter for our aged natives. Most of them have had fair shelter by the white man during their youth. Now in their old age they are left in a so called Government camp with no proper shelter from the rain in the wet season, which we must tell you is rain and wet in the North whilst it lasts. We also ask for soap for themselves to make themselves clean, all our natives are taught to use soap in the town, so why allow our old people to go dirty and unkempt, as the Department does.

One thing as half-castes we do wish to do is to thank the Medical Department for the better place for our natives at the hospital in Broome. Also the present doctor for his kindness and attention that we coloured people receive from him in his professional capacity.

Exemption papers: Another farce. We are told if we are good we could be granted a certificate. Again under the recommendation of the police who live here for a short period. After obtaining this desired paper, should we make just one mistake, that might only cost others a fine of 10/-, the power of the police could have [it] cancelled. So we call this a farce, for if we all were granted a certificate in January, the police could cancel all by December again. And some of us have no hope of ever getting those papers, because in past years we have refused favours to some of the police.

Now both natives and half-castes assisted in the great world war of other countries to overthrow the Hun, and it would surprise many did they know of the thousands that died for the British empire, yet we are treated as if the Hun were in power here.

Now as regards the paid lady Protector, we would like someone who understands us and our native women, one that we can go to when we are in doubt or confidence. One who would talk to us for our good. Not a person whose attitude and look would give us the shivers to look at only because she thought we might have done wrong that made us go to her. One that would listen and not try to put the fear of God into our hearts, before we have had time to speak to her. Some of us may want guidance also a little control, and we want someone that we could trust so that they would be out for our interest and not abuse.

The police supervision over us as our 'Protectors' in past years has been a very much abused power, and as they change every three years for fear of future years to come we pray that that will be ended. It would be a very long and shameful document if we described all their insults, nevertheless it is very real. Some of the police have not hesitated in forcing their way into our homes at any hour day or night, and grossly insulted us, they knowing full well that we are helpless and too frightened to retaliate.

We have many times been told on such occasions that we would be sent to some settlement or mission if we did not submit ourselves to them.

Finally. Many of us own our own houses and land, and many more of us could do so. We who do own our homes pay the rates when the rate time comes along. We can read, write, sew, crochet, laundry, also make our own clothes and for other people, also other domestic work. So that, Sir, on that qualification alone we think we should not be classed as natives and kept in bondage by the Act, knowing or at least hearing and reading about half-castes of other countries of the British Empire that they are not classed with their natives.

Again, Sir, we the half-caste population of Broome ask you to please consider our petition and give us our freedom and release us from the stigma of a native, and make us happy subjects of this our country.

Bessie Rischbieth Papers, NLA, 2004/12/234.

Document 2.10 Moving between ecstasy and despair

Dymphna Cusack was a novelist whose best-known work, Come in Spinner, *depicting women's lives in wartime Sydney, was written in partnership with Florence James. Her first published novel,* Jungfrau *(1936), concerned friendship between women, a sexual relationship between a student and her professor, abortion and the responsibilities of the modern woman. In this letter to Florence James she describes*

*the subject of her novel as 'women as they are', longing for wider
horizons, but held back by dragging anchors.*

My dear, I shall never save up enough money to get to England. Just as my
bank account begins to creep up, the exchange rate drops or I get some foul
disease, or one of the family gets chucked out of work—and then, I start all
over again. Not that life isn't terribly exciting in the meantime . . . as you'll
see by my address, I'm in the heart of things. I have a tiny flat . . . absurdly
cheap. Altogether I'm finding life as an independent woman so fascinating
that I can't conceive of wanting to change it for any other. Of course I'm
still teaching, and to my perennial amazement, finding it still interesting.
But scribbling is still my first love . . .

I am on my second [novel] now and hope to have it done by the end
of the year. It is still a bit of a strain combining *chef d'oeuvres* with training
the young idea. But it is worth it. I am growing increasingly to feel that
there is nothing so worthwhile as something that honesty reveals, some
phase, some experience, some idea . . . [this novel] is mainly concerned with
women as they are. Not as Galsworthy would have us believe they are, or
Aldous Huxley draws them or as Eleanor Glyn presents them, all wrapped
up in icing sugar—like Turkish Delight! but women as we know them.
Thinking, working, loving, desiring, growing weary of this freedom . . .
moving between ecstasy and despair. Full of longing for the wider horizons—and a little afraid of the snapped cables and dragging anchors.

Dymphna Cusack to Florence James, April 1933,
quoted in introduction by Florence James to *Jungfrau*
(reprint), Penguin, 1989

Document 2.11 How else is a girl to know she has found her soul-mate?

*As the idea of sexual freedom gripped modern women's imagination,
so sexual behaviour such as kissing was more closely scrutinized.
Kissing came to occupy a crucial place in many women's narratives
of discovery of 'true love', and this discovery in turn justified further
kissing. The kiss became a diagnostic gauge: from the kiss one knew
if it was the 'real thing', which had profound implications for one's
future. The editor of the* New Idea *invited readers to comment on the
subject.*

As a result of advice 'Margaret' gave recently in 'the Problem Club' to a
girl who wrote asking whether she should allow a boy, with whom she is

friendly, to kiss her goodnight, we have received letters from other readers questioning the advisability of recommending such a romantic procedure. We feel this is a problem that we should like other readers to express their opinion upon, although at the same time we fully realise that it is not a question that can be answered by a definite 'Yes' or 'No'. In certain circumstances a good-night kiss between a boy and a girl who have not reached any definite understanding may be very inadvisable; in others it may be beautiful and very desirable.

The Editor
New Idea, 26 May 1933

SHOULD THEY KISS GOODNIGHT? READERS' OPINIONS ON AN INTRIGUING SUBJECT

The following letters from readers are in response to a letter competition entitled, 'Should They Kiss Good Night?' This competition was announced in the issue for May 26, and a prize of 10s. was offered for the best letter received. The prize has been awarded to 'Kissus', South Camberwell, Vic., whose letter appears directly hereunder.

This competition has proved a great success, an enormous number of letters being received. A selection from them appears on this page, and a further selection will appear next week. A new competition is announced on page 9.

The Editor

THE PRIZE-WINNER

Dear Editor, You ask: 'Should a girl and boy, who have reached no definite understanding, kiss "Goodnight"?' Of course they should; otherwise how should they know they are in love?

Egbert meets Felicity several times at the Dance Palais. They are mutually attracted, and one night Egbert asks Felicity, 'May I see you home?' Does she haughtily tell him that she will send a snapshot of it? No, no! Thrilling to what might be love's young dream, she smilingly assents, and, later, is driven slowly homeward. Egbert's left arm around her shoulders.

Felicity is thrilled. Egbert is a nice boy, a good dancer, and has a good job and a car. He is her prince, and she loves him, or why else would she be thrilled? The car slides to a standstill, and Egbert murmurs in her shell-like ear, 'A kiss: just a little goodnight kiss!' She surrenders her lips to his. Horrors! it is like kissing a cod-fish! Crash goes her castle. Not if he were hung with diamonds would she marry him, for he is not her lover. She feels cold and tired. Good-bye, Egbert, except as a friend.

And so Felicity goes on from one man's kiss to another, until one day (or night) she meets Mr. Right. How does she know him? Why, by the thrilling sweet security of his *kiss*!

'Kissus.' South Camberwell. Vic.

YES AND NO

Dear Editor, To me, this question seems almost unanswerable, owing to different temperaments. One girl, who has had to battle for herself in life, and has become hardened, treats a kiss in a matter-of-fact way. She goes to a dance, meets a boy; he is fascinated, takes her hand, and the usual kiss is indulged in. After the kiss she is wise enough to say 'Good-night', and to go inside immediately.

However, another girl, from a sheltered home, perhaps an only child, when placed in the same position would not be so wise. She would probably be thrilled regarding the dance, and the modern youth would seldom be satisfied with one kiss from this inexperienced girl, and being a novelty to her, she would not wish to go inside immediately, and I think that is where the negative answer should be strongly applied.

A friendly kiss between a boy and girl can be very beautiful, but too many are willing to exchange with casual acquaintances the kiss which should be reserved for the partner in life.

'Happily Married.' Geelong West. Vic.

IN HUMOROUS VEIN!

Dear Old Ed., I nearly died laughing, if you know what I mean, when I read about this 'Should they kiss' argument. Where have you been this long time, and don't you ever go to the talkies? Of course they should kiss! How else is a girl to know she has found her soul-mate? None of this chaste, virginal modesty for me; it won't work nowadays. Look at my married sister. Her husband never kissed her until he bought the engagement ring, and then he only pecked her on the cheek, and started right in to talk about time-payment furniture and bassinettes.

No, I would rather be kissed under the rose trellis by a perfect stranger than be treated like that. Kisses are the small goods in the bargain basement of love, and a girl's got to be a wise shopper these days. I am sending you a week's notes from my diary, so that you can see what I mean.

Monday—Came home with Tom. Glamorous night, little shy moon. Tom kissed me—just like Clark Gable. I ran into the house like a frightened fawn. One must play up to this he-man stuff.

Tuesday—Tom tried to kiss me again. I slapped his face. What does he think I am?

Wednesday—Albert took me to the flicks. He said I was like Norma Shearer, only I had a better figure. Going home he kissed my hand. I can't help it if those sticky chocolates get on my lips. He's a bit slow, anyway.

Thursday—Tom telephoned me. I was cold. Albert rang me—I was an iceberg!

Friday—Met Tom in the street. He bought me a lovely box of powder. I wonder will he try any of his Clark Gable stuff to-night? If so I shall scream—or shall I?

'Freda the Flapper,' Wagga, NSW
New Idea, 23 June 1933

Document 2.12 An individual life unswallowed in domesticity and motherhood

Numerous women responded eagerly to modernity's promise of individuality and freedom. Some found a tension between their experience of modern sexual romantic love, their interest in marriage, and their dread of enveloping 'hominess'. Norma Bull, an artist living in Melbourne in the 1930s, recorded in her diary her thoughts on the ambiguities of freedom.

Fri 9 April 1937 *'L'AMOUR'*
Late night; Th[Theon, her lover] didn't properly underst. I had long ago been engaged to M[Mark] when I sd. engagements were unhappy times, so thought he'd better give me up to M. His heart stood still, it was an awful moment. Had he read that I still hankered after M. after deciding that our lives were too dissimilar? I sd. it somehow didn't work. He was relieved, sd. he couldn't let me go, nearly broke his heart with the strain wh was immense, what can I do? I wish I knew what thoughts went through his mind. I sought to pacify him; I did; it took time; he didn't care if we were here all night; it would be so easy to marry; or so it seemed to me, but it must not be, now. He kissed my hand & marvelled at it . . .

He thinks that women have far less passion than men, that a man desires marriage before 35. I say what about women? They have sobering influences which in no way proves that many find restraint easy. For many it may be as hard as for men but it is not 'done' for them to admit it.

Sun. 9 May, 1937

[Mother's Day, spent visiting a family with young children.]

Here was blissful home life at its most idyllic. The perfect father, the perfect mother, & 2 fine healthy children, full of devilment. This is marriage . . . [sic] a happy, idyllic, successful marriage. It makes one a little wistful, a little lonely, all this happiness. Almost envious, & yet— would this fill one's whole life?—What if it did not & left one yearning still? We who crave for an individual life unswallowed in domesticity & motherhood, we would have one part of ourselves free from all enveloping hominess to satisfy the other cravings that must inevitably come.

Mon 12 July 1937

Continue printing & reading. Finished part 3 [of *Sex Ethics*], a brief, high-handed unscientific essay without any attempt at references or proofs or authorities quoted. Primitive races are regarded as lacking moral suppression. Does this correctly apply to the aborigine who has rigid laws concerning marriage into the right tribes etc. Christ is regarded as sanctioning some sex freedom & seems to be strangely misrepresented perhaps due to the fact that he did not condemn unfortunates who were brought to him, eg. the woman taken in adultery. Nevertheless he made the distinction of 'becoming one flesh' as a reason for life-long partnership & loyalty. Surely no sex freedom could be deducted from any of his reported statements when he did not even favour divorce of the unhappy.

Typically medical in outlook, the book does not appear to acknowledge good derived from the power of self-control, & with them sublimation seems unheard of. Whereas they probably overestimate the ill-effects of sex-starvation as well as the beneficial results to the physical system of fulfilment. It is likely that romance & love in its most spiritual, ennobling, & sublimated forms is as rejuvenating & stimulating & beneficial to mind & system, or very nearly so than the not more idealistic form that love takes in complete physical expression. Can this latter ever suppress the first careless rapture?

Wed. 14 July, 1937

Read some of Marie Stopes' 1934 book. How different in style from *Married Love*! This is hasty & blatant but for the working man . . . We [with mother] talked by the fire over breakfast for hours on marriage & sex. It is a fine art I am assured.

There are complications unproved I think such as a possible 5 or 6 monthly cycle wh. may explain many struggling couple's desire for divorce in between times of warmth. This if it were so would be a strong reason for at least 6 mths mature decision on any act of separation. Is there any way of retaining romantic love thro' marriage?

Thursday 15 July, 1937

Read part of Marie Stopes' 1918 book written for medical men in a different vein and more delicately handled also much more scientific than the book written by the medical men wh. is high handed, making sweeping statements sans references. Stopes refers everything and gives sources. All married people should study the book even if they make their own diagnoses without reference to medical advice of her clinics. Further book ought to be written to give all details to enable intelligent women to understand their requirements without attempting to force them to clinics. Most healthy individuals resent attention of this nature & it is psychologically injurious to sensitive types.

The book is crammed with sensible information & confirms many instinctive opinions I had held re flora & secretions (chemical interchange not mentioned, only on the part of the woman), douches etc interfere with natural contents. But further, foreign matter I consider is offensive & ruins spontaneity particularly for the woman since nature has been unkind in forcing the precautions on her in particular.

Fri 16 July, 1937

What a strange & wonderful thing love is if it is earned & won & reearned and rewon in happy round; the wonder of thought transmission without words, the inspiration of perfect unity of idea, desire, vision, of the very breath of life, a new rhythm to live for, a fresh impulse to infuse into exalted existence. I could go on for ever under its radiant influence. I do not wish this beauty to depart from me, ever . . .

These moments were not meant to last, except as memory. I snatch at them in half waking flashes as if they were beside me, as if I could stay their fast flying wings.

Tues 27 July, 1937

Read most of 'Contraception' by Marie Stopes, part of the same, small book for the working woman, written later, with no new advances. The former is a readable book with many good references, the medical book *Sex Ethics* was disappointing in its unreasoned statements tho' written by 6 or more of the cream of the profession.

Diary Extracts of Norma Bull,
LaTrobe Library Collection, State Library of Victoria
MS 12481 Box 33369/1–7

Document 2.13 Attacks on women workers

The 1930s depression gave rise to a new wave of antagonism towards women's paid employment, which was interpreted by many commentators as an invasion of men's jobs. In 1932 the New South Wales Government passed legislation dismissing married women teachers and lecturers. The attacks on working women often concentrated on the working woman's appearance, her dress and lipstick—symbols of feminine excess. Jessie Street and other feminists such as Muriel Heagney spent much time defending women's right to work.

LETTER TO EDITOR, *THE SYDNEY MORNING HERALD*, 20 FEBRUARY 1934

The disparaging attacks on women workers by your correspondents are most unfair. That they are cheap labour is not the fault of the women workers who have repeatedly stressed their claim for equal pay. The lower wage which women are paid is imposed on them by the laws of the State. The declared basic wage for men being £3.6.6 and for women £1.16.0. As for the accusation that the girls are 'scarlet lipped' and 'overdressed', I would draw the attention of your correspondents to the fact that girls have to compete in the open market for jobs, and that if they are as described it must be that the employers prefer them so. Unemployment is a tragedy. It is more of a tragedy for a man with dependents and a woman with dependents than for men and women without. Let us not forget that the money earned by a man is necessary for him and his family. The tragedy of unemployment will exist as long as there are men and women wanting work who cannot get it. Turning out women workers will not cure unemployment, it will only shift the burden of it on to the shoulders of a class which is already handicapped by prejudice, custom and lack of status and opportunity.

For the first time in history women can keep themselves honestly and decently so let us think hard before we prevent them earning their living by legitimate means.

Jessie Street papers
National Library of Australia,
MS 2683/38

Document 2.14   The problem of abortion

As women sought more control over their lives, in circumstances where poverty often seemed to render good motherhood an impossibility, many tried to limit their number of children by illegal means. This report to the National Health and Medical Research Council published in 1937 suggests that the incidence of abortion and deaths associated with abortions had steadily increased during the 1920s and 1930s. By 1935 it was estimated that there was one abortion for every two confinements admitted to the Women's Hospital in Melbourne. Most women obtaining abortions were married and gave poverty as their reason—but there was also the modern desire for 'pleasure and freedom'.

THE PROBLEM OF ABORTION

by R.G. Worcester, M.D., B.S., D.G.O., M.C.O.G., F.R.C.S., Hon. Clinical Assistant to Out-Patients, Women's Hospital, Melbourne.

The increasing incidence of abortion is causing concern throughout the world. In view of the decreasing birth rate, this problem is even more serious in Australia. In Victoria alone, 40 to 50 women die from abortion every year; more than ten times that number have chronic ill-health afterwards, and an even greater number are left sterile.

1 *Incidence of abortion*
Taussig estimated that 40 years ago there was one abortion to every seven births, but in the United States of America to-day, there was one abortion in every three births. In Williams' textbook of Obstetrics, the ratio is given as one abortion to every four or five births. Kopp, Macomber and Plass of America estimate that the ratio is one to two and a half in the cities, and one to five in the rural districts.

In order to form some estimate of the incidence of abortion in Melbourne, the family histories of 100 consecutive patients at the Women's Hospital, Melbourne, were investigated. They were all married women who had not been admitted suffering with an abortion, or any pelvic inflammatory condition. (In this series, one case was discarded, a woman who stated she had had twenty miscarriages!) The total number of pregnancies was 306, of which, 248 resulted in the birth of a child, and 58 were abortions, giving a ratio of one abortion to four births. In a further series of 208 patients who were all admitted following an abortion, there were 183 married women. These women had a total of 441 children, and 372 abortions, showing a ratio of four abortions to every five births!

This latter series is probably abnormal, consisting of a group of women who suffer from habitual abortion, or who frequently resort to illegal interference, but there are thousands of such women in Victoria.

Hence, the actual ratio of abortions to births is between the two estimates.

One is of the opinion that the actual ratio is about one abortion to every three and a half births. This means that 8,000 abortions occur annually in Victoria.

The incidence of abortion is increasing

At the Women's Hospital, Melbourne, the average admissions over the past five years show that 21.5 per cent of the total patients admitted were suffering from abortion. In the table of statistics shown, it will be noticed that the admissions for abortion were trebled between 1910 and 1920, and that since 1920 they have been doubled. Coinciding with this, there has been a marked increase in the number of births at the hospital. This increase has not been proportionate.

In 1900 there were eight times as many births as abortions.

In 1910 there were five times as many births as abortions.

In 1920 there were twice as many births as abortions.

In 1920 to 1931, the births increased slightly more in proportion to the abortions. Since 1932, the abortions have increased, until, in 1935, there was almost one abortion admitted to every two confinements.

The deaths from abortions in Victoria have steadily increased, until last year the total was double that of eleven years ago. Hence, we may assume that the incidence of the total number of abortions has also doubled during this period.

2 The relation of abortion to puerperal sepsis

The deaths from puerperal sepsis in Victoria have shown a decrease, falling from 43 in 1926 to 19 in 1935, but rising again to 40 in 1936. On the other hand, the deaths from abortion have increased from 28 in 1926 to 43 in 1935, and totalled 56 last year. During the five-year period, 1931–35, 142 women died from sepsis following childbirth, yet there were 190 deaths following abortion. In 1926 the deaths from abortions formed 14.2 per cent of the maternal mortality. Since this, there has been an increase, until, in 1936 they formed 31 per cent of the maternal mortality.

Therefore, these deaths from abortion are masking the very real improvement which has been achieved in reducing the death rate from childbirth, during the past decade.

3 *The frequency of criminal abortion*
Taussig estimates that 60–65 per cent of all abortions in America are illegally induced. Parish of London, in a study of 1,000 cases, found that 48.5 per cent of abortions were criminal. Passmore (British Post Graduate School) has recently published a series of 117 cases of abortion, of which 43 per cent admitted criminal induction, and a further 17 per cent were presumed to have been criminally induced.

The recent Committee of Inquiry into the problem of abortion in New Zealand estimated that nearly two-thirds of all abortions were criminally induced, adding that the impression of the Committee was that this was an underestimate.

In a series of 1,069 cases of septic abortion, which I investigated at the Women's Hospital, Melbourne, 1930–33, 41.4 per cent. admitted that criminal interference had been committed. In the present series of 208 cases which have been interrogated at the Women's Hospital during the past few months, 89 or 42.8 per cent admitted criminal induction. A further 35 cases, or 16.8 per cent were presumed to be similarly induced. Thus, of this series, 124 or almost 60 per cent admitted or presented evidence of criminal induction. This, in my opinion, is an underestimate. Many of the women forming the 40 per cent of presumed spontaneous abortions were in circumstances of extreme poverty, and stated that they did not want more children.

4 *The methods employed in criminal abortion*
Fifteen of the 89 women who admitted illegal induction of abortion stated that they used drugs alone. A large number of them stated that drugs were used, and these failing, some mechanical method was adopted. It is the experience of most authorities that drugs are successful in only a small proportion of cases, and then only when taken in poisonous doses. The Committee of Inquiry in New Zealand investigated a number of drugs advertised as for the 'correction of women's ailments' or 'correction of irregularities'. They analysed some of these drugs and found they had no value for their alleged purpose of correcting menstrual irregularities, and as abortifacients they were useless. Furthermore, the gross profit on their sale was, in some cases, over 900 per cent.

Of the mechanical means, syringing of the uterus is apparently the most common in Melbourne, while the insertion of a catheter or tube is also common. The insertion of a knitting needle or slippery elm bark is, fortunately, used less frequently.

Persons procuring the abortion

In 71 cases, the patient stated that she herself performed the illegal interference. While it is probable that a few women can feel or see the cervix and introduce an instrument or the beak of a syringe, it is obvious that the above figure is much too high. In most cases, these women have been made to promise that they will say the interference has been performed by themselves. Thus, in the majority of cases, the professional abortionist is shielded. In the majority of cases, the abortionist is a nurse or lay person. In two cases of this series, a medical man was responsible.

5 *The underlying causes of abortion*

A. *Criminal abortion*

The reasons which have led to the present alarming number of criminal abortions may be grouped under the following headings:

(i) Pregnancy in the unmarried.

(ii) Unsatisfactory domestic relations.

(iii) Economic distress.

(iv) Changes in the social outlook.

(v) The spread of contraceptive measures combined with ignorance of how to use them.

(vi) Fear of confinement and ignorance of the dangers of abortion.

(i) *Pregnancy in the Unmarried.* Illegitimacy is no longer the dominant fact in induced abortion as it was a generation ago. Of the 208 women in the series presented, only 24 or 11.8 per cent were unmarried. In spite of the increased knowledge of contraception, the illegitimate births in Victoria have fallen very little since 1910, from 5.77 per 1,000 births in 1910 to 4.25 in 1935. Although the hospital statistics show only a comparatively small percentage of single women admitted for abortion, it is considered that single women tend to conceal their condition and are not seen by a medical practitioner unless they develop complications, when they are sent into hospital. The total deaths from abortion at the Women's Hospital for four years amounted to 99, of which 72 were married and 27 were single. Previously, it has been shown that of the total abortions admitted, only 11.5 per cent were single women, yet about 27 per cent of the deaths are unmarried women.

The increasing freedom of the sexes, the influence of alcohol, and the false sense of security fostered by the use of contraceptive measures are factors in the causation of illegitimacy and abortion in the unmarried.

(ii) *Unsatisfactory Domestic Relations.* Domestic unhappiness, or the refusal of the husband to support his wife occurs in a small percentage of cases (5 per cent). In some cases, there were instances of the husband ill-treating his wife, who sometimes had to work to support the family. Sometimes the husband obtained his sexual gratification with no thought for his wife, leaving her the worry of preventing any possible pregnancy. If pregnancy ensued, the woman, being the sole support of the family, and often in ill-health herself, had no option but to induce an abortion.

(iii) *Economic Distress.* Economic distress is the cause of the largest number of abortions. In Russia, where each woman must give the reason for the interruption of pregnancy, the records show that poverty was emphasized in one-half of the cases. The majority of our series, 49 out of 89 admitting criminal abortion, stated that poverty and bad living conditions were the reasons which led them to induce abortion. Some of these women had several very young children, in some cases still on the breast, and with a husband out of work, could not face the thought of bringing another child into the world.

In the homes of 86 of the 184 married women interrogated, the breadwinner was out of work, on sustenance, or only obtained work occasionally. This means that in almost half of the homes the family had barely enough to live on. Can we wonder, that, when these women are faced with a new pregnancy, they grasp at any means of terminating the pregnancy. Under social conditions such as these, one is not surprised that there are so many abortions.

(iv) *Changes in the Social Outlook.* In not a few cases the statement that the family was already large enough was given as the reason for not wishing to have another baby. It will be noticed from the tables shown that 114 or 62 per cent of women in the series had two children or less, and that only fourteen or 7.8 per cent had five children or more. In many of these families, the income was sufficient for a small family, but an addition would have meant hardship.

This outlook is not limited to the poorer classes. Large families are not fashionable even among the middle classes and the wealthy. The modern desire for pleasure, and freedom from household responsibilities has led many to limit their families. In our community, the single man or woman, or the married couple with no children, are in an infinitely better position than the married couple with four or five children. The single man earning £4 to £6 per week has much more freedom and pleasure than the married man earning the same amount, even if his family is small.

Can we blame a woman who has been earning almost as much as the man she marries, not wishing to give up her freedom and pleasure to rear a large family? Occasionally the unwillingness of the wife to give up her remunerative work is a factor in a desire to limit her family, and when contraceptives fail, to seek an abortionist.

(v) *The Spread of Contraceptive Measures and Ignorance of How to Use Them.* Contraceptives are largely used and, judging by the marked decline in the birth rate in recent years, are, in many cases, successful. In many cases however, they are unsuccessful, and then the women frequently resort to abortion. From the table shown, it will be seen that of the women admitting criminal abortion, 82 per cent practised contraception; and of the cases of presumed interference, 68 per cent used contraceptives. In the cases presumed to be spontaneous abortions, only 22 per cent were in the habit of using contraceptives.

Many women complained of the ineffectiveness of the contraceptives. In most cases the use of defective methods owing to their cheapness, and the lack of knowledge of how to use them, were responsible for their failure. Effective appliances are unnecessarily expensive; and further, we all know that even the best contraceptive is likely to fail. Do the public realize this? Is not too much reliance placed upon the use of contraceptives? At any rate it appears that contraceptives tend to produce a false sense of security, and when they fail abortion is resorted to.

The New Zealand Committee of Inquiry have drawn attention to advertisements appearing in certain periodicals advertising contraceptives, and also the practice of certain so-called 'mail order chemists' who send out price lists of contraceptives and abortifacients indiscriminately through the post.

(vi) *The Fear of Childbirth and the Ignorance of the Dangers of Abortion.* The fear of childbirth is uncommon to-day, but the dangers of abortion are not realized as widely as they should be. Many of the patients questioned stated they did not consider that there was much danger in having an abortion. Some of them stated that they had experienced other criminal abortions without any complications.

B. Spontaneous Abortions

While in numbers spontaneous abortions present the smaller problem, we, as physicians, are deeply interested in these cases because they include that large group of women who crave the joys of motherhood, but through untoward circumstances, in spite of repeated pregnancies, are denied its consummation.

The spontaneous abortions in the cases presented, formed about 40 per cent of the total abortions, although this is probably an overestimate. Taussig considers that one in ten of all pregnancies end in spontaneous abortion. Time does not permit me to deal with this problem at length.

Dr. Streeter at the Carnegie Institute in Baltimore has shown that defective germ cells, either before conception or shortly after, play an important part in the etiology of spontaneous abortion. These cases, often associated with the so-called 'missed abortion', constitute practically one-third of all the cases of spontaneous abortion. Disturbed endocrine secretions in the man, and even more so in the wife, play a large part. Pelvic factors such as infantile uteri, inflammatory conditions, tumours such as myomata, polypi and ovarian cysts, deeply lacerated cervices, and markedly relaxed pelvic floors are occasional factors. Retroversion of the uterus is more often accused than it should be.

The general physical condition of the prospective mother is often to blame. Cases with low sugar tolerance, low renal reserve, or active spirochaetal infection, are likely to have spontaneous abortions. According to Curtis and others, foci of infection sometimes produce placental lesions which terminate in abortion.

6 Possible measures to reduce the incidence of abortion
One does not propose to deal with this aspect of the problem at length. The following remedies are suggested:

(1) *Relief of Economic Distress.* Of the married women admitting criminal interference, 31 or 44.4 per cent stated that, with some financial assistance, they would not have interrupted the pregnancy. Forty-one or 55.6 per cent stated that financial assistance would have made no difference. This does indicate that a large proportion of criminal abortions would be avoided if there were some financial assistance obtainable for these women.

(2) *Increase in tax Exemptions for Children.* This remedy was suggested by Professor Marshall Allan in the Anne MacKenzie Oration, 1936. These exemptions should be made more liberal, and could also cover a wider range of income limit than at present. At the same time, taxation of single persons and childless married couples should be increased.

(3) *Direction of the Knowledge of Birth Control Through More Responsible Channels.* In this way, the uses of contraceptives may be controlled.

(4) *Prohibition of the Advertisement of Contraceptives and Abortifacients.*

(5) *Education of Women Concerning the Dangers of Childbirth.* Maternal mortality is always being discussed, but do the public know that abortion is responsible for more deaths than puerperal sepsis?

(6) *Intensive Study of the Underlying Causes of Spontaneous Abortion and its Prevention.*

Summary

1   It is estimated that 8,000 abortions occur in Victoria every year, and that the incidence is one abortion to every three and a half births.
2   The number of abortions is increasing rapidly, having doubled during the last ten or twelve years.
3   The death rate from abortion is increasing, and is now more than that from puerperal sepsis.
4   Deaths from abortion form more than one-quarter of the maternal mortality.
5   Criminal interference is responsible for more than 60 per cent of all abortions.
6   The chief causes of criminal abortion are economic distress, and the changes in the social outlook.
7   Contraceptives are widely used, but owing to lack of knowledge in their use, many failures occur, and abortion is resorted to.
8   Spontaneous abortions occur in about 30–40 per cent of cases, and are due to various physical causes which could be corrected.
9   Remedies to control criminal abortion consist mainly of measures to relieve economic distress, and the education of women in the dangers of induced abortion.

Acknowledgements

I wish to express my thanks to Professor Marshall Allan whose advice and active interest has been of the greatest value. I would also like to thank the Senior Honorary Staff at the Women's Hospital for allowing me to interrogate their patients; also the Medical Superintendent, Dr. Lawson, and the Senior House Surgeons who have helped me in this work.

Report of the National Health and Medical
Research Council 3rd Session Nov 1937
Cw Parlt Papers pp. 25–27

Part 3
Imagining equality, 1941–1968

World War II had far-reaching implications in the lives of Australian women. For younger women in particular, participation in wartime service brought new experiences of independence and earning power, and opportunities to explore sexual relationships—with women and men—in less restrictive environments. The behaviour of younger women was frequently misunderstood by a generation of feminists for whom morality and the dangers of sexual activity, especially venereal disease, had long been matters of great concern. The meeting of these women in November 1943 to draw up the Australian Women's Charter reflects their incisive analysis of women's subordination, and their belief that the 'double moral standard' was reflective of it. Their recognition of national and international racism also demonstrated their ability to analyse the plight of other groups—calls for Aboriginal self-determination, for example, were falling on deaf ears in the white community.

War raised other concerns in the Australian community, especially fears about the declining birth rate. Politicians and leaders appealed to women as mothers to increase the population: on their shoulders rested Australia's ability to protect itself from enemy attack and staunch the threatening flood of undesirable immigrants. Those advocating the selective breeding of only fit and healthy children reflected a similar kind of racism. Although such calls were not heeded by the white community, the policy of taking Aboriginal children from their families was maintained on the assumption that the Aboriginal race would thereby die out. Aboriginal mothers were actively discouraged from having children, and the legitimacy of those they did bear was seldom recognised by formal registration.

Despite the encouragement of white women to bear more children, the women themselves acted otherwise. With reliable birth control available, especially to middle-class women, they resisted further enslavement to domestic drudgery and relished the opportunity to record the reasons for their decisions. Women realised that despite the rhetoric, motherhood did not win much recognition or support. Dame Enid Lyons, the first woman elected to the House of Representatives, was also well aware of this and became a staunch advocate of motherhood. Along with others, she believed women's reluctance to bear more children stemmed from selfishness and the influence of advertisers: women were too preoccupied with what they looked like and with acquiring consumer items.

A partial solution to Australia's population problems was found in large-scale post-war migration policies. While men were desired for their labour, women were sought as childbearers and as restraining influences on their husbands. Many women followed their husbands out to Australia, or were married by proxy and arrived in Australia to meet a man they knew only from photographs. The separation from home, family and country was devastating, while the racism they encountered daily in the workplace, streets and hospitals, left many migrant women desperate and depressed. They turned to other women from their communities for support and understanding. Many returned to their own countries.

The end of the war did not bring an end to feminist agitation. The United Association of Women remained strong and active throughout the 1950s, especially in campaigns for equal pay. The energy of the feminist movement, captured so well in the UAW song 'Wild, Wild Women', did, however, wane. A new generation of women were not convinced by the feminist analysis of their oppression. Marriage and the home enticed women of the 1950s with the promise of lasting happiness, and they increased both their marriage rates and their childbearing.

The suggestion that not all was well behind the romantic dream was recognised by the founders of the Marriage Guidance Council. The Council remained a strong supporter of the institution of marriage, but advocated more realistic expectations. The earlier feminist critique of marriage became lost in the familial discourse of the 1950s.

In individual homes, however, women were challenging the imperatives of heterosexuality and endless childbearing, Such challenges came in the form of lesbian relationships, or individual resistance to male violence and power. Abortion, though rarely spoken of during this time, remained for many women a necessary, though traumatic, means of limiting their offspring. Economic imperatives forced many women to terminate their pregnancies, and others were strongly advised to have their babies adopted to avoid the financial problems and social stigma of the 'unmarried mother'. It was a decision that brought profound grief to many women.

The 1960s marked a decade when women again began to organise collectively. The introduction of conscription in November 1964 sparked the founding of Save Our Sons, a group of mothers opposed to compulsory military service, especially for action overseas. As the movement grew, SOS's opposition to the Vietnam war became stronger and SOS became a significant part of the large anti-Vietnam war movement.

From their experiences in this movement and in New Left groups, a new generation of white women began again to assess the position of women in society and to understand that individual experience has a political dimension.

Document 3.1 'I expressed a desire . . . for a Yank'

World War II opened up many possibilities for women. Their entry into the services was greeted warmly by a government requiring their labour, but their active pursuit of sexual pleasure provoked fears of declining morality. Australian women responded readily to the presence of large numbers of American servicemen, who seemed better dressed, better paid and better mannered than Australian men. This excerpt from the 1942 diary of a 19-year-old woman studying at Melbourne Teachers' College captures the mood of experimentation, the importance of kissing in the dating ritual, and the willingness of the writer to 'seek, sample and enjoy', even if to her own cost.

EMERGENCE INTO FULL YOUTH

I expressed a desire to silly Jack P for a Yank boyfriend (Melb. & fact all Aust. is swarming with them—since Xmas—& I felt I'd missed life, not having even met one. Elsie & I spoke to some one night in the dark of Swanston St. but didn't pick them up as most girls do now) & he is one who takes up any remark or action, jokingly threatened to do so all afternoon, till he finally did bring into our party a lonely one he found. I was furious for a time, but calmed down & the four of us—Stanley Dyjak his name—ugly, big, quiet, studious & apparently sincere—from New Jersey—went to tea in town—then joined the Sunday night lovers throng who make Melb. a queer old wild place now. We sat & watched the Yarra from the Alexandra Gardens & following Jack's example Stan got romantic & kissed me once (I objected on principle, of course). Gosh, two bench episodes in a week end—when the only other time I gave in as far as that to Doug—usually I walked slowly & steadfastly almost all the time! Stan came home with me, took my address & promised to ring that week. There, I had 2 possibilities. Would they eventuate? . . . Thurs. arrived—Patricia working busily in Study about 1/4 past 8 was informed of a visitor outside—'Twas Stan at the ungodly hour wanting me to go out. I felt reckless . . . We went to Capitol, got in in time to see the last picture Dive Bomber, had supper & managed to get back just after 1/2 past 11. Promised to go out with him somewhere on Sunday. That was a success! Next evening . . . heard yells of telephone! from below—thinking—Stan! I rushed down, to be met outside S. C. Office by Jack, who startled me, by asking would I come, there and then to pictures at the Union Theatre—University! What could I do—I said yes, rushed upstairs . . . lost my nerve—sat down—got up, went in to Marg next door, told the tale—asked her to pretend another call came (silly of me) & when she did so, bolted down leaving a bewildered Crossie & girls. Was ready & away without leave, without scruples in 5 mins. Did not enjoy the programme, but the company—yes! we strolled again in Uni. grounds, sat again, & this time Jack finally kissed me—then apparently remembered he should not have—and we rose & went home. He weakened again at the last moment & we laughed over my playful rebuke. But I did enjoy it! More than Doug's technique—more experience I suppose . . .

Will this tale ever end.

[After a day's outing to Macedon] and returning at 9 o'clock, I actually let myself in for another walk with Jack—just a brisk walk of less than an hour round good old Uni—but what an interesting, satisfying evening. I held off a little from him—feeling that I didn't want to get too keen on him. Instead we had most intriguing talks about 'Bouverooing' the practice of boys last year, of following couples each Sun. evening—somehow connected mysteriously—no-one will tell how or why with a certain disreputable Bouverie St. near here—I found that although I had never been in Love—Jack had many times—with all sorts of things: Music, Poetry, Clouds, the Country— . . . I glowed to think how well we could get on. We discussed religion & such deep things freely while my hand was held & occasionally kissed. But when he kissed me, in fact apparently when I spoke of never having been in love, so emphatically I made a mistake—I said we'd better go in because I didn't quite understand what he meant by that kiss. As we parted on the door step, Jack said some quite strange things about the rut we humans get into— only one in a million get above his environment—all as much, so much the same. Then he kissed me gently & went. I was elated by the evening & stimulated, thought—all's O.K.—I'm not in love but I have found a very nice romantic friend, as I call them. I looked forward to the Ball on the Friday. But something happened—I'm not being dramatic. That week Jack scarcely came around the College & when he mentioned the Ball said didn't think he'd take a woman because couldn't eat as much as he liked at supper & other hooey.

On the Wednes.—I, very puzzled by the definite change . . . asked Elsie what she thought had changed him. With diffidence, she told me this. Her opinion was that J. wasn't quite as good as he tried to make out—that when he was with me, he was as I was but the effort to be always like that was too much, he turned to other types of girls. I strangely enough couldn't either verify of deny this charge, for nothing he had said pointed that way. I decided however, to go to the Ball alone & just 'lay low & see'. It was hard to take the teases of the girls when I swore I wasn't going with any-one—they, by this time were quite convinced that we were a twosome. The Ball was a great success—but emotionally a failure. Jack arrived, danced twice with me & devoted rest of time to Kathleen Davies & Bruce Miles, Jack's friend, took me to supper—I had every dance—but went home alone. Jack apparently was still quite friendly but definitely shearing off. That evening (Sat.) I promised Stan I would go out (rang Thurs) but there was another blow—he didn't turn up so I tortured myself by going to a mystery night at Palais with Elsie & confirmed my earlier fears. I said I didn't care, but was just hurt in my pride, which was partly true—I had lost a good deal of self confidence that week-end. Poor old Else was quite convinced my heart was broken— but occasionally I still doubt whether I have one or not. Jack's affair was resolutely declared also closed for the following week & Stan, a complete wipe-off—I thought my judgement of people must be punk. Until this day I have heard nothing directly from Stan but Elsie's Jack—now back in uniform, declares he saw him during the hols. Stan said he was going up North—everyone goes up North—to Wyndham & casually enquired

'How's the little blond at the School?'—No further remarks needed. Anyway I can tell my Grandchildren at least that during those momentous days when Aust. was rapidly accumulating thousands upon thousands of Yanks, when Melb. went bad, & every girl discussed her 'pick-ups' I too had a little experience.

The Yanks are rather nice though, as a whole, either very talkative & extremely quaint humoured—frank—or quiet uncommunicative slow chaps. We were surprised at how slow so many are—lazy of speech & movements & rather well fed looking—& the variety of uniform & race! One thing I have noticed the high standard of Education & the great interest in such matters—you'd never get an Aussie to discuss school etc.

Is it worthwhile? this hooey one goes through when young. Men seem to think so. At least I understand why it is written about so much it's true—as I never believed before, and so prevalent. Human kind just continually suffering from a Grand attack of Imaginitis over one branch of its life. I read a Psychology book this year with some rather startling ideas on Sex.—Sacrifice to Attis it was called, in reference to the anti-sexual rites performed to the god Attis in ancient days. It said that in no other animal does sex occupy such a large part of time & interest—our entertainment, clothes, etc. centre round it, yet it is repressed & thwarted, disguised & dished up as other things. From something comparatively simple it has became one of the greatest problems, especially for young people. Everything is calculated to inflame them, but the thing is forbidden them. I could not imagine it being any other way. The last chapter was call 'Liberty—or Extermination?' I cannot give any opinion on this yet—it hasn't touched me enough.

Document 3.2 'Homely metaphors of the kitchen'

Dame Enid Lyons, the first woman in Federal Parliament, was elected to the House of Representatives in 1943. Lyons recognised the import-ance of having women in Parliament and stressed the need to keep the affairs of the home in public view. In her maiden speech she discussed the complex ties between nationhood, citizenship and family life, a theme she maintained throughout her public career. As a mother of eleven children she believed she spoke with authority on the subject of maternity and the needs of mothers.

Dame ENID LYONS (Darwin)—It would be strange indeed were I not to-night deeply conscious of the fact, if not a little awed by the knowledge, that on my shoulders rests a great weight of responsibility; because this is the first occasion upon which a woman has addressed this House. For that reason, it is an occasion which, for every woman in the Commonwealth, marks in some degree a turning point in history. I am well aware that, as I acquit myself in the work that I have undertaken for the next three years, so shall I either prejudice or enhance the prospects of those women who may wish to follow me in public service in the years to come. I know that many honorable members have viewed the advent of women to the legislative halls with something approaching alarm; they have feared, I have no doubt, the somewhat too vigorous use of a new broom. I wish to reassure them. I hold very sound views on brooms, and sweeping. Although I quite realize that a new broom is a very useful adjunct to the work of the housewife, I also know that it undoubtedly is very unpopular in the broom cupboard; and this particular new broom knows that she has a very great deal to learn from the occupants of—I dare not say this particular cupboard. At all events, she hopes to conduct herself with sufficient modesty and sufficient sense of her lack of knowledge at least to earn the desire of honorable members to give her whatever help they may be able to give. I believe, very sincerely, that any woman entering the public arena must be prepared to work as men work; she must justify herself not as a woman, but as a citizen; she must attack the same problems, and be prepared to shoulder the same burdens. But because I am a woman, and cannot divest myself of those qualities that are inherent in my sex, and because every one of us speaks broadly in the terms of one's own experience, honorable members will have to become accustomed to the application of the homely metaphors of the kitchen rather than those of the operating theatre, the workshop, or the farm. They must also become accustomed to the application to all kinds of measures of the touchstone of their effect upon the home and the family life. I hope that no one will imagine that that implies in any way a limitation of my political interests. Rather, it implies an ever-widening outlook on every problem that faces the world to-day. Every subject, from high finance to international relations, from social security to the winning of the war, touches very closely the home and the family. The late King George V, as he neared the end of a great reign and a good life, made a statement upon which any one may base the whole of one's political philosophy, when he said, 'The foundation of a nation's greatness is in the homes of its people'. Therefore, honorable members will not, I know, be surprised when I say that I am likely to be even more concerned with national character than with national effort . . .

I have been delighted, since I came here, to find the almost unanimity that exists in respect of the need for social service and in respect of many of the other problems that have been discussed in this chamber. In the matter of social security one thing stands out clearly in my mind. Such things are necessary in order that the weak shall not go to the wall, that the strong may be supported, that all may have justice. But we must never so blanket ourselves that those fine national qualities of which I have spoken shall no longer have play. I know so well that fear, want and idleness can kill the spirit of any people. But I know, too, that security can be bought at too great a cost—the cost of spiritual freedom. How, then, may we strike a balance? That, it seems to me, is the big question for us to decide to-day. There is one answer. We know perfectly well that any system of social security devised to-day must be financed largely from general taxation. Yet I would insist that every person in the community in receipt of any income whatsoever must make some contribution to the fund for social security. I want it to be an act of conscious citizenship. I want every child to be taught that when he begins to earn, then, for the first time, he will have the first privilege and right of citizenship—to begin to contribute to the great scheme that has been designed to serve him when he is no longer able to work and to help all of those who at any period of their lives may meet with distress or trouble. In such a scheme, I believe, there should be pensions for all; there should be no means test; those who have should contribute according to their means. But every one, however little he or she earns, should contribute something, be it only a three-penny stamp, as a sort of token payment for the advantage of Australian citizenship. In passing, let me say this: There is one reform, at least, that could be applied to our present pensions system, which would have the greatest effect in making a little brighter the lives of those upon whom the years are already closing in. I consider that every pensioner should have his or her pension posted to him or her in the form of a cheque. At the present time any pensioner who so wishes has the right to have the pension sent in that way, but few pensioners are aware of it. If that were done, I believe that not only would congestion in post offices be relieved, but also that a small contribution would be made to easing the burden of those who have come to old age or illness.

I am delighted that the honorable member for Denison [Dr. Gaha] should have secured the honour of having introduced to this chamber, in this debate, the subject of population. Other members also have seized upon that subject, apparently with a very great deal of pleasure, and have dealt with it at some length; but to the honorable member for Denison go the honours. I, like him, have pondered on this subject—not with my feet upon the mantle-piece, but knee-deep in shawls and feeding bottles. I have pondered it, surrounded by those who, by their very numbers, have done quite a good deal to boost the population of Australia. I believe that I have at least tried out some of the theories which would make for a better population, and that I know some of the difficulties that present themselves to any person who, in these days, desires to rear a family. One honorable member has spoken of the need for a greater population for reasons of defence. That, of course, is something that has to be considered. But there has also to be considered the fact that, unless we fill this country we shall have no justification in the years that are ahead for holding it at all.

I consider that something more than decentralization is necessary if the population of Australia is to be increased. It would be well to go back a little while and look for the reasons for the decline of population during the last 50 or 60 years. Two main reasons are ascribed, the first the growth of industrialism and the changed conditions resulting therefrom. Population became urban instead of rural, and the conditions in which children were brought up became less and less suitable. People were crowded. Housing was inadequate, and the large families went to the wall. The incidence of disease increased, and industrial disease came with the development of new occupations. The workers were unmercifully exploited. State paternalism became necessary, and even in State paternalism certain reasons for the decline of family life can be found. At the other end of the social scale other reasons can be found for the declining birth-rate. New inventions, and the provision of luxuries, provided new ways of spending incomes and leisure. There was less domestic help to be had. Finally, people began to think that the woman who became the mother of a family was something of a lunatic. About 30 years later she began to be regarded as something of a criminal lunatic. In the end the belief developed that it was a social virtue to produce fewer and fewer children. Where such a state of affairs exists, it is a matter of courage, even of hardihood, to have a family of more than two or three.

Still another reason for the declining birth-rate is sometimes advanced, a reason belonging to the moral rather than to the economic sphere. It is to be found in that strange reluctance to reproduce themselves that has overtaken the peoples of the past in the final years of their decline. That is a picture which none of us cares to contemplate. I agree with the honorable member for Denison that we cannot hope, merely by economic measures, to increase the birth-rate. Certain things are necessary to be done in order to ease the burden on families, but they must be looked upon only as measures of justice to those who are prepared to face their responsibilities. We need maternity and nursing services; we need some kind of domestic help service; we need better houses. But those things cannot in themselves revive the falling birth-rate. We must look to the basic wage, which at present provides for the needs of three children for every man who receives it; yet how many thousands of men in this country have no children at all? How many have fewer than three—yet the three notional children of the man who has not any militate against the success in life of the children in other families of six and seven and eight. The basic wage is meagre enough in all conscience—too meagre—but it should be estimated upon the needs of a man and his wife, or of a man who must provide later for a wife, and the children should be provided for by an extension of the child endowment system. Let the man's wages be a direct charge upon industry, but the children should be a charge on the whole community. If we hope to increase the birth-rate we must look to a resurgence of the national spirit, a resurgence of national vitality. We must look to a new concept of the dignity and worth of the family in the social order. I agree with Paul Bureau that the family is the matrix of humanity, the secret laboratory in which every unit of human society is prepared, organized and maintained, and if that laboratory is disorganized or chaotic, the most serious disorders in social life must be expected.

29 September 1943
Commonwealth of Australia Parliamentary Debates,
vol. 176, v, pp. 182–4

Document 3.3 Debuts in Canberra

The Parliamentary debuts of Dame Enid Lyons and Dorothy Tangney provoked much comment. While Senator Tangney made a point of denouncing feminism, the attention the press gave to the dress and 'quiet' demeanour of the two women indicates how readily their parliamentary talents were deemed secondary to their gender. The femininity of both politicians apparently had to be reasserted in their entry to political life.

AUSTRALIA'S FIRST WOMAN SENATOR

It seems fairly certain that Miss Dorothy Tangney, who was the selected member of the Labour Senate team for Western Australia, will be elected. In that case she will be the first woman Senator in Australia. Miss Tangney is a teacher by profession and in her early thirties. She worked her way through school and Perth University on scholarships and is described as a woman of great energy, very friendly and a good mixer. Her father is an engine driver on the State Engineering Works, Perth; one of her brothers is in the R.A.A.F. and another brother in the A.I.F.

When interviewed by our Perth representative, a few days ago, Miss Tangney declared that she was not a feminist and did not believe that women would re-make this world of ours in a hurry, but should co-operate with the men in re-shaping it. She has all the makings of a sound legislator, and her first appearance in the Senate will be an interesting event.

British Australian and New Zealander 4 September 1943

DEBUTS AT CANBERRA

Senator Tangney; Dame Enid

Canberra, Sept. 23—With the historic advent of Dame Enid Lyons as Australia's first woman member of the House of Representatives and Miss Dorothy Tangney as the first woman Senator the official opening of the 17th Federal Parliament today was of special interest to women whose numbers and smart frocking heightened the colourful spectacle.

For the swearing-in ceremony in the House of Representatives Dame Enid Lyons took her seat beside Sir Earle Page in the position usually occupied in the last Parliament by Mr R.G. Menzies, then merely a back-bencher. Dame Enid took the oath on the Bible formerly used by her late husband. She wore a short-sleeved, tailored black frock and a wide-brimmed, black velour hat. Her frock was relieved at the neckline with a lace collar. Quiet and unobtrusive in all her movements, Dame Enid received the good wishes of all. She repeated the oath of office in a very strong voice and perhaps received most applause of all the new members.

Miss Dorothy Margaret Tangney was warmly welcomed by the Senate. Senators came over to her seat, next to Senator Aylett (Tas), to be introduced by a fellow-West Australian, Senator Clothier. She wore a deep blue frock with short puffed sleeves and a gored skirt. Her suede shoes were in a matching blue and she was hatless, her curly fair hair parted at the side in a short shingle.

Senator Tangney showed a little nervousness as she waited her turn to be sworn in, clasping and unclasping her hands, but she took the oath in a firm, clear tone while her parents proudly looked on. She made her maiden speech when she spoke to the motion of condolence for the late Senator Cunningham, former President of the Senate. Her voice was husky with influenza but at this stage she did not betray the nervousness to which she later confessed. Many women rushed to congratulate her as she left the Senate. She said she had been greatly impressed by her first day in Parliament. Tomorrow Senator Tangney will move the Address-in-Reply.

British Australian and New Zealander 24 September 1943

Document 3.4 'Rights earned and abilities proven'

In 1943, in the midst of war, 90 women's organisations gathered to draw up the Australian Women's Charter. Calls for anti-discrimination legislation, child care and racial equality heralded many of the concerns that emerged with women's liberation in the 1970s. The Charter also addressed many of the issues that had concerned feminists for decades: equal pay, economic independence for mothers and the double moral standard. Calls for land, education, health care, economic independence and wage equity for Aborigines suggest a sensitivity to the effect of systemic racism on Australia's indigenous population. The final resolution, made in recognition of the persecution of the Jews, indicates how early and widespread was the knowledge of Hitler's barbarism.

AUSTRALIAN WOMEN'S CHARTER 1943

(1) Woman in war and peace

This Australian Women's Conference, representing every State and 90 organisations in the Commonwealth, called after four years of war, affirms its unshakeable belief that the hopes of all women for a world in which justice and liberty and equality will exist depends entirely upon winning the war and eradicating Fascism in any form in every country.

Therefore, this Conference calls upon every woman to take her full share in the war effort by either enlisting in the defence forces, undertaking work on the land or in industry, or enrolling as a voluntary worker, and by subscribing to war loans.

This Conference further affirms its belief that if we are to win the peace it is necessary to plan for peace while carrying on the war, and while noting with satisfaction the action of the Government in creating a Ministry of Reconstruction, exhorts the Government to make fuller use of the vision, enthusiasm, practical wisdom and capabilities of women in the planning of reconstruction.

(2) Woman in public life

The Australian Women's Conference affirms its belief that women have a special contribution to make in public life, as citizens of a democratic community, and in order that their capabilities may be developed and utilised for the national good.

We recommend that

(a) every encouragement should be given to women to stand as candidates for all elected legislative bodies;

(b) women be appointed in adequate numbers to national and international conferences, diplomatic posts, to administrative positions of authority and responsibility, and on boards, commissions, etc.

(3) Women at the Peace Conference

Whereas in every country women have taken a full share in their country's struggle to win the war, and in all the war centres shared the dangers and privations of war and have shown courage, resource and endurance.

This Australian Women's Conference affirms its belief that women have earned the right and proven themselves capable to take an active and comprehensive part in every aspect of the making of peace and the subsequent planning and control which will be necessary to win lasting peace.

We declare that qualified Australian women with full status as delegates should be included in sufficient numbers to participate effectively in the delegation attending the peace settlement as representatives of the Australian people . . .

(5) Equal rights legislation

Whereas past history and contemporary conditions demonstrate that many laws, regulations and statements purporting to confer rights, status and opportunity on all people are, in fact, only applied to male persons;

We request the Commonwealth Government to introduce a Blanket Bill, designed to abolish sex discrimination and to establish and maintain equality for all citizens without distinctions based on sex, and to provide that any sex discriminations embodied in any laws or regulations be invalid;

We further request the Commonwealth Government that when the Referendum is held for the amendment to the Constitution an amendment shall be submitted to provide that women shall be entitled to equal rights, status and opportunity with men, and to provide that any sex discrimination embodied in any laws or regulations be invalid . . .

(7) Employment of women, wage earners and professional women

We believe that the standard of living of the whole community is threatened, and animosity between men and women wage-earners is engendered by cheap female labour within the community.

We believe that experience has shown that whenever women have been given the opportunity to do work previously performed by men in the professions, in the Public Service, in industry, etc., they have proved themselves capable of measuring up to the established standards.

We recommend that
(a) there should be no sex discrimination limiting the opportunities
     for women, and that they should be given equal pay, equal status,
     equal opportunity and equal responsibility with men in all
     appointments and spheres of employment:
(b) all restrictions be abolished on the right of women to work [i] at
     night, [ii] in any specific occupation, [iii] at any particular period,
     and [iv] when they marry;
(c) in all laws and awards, adult female labour should be classified
     with adult labour instead of being classified with the labour of
     young persons;
(d) all sex discrimination in the Public Service be eliminated and the
     principle established throughout the Public Service of equal pay
     and equal opportunity for men and women;
(e) the Government eliminate in its plans for training for post-war
     employment the sex discrimination introduced by fixing lower
     rates of sustenance allowance for women than men, and give to
     men and women the same rates of sustenance allowance;
(f) canteen services be provided in all industrial establishments
     where the number of employees is in excess of 250;
(g) provision be made for domestic workers in private homes to
     obtain an award governing their wages and conditions . . .

(13) Woman as mother and/or home-maker

We believe the indispensable service rendered to the community by
mothers, accompanied as it is by inevitable and specific handicaps, and
responsibilities, demands special consideration and provision;

We further believe that economic independence strengthens character
and develops a greater sense of responsibility, whereas dependent economic status denies liberty and opportunity and justice to the individual.

In order to alleviate these disabilities, we recommend that
(a) the mother and/or home-maker be remunerated for her work in
     the home by a personal endowment of a minimum of 30/- a week,
     operated on the same principle as child endowment;
(b) the existing system of Child Endowment apply to all dependent
     children in a family and be increased to an adequate sum . . .

(18) Child care

As experience has shown that the mental and physical well-being of
children is developed, and delinquency prevented by the existence of day
nursery and nursery schools and supervised playground facilities,

We recommend the Commonwealth Government to

(a) establish a National Children's Bureau with Headquarters at Canberra, under the aegis of either the Department of Reconstruction, of Health, or of Social Services to

    (i) formulate a National Programme for promoting the welfare of children;

    (ii) assemble information from scientific sources;

    (iii) interpret this information for the public;

    (iv) disseminate this information throughout the Commonwealth;

    (v) educate systematically public opinion in the best standards of child care;

(b) subsidise a national scheme for the establishment of a network of child centres wherever needed and provide that Education Departments, local Councils and elected citizens' bodies in each State co-operate in the development and administration of these Centres in order to develop local interest and effort to the maximum . . .

(21) Moral standards

Whereas the experiences of many countries over the last 100 years has demonstrated that the regulation of prostitution encourages vice, stimulates the white slave traffic, creates a false sense of security from venereal infection, and imposes cruel injustice and humiliation upon the women concerned while allowing men to go free; and

Whereas the economic inequality of women tends to lower their dignity and status;

Therefore we declare our unswerving opposition to the licensing of vice by the registration of prostitution, registration of brothels, or any other form of regulation, including the compulsory examination and detention of women on suspicion, and

We recommend

(a) an equal moral standard for men and women;

(b) a widespread publicity campaign on (i) the need for early treatment of sufferers from venereal disease; (ii) the causes of venereal disease such as promiscuous sex relations, ignorance about sex matters, bad housing, economic insecurity, the existence of undesirable places of amusement, abuse of the use and sale of alcohol, etc.;

(c) that sufferers from venereal disease be under the supervision of officers of the Health Department, assisted by social workers and almoners, instead of the Police Department;

(d) the provision of adequate facilities for the free and secret treatment of venereal disease;

(e) the adoption of scientific methods for the rehabilitation of girls and women who have contracted promiscuous habits;

(f) the education of children in the laws of reproduction through the scientific approach of botany and biology, leading up to education of adolescents in the emotional and ethical aspects of sex relations and the significance and responsibilities of family life;

(g) that men partners in immorality and patrons of prostitutions be regarded as equally guilty of an offence under the law;

(h) that ample facilities for healthy recreation be provided;

(i) that the sale of liquor be strictly controlled;

(j) the prohibition of the publication or distribution of literature calculated to stimulate crime, sexual laxity and other anti-social behaviour.

(24) Aborigines

This Conference deplores the continued neglect of the native race and demands immediate measures by the Federal Governments to arrest the process of extinction and to provide the Aborigines with all the means for a secure and prosperous life. These immediate measures to include the following:

(a) Federal control over all questions concerning the welfare of the Aborigines;

(b) Tribal Aborigines to be given reserves; such native reserves to be inviolable, the land and natural resources to be the property of the Aborigines;

(c) adequate medical services to be provided for the Aborigines throughout Australia;

(d) no contact with the natives in the reserves to be permitted except by members of the Medical Services and other specially qualified persons responsible to the Government;

(e) the potential equality of the Aboriginal Race be recognised; education be directed to preparation for full citizenship rights and responsibilities, including technical and other training and the opportunity to use this training;

(f) the term Australian Aboriginal be interpreted in the law to mean full blood Australian Aboriginal;

(g) suitable advisers be appointed to assist in the gradual economic development of the Aborigines. Native enterprises to be developed on a co-operative basis;

(h) the abolition of the system of employment by license; the aboriginal worker to be entitled to receive the full amount of his or her wages as a legal right;

(i) that women be urged to use their influence to eliminate colour prejudice from the social life of the nation.

RACIAL PERSECUTION

In view of the urgent need for immediate action to be taken to rescue the Jewish race from the systematic massacre being perpetrated by the Nazis in Europe, the following special resolution was passed at the Australian Women's Conference:

Realising that the Jewish people were the first victims of Hitler's barbarism; that already over 4 000 000 Jewish men, women and children have been massacred; and that the Jewish people alone have been selected by the Nazis for complete annihilation [we] Australian women, in conference assembled, urge that in accordance with uprooted European Jewry's desperate need, relief and rehabilitation be provided, and equal status restored to them by the United Nations at the earliest moment possible.

Further, we urge, in the name of justice and mercy, that those who can escape shall be provided with opportunity for migration and settlement in Palestine and elsewhere, and that the Australian Government be asked to approach the authorities concerned to further these purposes.

Document 3.5 Wild, wild women

The time, energy and commitment that hundreds of women devoted to campaigning for women's rights is captured in this United Associations of Women song.

WILD, WILD WOMEN

1.   Once I was happy and was a good wife,
        I joined the United to learn about life,
        I met with a gal and she said 'Come with me,
        We'll work day and night to gain equality.'

Chorus Jessie Street and meetings and wild, wild Women,
        They drive you crazy, they drive you insane,
        Market Street and Charters and wild, wild, women,
        You get nicely finished, then start off again.

2.   To sit on a jury we'd very much like,
        So asked Mr Martin to make it alright,

He said that a seat on a jury he'd find,
But we'd first need a seat of a different kind.

Chorus Ministers and meetings and wild, wild women,
They drive you crazy, they drive you insane,
Deputations, minutes and wild, wild women,
In Melbourne or Canberra, it's all the same.

3. Now I am feeble and broken with age,
The lines on my face make a well written page,
I'm leaving this story so sad but so true,
On what the United can do unto you.

Chorus Market Street and meetings and wild, wild women,
They drive you crazy, they drive you insane,
Ministers and Charters and wild, wild women,
You find that you get equal pay on the brain.

4. Write on the cross at the head of my grave,
For women I worked like a so and so slave,
Take warning dear stranger, take warning dear friend,
Then write in big letters those words at the end.

Chorus Jessie Street and meetings and wild, wild women,
They drive you crazy, they drive you insane,
Conferences, minutes and wild, wild women,
(*Slowly*) If we come back on earth guess we'd do it again.

Document 3.6 Population unlimited

The widespread concern over Australia's declining birthrate indicates how successfully women were controlling their fertility. Politicians and planners urged women to have more children and put the nation's interests above their own. In this radio broadcast four public figures discuss the reasons for the declining birthrate and the moral and social impact of widespread birth control.

Dame Enid Lyons:
Mr Chairman, Ladies and Gentlemen. The guilty secret is sure to come out, so perhaps I had better mention it now. I am the mother of eleven children, and I feel that I am under a very grave handicap in entering on this discussion.

Now, the first thing I wish to ask you to agree on this—that the most important person to be considered in such a community is the mother.

(Applause.) To assist the mother in every possible way we shall agree is one of the things that is necessary for any civilised community, and so we will say that all the care that can possibly be given to mothers is something that this country has got to give as a measure of justice to its women, who are going to do their duty to the nation by producing families . . .

There is one other point of importance which I think women find to be a great deterrent to having many children. That is our standard to-day of feminine beauty. Who are the people who decorate the magazine covers? The ladies of three husbands and no children—(laughter)—or at the best, two husbands and one child. It is not good enough. Who are those whose beauty to-day is extolled? Those who have kept the extreme slimness and suppleness of early youth. And really there is no beauty greater than that soft roundness of a young matron, and yet we cast it aside and regard it as nothing. I want to see the magazines refusing articles that exalt sex as an end in itself, and regard the child as being after all of not very great importance. In any event it appears to me to have a very great deal of bearing on the point. The Greeks laid very great stress on physical beauty and physical perfection. We are going to the same extreme, and we feel that unless a child is 100% perfect it is better for it not to be born. But how much of the world's work is done by people who have false teeth and flat feet? Mr. Churchill is distinctly over-weight, and Mr. Roosevelt, I believe, has suffered from infantile paralysis. I tell you this, that caution, if it is urged upon parents to let us bring only children who are 100% fit into the world, is not the only thing to be considered. It was not caution that inspired Mr. Churchill at Dunkirk or when he asked the people of England for their blood and tears and sweat. It was not caution that moved Joad when he said that we were losing our instinct for paternity because we had found a means to frustrate it without denying ourselves the pleasures of sex.

Dr Norman Haire [sexologist]:
Limitation of population wisely applied is a social necessity in every society no matter what the economic set-up may be, but of course, like everything else, it may be applied unwisely to the detriment of the community. We are all, I suppose, agreed that Australia needs to increase its population, but to suggest that the increase should be unlimited and uncontrolled seems to me very stupid. Any country which was to set out to attract physically or mentally inferior migrants from overseas—syphilitics or lepers or lunatics or epileptics, or migrants otherwise unlikely to be successful citizens, would be regarded as very short-sighted and foolish.

It is just as important to choose suitable migrants from the womb as it is to choose suitable migrants from overseas. It is not only the quantity of births that matters. We must also consider the quality of the children born, and the likelihood of their growing up as healthy, happy and useful citizens. The idea of mere life as life is not to be worshipped blindly. A maggot is not as valuable as a cow, nor a poisonous snake as an edible eel, nor a physically or mentally defective child as a healthy one. It is obviously stupid to offer the same baby bonus to parents of bad stock to provide us with healthy children. The same is true, of course, of income tax rebates and other inducements to parenthood. We should be as careful to dissuade parents of bad stock from producing children who are likely to be a burden on the community as we are to induce parents of good stock to provide healthy children who are likely to be an asset to it. And now I should like to make a suggestion. I suggest that the Government should immediately offer a No-Baby Bonus for parents of bad stock, while the present baby bonus should be restricted to healthy and otherwise desirable parents . . . It is not the number of children born that is important but the number which survive to become healthy, happy and useful adults and to produce children in their turn . . .

It is our business to improve social conditions so that parents will not be deterred from having children by any difficulties such as inadequate housing, lack of domestic help, or feeling generally insecure. All potential parents should be instructed in the way to have these children born under the best conditions. Where contraceptives are easily available, abortion becomes infrequent. If these facilities are denied, abortion flourishes. Facilities should be provided for the surgical sterilisation at their own wish of parents of bad stock, or of mothers whose health makes pregnancy always a danger to them. Thousands of married couples long for children, but are sterile. Often this is the result of venereal disease. Often it is the result of illegal operations, abortions, and of course it may be due to other causes. Facilities should be provided for the investigation of all cases of infertility, so that the cause may be determined and proper treatment instituted for each individual case.

Mr Colin Clark [Director of Bureau of Industry, Qld]:
The natural sexual love between men and women and its natural consequence, the bearing of children, is one of the finest and most beautiful things on this earth, and that is why its perversion is so unnatural.

What Dr Haire described as contraception involves acts which are filthy, vicious and disgusting. They constitute one of the worst forms of sexual immorality. The practice being so widespread does not make it any more moral; rather the reverse, and I think we look pretty foolish when we stand round solemnly and learnedly discussing whether people should commit such acts or not. The only moral act by which the births may be restricted is partial or complete abstinence . . .

When people say 'We cannot afford to have more children,' it does not mean that they are short of the necessities of life, but that they cannot have any more children and keep up the comforts to which they have become accustomed.

Although many people are in different ways responsible for this state of affairs, I want to place particular blame on the advertisers, and the advertising profession who have made it their vocation to persuade people to try to buy things they would never have thought of it left to themselves; persuaded them to buy all this stuff which they do not really want, and generally the family suffers. Advertisers make profit at the expense of the security of married life and at the expense of the nation's future. Then, several stages worse, we have commercial interests who make profits out of the direct exploitation of the sexual instincts, publishing indecent books, periodicals and pictures; also the producers of contraceptives and traffickers in abortion who have built up a definite vested interest in sexual vice.

In conclusion, let me say that unless there is a radical change in our attitude towards children, this will not be our country very much longer. At best we are going to be partially submerged under a flood of uninvited immigrants, but more probably the country will be taken over from us by violence. However sympathetic other white countries may be towards us, they will not permanently be willing to incur the danger and expense of warding off potential attackers against the country which we ourselves are making no attempt fully to utilise.

Mrs. Jessie Street:
Mr. Chairman, Ladies and Gentlemen and Listeners—When we remember the sacrifices that a woman is called on to make when she becomes a mother, and the burdens and responsibilities of fatherhood, we must marvel that there are so many who face parenthood as willingly as they do. It is a triumph of instinct over all obstacles and handicaps, and it is just because the desire for parenthood is such a strong instinct that we can hope to increase the birthrate by removing many of the difficulties and handicaps with which it is at present surrounded.

Although civilisation and large cities have brought many benefits, they have complicated life considerably and many of the burdens of civilisation fall upon mothers. Take the present standards of cleanliness alone. They entail a tremendous amount of washing children and clothes and cleaning homes. The variety of foods we now consume needs frequent and expert preparation, upon which much time and energy is expended. Food must also be purchased and transported from the shop to the home.

The very admirable but at the same time very recent development of independent homes for all married couples also makes a lot of extra work for the wife and mother. She must do her own shopping, cooking, housework and laundry work. She must stay at home to look after the child or children, or take them with her wherever she goes, whether it be shopping, visiting, the pictures or anywhere.

When people lived in communities many of the children were looked after by some of the older women. The strain and responsibility on mothers was not as constant or varied as under present conditions. Glorifying motherhood has brought about the result of doubling the birth rate in the Soviet Union, and there is reason to believe that a similar approach in Australia would have a similar effect. Anyway, I believe there would be no harm in trying it.

'Population Unlimited?'
The Nation's Forum of the Air, vol. 1, no. 2
Australian Broadcasting Commission
23 August 1944

Document 3.7 'I found more satisfaction and happiness than I ever thought possible'

The protestations of politicians did little to entice women into repeated childbearing. Dr Wallace was a Melbourne doctor who provided many women with their first reliable method of birth control in the form of diaphragms such as 'dutch caps'. This letter to him gives a very personal insight into how much birth control meant to one woman. Freed from the terror of repeated childbirth—or abortions—she was able to enjoy sex in ways she had 'never dreamed of'.

West Brunswick, 12 October 1943

Dear Dr Wallace,
Re your letter of the 4th inst. I am only too willing to help you in your research work. First let me say I have found your method more than satisfactory. It must be about three years now and I have not had a moment of anxiety and can honestly say that it has taught me more happiness than I have ever dreamed of. I'm sure my whole life would have been different if I had known about this when I was first married. Can I give you an

account of my married life? It has been a mystery to me and perhaps you can account for my reactions. I married and had my baby after a few months. Very sick for the first five months and a forced birth, leaving my womb open and protruding. I just lived in fear from then on. When my daughter was seven months I became pregnant again. I was terrified and finally had a 'miscarriage' by means of a syringe. A curette followed and later an operation to put my womb back. After that it was a nightmare and although my Husband was the most careful and understanding man, we just drifted apart sexually. Nothing he could do could revive any feelings and our life was very unnatural. I didn't want it to be, but couldn't help it. So he went his way and I went mine. We didn't blame each other. After many years of living more or less as 'Pals' he found someone else and strange to say I did. It was then I saw you as I was still too nervous about it. Think me immoral if you like, but I hope to marry him when he comes back from New Guinea. And that is the strangest thing that happened to me. I got confidence and so much happiness that even if I had become pregnant (under proper circumstances) I'd have loved it for love's sake and thought it worth it. My first start off in marriage was so different to what I expected that it killed what should have been the most wonderful thing in the world. And through no fault of my Husband, just lack of knowledge. If I make a success of my life later I have you to thank and even though I may and probably will not ever have more children as I am nearly forty, I found more satisfaction and happiness than I ever thought possible.

Wallace Collection, Letters re Contraception
University of Melbourne Archives

Document 3.8 A 'freemasonry' of women

When the National Health and Medical Research Council called on women in 1944 to give their reasons for limiting their offspring, they responded readily. The resulting NHMRC Report drew heavily on the letters received. Economic hardship was the reason most women gave for the use of birth control, but they also drew attention to the inadequacy of the child endowment, the basic male wage and the impossibility of domestic help. Many also cited the misery of their mothers' lives as a deterrent to having large families, along with the physical disabilities brought about by pregnancy and repeated child-bearing, and the expectations that they be 'good wives' to their husbands.

'Your invitation to young married women to give you a reason why they will have no children. I have one child, a boy two years, and that's all I intend to have. My mother reared a family of fourteen children, ten of us and four orphans of her sister's. Father worked long and hard, and will I ever forget 1930–33. We were half starved. Father tried everywhere to get work; there was sixteen of us had to live on 25s. per week. My parents were honest, law-abiding citizens; they were pushed around and looked down on, and had to watch their children go hungry, barefooted and ill-clad to school every morning. Was enough to break any woman's heart. All us boys and girls of our family resolved we would not bring any children into this world above two. Until we get in power in Australia a human and competent government, that is my answer. Give young people security, and you won't have to rave about babies. There will be plenty, when the Government desires to keep the food for the people who produce it and pay for it, instead of destroying it and wasting it. The Government has the remedy; don't blame the young mother.'

'I have nine children and consider myself the greatest advertisement for birth control. I advise all my young friends not to have babies. Give the mothers somewhere to bring their babies, homes to clean and be proud of, with large rooms and verandahs, rent in proportion to income, give them homes that the children can bring their friends to, and you will restore the beauty of home life and our falling birth-rate. I think Australia is the greatest country in the world and the worst handled.'

'I heard over the wireless to-day that you wish to know why we women won't have children or only one or two. I have two children, I would hate to have any more, and I have no intention of having any more. I love my children and I feel I would like others and have lots of love to lavish on them but the drawbacks far overrule the so-called joys of motherhood because the average mother has to do everything for them and her husband, and in lots of cases also look after aged parents. Motherhood means giving up outings as by the time one is ready to go out, finished the house-work and dressed and bathed the children, &c., I feel too tired to go out, but have to drag out to do the daily shopping and come home laden like a pack-horse with parcels, dump the parcels, then rush round and get tea and wash the children ready for tea and bed after, to the accompaniment of fights among the children, &c., then, tea over, washing up, wiping up, and a spot of darning, &c., then bed, feeling as if you could only fall into bed and sleep, but have to be a good wife to husband, wishing one could sleep, instead of having to worry, then perhaps to sleep if you are lucky enough not to be disturbed by child awake or crying with tooth-ache, &c., or some other thing; when morning comes too soon, six o'clock up to the grind again, wondering how the weekly wage will cover wood this week and if the woodman can bring it, with other worries of someone wanting new clothes and only rubbish to buy that looks alright but has no lasting quality; no amount of screwing can run to a holiday as the fares for husband, wife and two children are too much, so think to myself how on earth could we have holidays or go to the pictures now and again, as each child means another 1s. 3d. each time for pictures, or another fare for holidays; more children mean more bed clothes, blankets, sheets, and every other thing with a house with two bedrooms, all the children in one bedroom, or the boys outside and girls in only other bedroom. The present way of running things will never be any better until a woman is allowed to have the advising of those in charge of things—some one who knows just what it is like to have them and look after them. It is just unpaid drudgery, never ever getting a day off, or never having a penny to spare because there is a use for every penny, so why increase the drudgery by having more children; every one extra means more years spent in rearing them, being overtired all the time generally makes the husband wish to go out instead of staying home watching you work after tea, you wish sometimes when you aren't so tired you could go out too, then you know you can't as you wouldn't, if you loved your children, go out and leave them alone, and so you don't go out, but it makes you see the drawbacks of children.'

'You have asked the women to write to you and give you their reasons for limiting their families. To me there is only one reason—fear. Dread of the unmitigated torture and indescribable agony a woman has to go through to produce a child. I have one child of three years and as much as I would like at least one other, whilst I have means to prevent it, I could not bring myself to face the actual child-birth again.

Until something is done to make child-birth 'bearable' no noticeable increase will be possible in the population. I have been very interested in this question and have listened with interest to a recent discussion by a lady doctor on the wireless on the declining birth-rate. Her reasons, I thought, were good, but the main one, naturally, was omitted. No woman tells another who has not borne a child what she goes through . . . I have a university degree and have travelled in most countries of the world and women are the same the world over. I think a great deal has yet to be done in the field of obstetrics and that must be the beginning.'

'I believe you desire the reasons of mothers for only having a limited family. Well, one of them is this: What do we owe to Australia? It starved us and our children after the last war and it will do the same after this *if we let it.* Therefore, we have decided that there won't be so many of us to starve this time. It is better to gaze on one or two hungry children than, say, eight or nine and if one can arrange to have none so much the better. We, the mothers, hold this power in our hands. We have a freemasonry among ourselves that is colossal. If we find out any birth-control hint, we pass it on. I myself know of an easy, safe method of abortion. I know of hundreds of other ideas that have been passed on to me by desperate and despairing mothers of hungry children. Things will have to be mighty attractive in the New World before we consider the inconvenience of big families.'

Report of the National Health and Medical Research Council
Eighteenth Session
22–24 November 1944

Document 3.9 'The lion that tasted blood'

The assumption that women would return to the kitchen once the war ended was soundly rejected by many women. Women had proved their abilities and would continue to participate in public life. Women in the labour movement called for improved conditions for working women, but they also acknowledged the importance of attending to the needs of mothers and the inequities of family life.

MUST WOMAN RETURN TO THE KITCHEN?

By Clarice McNamara

This war, like the last, has done strange things for women. Kingsley's refrain that 'men must work and women must weep' no longer holds true. Women now, and of the post-war world will weep all right; they will weep for menfolk killed on the battlefield or maimed, and many will weep for the experience of love, marriage and motherhood the war has denied them. But above all they must work.

Never before have women experienced such opportunities for showing what they can do; and in the post-war world they will be needed more than ever to fill jobs for which, during these war years, they have served a meteor apprenticeship.

Obviously, there will be much readjustment when peace is declared. War service and war industries must be changed to peace activities. But there will be many reasons why thousands of women all over the world will remain in their present or other socially useful occupations.

Apart from the need for women workers to replace male victims of war in factories, farms, businesses and professions, there is the added reason that women now are like the lion that tasted blood—they have savored the sweets of economic independence, of public responsibility, of some measure of equality with men in the workaday world, of the refreshing wider contact that comes with interesting employment outside the home.

All these things are not going to be renounced overnight for the previous order in which woman's main role was that of home-maker and child-rearer, while she was frowned upon or tolerated in any jobs save those of teacher, nurse, shopgirl or typist.

Now that women have proved themselves successful land-army workers, tram-conductors, engineers, oxy-welders, ship-repairers, signallers, accountants, veterinary surgeons, psychiatrists, social workers, editors, administrators in parliaments and local councils, it will be impossible, in a post-war world that makes any serious attempt at democracy, to dismiss them from their posts, and suggest that they occupy themselves with domestic affairs only, or be satisfied with the pre-war limitations of a woman's job.

I think women will fight to keep the measure of emancipation and economic independence they now enjoy—and they will fight till they have attained full equality with men of payment and conditions . . . An efficient woman worker brings attention to detail, adaptability, deftness of fingers, conscientiousness and courage. Her traditional pre-occupation with the personal in contrast to the abstract can be redirected from absorption in self or from catty gossip, to the unobtrusive organising and smoothing out of personal relations that is part of the work of a good forewoman, a social worker, a secretary, or even a good shop assistant or bus conductor.

Entry of women into jobs where formerly only men worked has brought with it that salutary good fellowship and atmosphere of graciousness which is on the staff of a co-educational school, in contrast to the atmosphere of schools staffed by women or men only.

What, then, is to become of the home? If so many women are to be breadwinners, is not our national home-life threatened? Will not our birth-rate decline to the point of national suicide? Will not the young children be neglected?

The answer to these questions is that love of children and home-making is far too deeply inlaid in a woman's nature to be fundamentally upset by modern changes. But, at the same time, I think we have to face frankly the fact that the home as we of the older generation have known it is threatened. The Labor Movement must fight especially for a better deal for wives and mothers.

Education and preparation of young people for marriage and parenthood is so intimately interwoven with all other social questions that we cannot much longer dodge it. If the Labor Movement is to strive for equality of opportunity of every citizen and the greatest good of the greatest number, it cannot shut its eyes to that part of our personal and communal life which is fundamentally important to our social well-being—the sexual and parental life of individual men and women.

If we have courage and calmness to examine this question, we must at once see that all the economic reforms in the world will be of little benefit to the masses of the people unless we also fight for reforms in the sphere of marriage (*and* divorce) and parenthood. Among these reforms I would list these, as most urgent and fundamental to women's welfare:

- *Education of young people* for wise, well-adjusted marriage and parenthood, and against the curse of venereal disease. This education should take the form of advice by experts in Bureaus of Family Advice, free literature, a campaign of lectures and radio talks, and special courses of training for parents, teachers and all who have care of young people.
- *Reform of the Divorce laws* to abolish the farce, misery and hypocrisy of incompatible couples being forced to live together unless they are willing to endure the publicity and stupid conditions of our process of obtaining a divorce.
- *An independent minimum income* for all wives without children, in return for efficient home-making and part-time work for the community. It is time we declared ourselves against the traditional idea that because of her marriage, a girl may automatically be free of all responsibility to society. Conversely, this reform would put an end to the abominable mid-Victorian hangover of the young wife being dependent on the husband for all money, however niggardly or unjust he might prove to be.
- *Part-time work* to a certain age (and conditional upon good health) for older women with no remaining family responsibilities, who could devote a few hours daily (as so many do now) to such splendid work as relieving in children's play centres, day nurseries, libraries, community centres, hospitals, factories and farms.
- *A complete network of nursery schools* and kindergartens with trained staffs, in every area, suburban and country. This is an urgent necessity for modern mothers with little domestic help, and for modern children of small families.

Labour Digest, April 1945

Document 3.10 'My heart is going to burst from the agony'

When Ben Chifley's post-war Labor Government introduced a mass migration policy it was concerned to populate Australia's expansive continent and to find a labour force willing to carry out large scale public works; the 'whiter' the migrant the better. Most migrants left their own countries with no idea of what lay ahead. Women in particular faced experiences of intense loneliness and isolation, and often suffered terrible humiliation at the hands of doctors and nurses. A. Marino wrote her memories of her early years in Australia in the form of a journal.

Autumn 1951, Paese, Italy

Finally, Mario has sent the immigration papers for me to join him in Australia. But I am so angry with his mother and sister. They actually received the letter a week ago and of course opened it, as they usually do with my letters. Mario's mother came to me and asked if I wanted to go to Australia. What a question! I am dying to get out of her house.

I was so excited, I raced over to my parents' home and gave them the good news. They were happy for me, but mamma started to cry, and papa's voice wavered as he wished me well. Rosa too was crying, as were the other young ones. Silvio is also expecting an invitation from Mario to migrate to Australia. I'm happy Silvio is coming with me. I'll feel a lot safer having him on the ship with me and I won't be so lonely. Poor mamma. Silvio was always one of her favourite sons. I think that losing her two eldest children will be really difficult.

The truth is, I don't really want to go to Australia. I love my family so much. I love my village. Oh, how I love this country! I think about Australia sometimes and the stories about kangaroos in the streets. Although Mario has told me that Australia is a country of great opportunity, I know in my heart I won't be happy there . . .

I hope when I get there and Mario and I are alone that he will stop throwing things around and hitting me. I think I just couldn't stand it if he didn't stop. Damned honour! That's what's really causing the problem. What will people say? Shush. Pretend all's well. Pretend you're really happy. *La vita è una lotta*—life is a struggle. Do other women have these problems or am I just the unlucky one? Once I get to Australia I'll know for sure. God help me! . . .

May 1952, Melbourne, Australia

Mario is fast asleep. It's now 2am. Our ship docked this morning. I was so scared. Everyone hurried to get off to meet their loved ones. I saw

Mario waving frantically to catch my attention. He was alone. He was so happy to see Silvio and me, he just couldn't stop chattering and asking questions. We caught a taxi to our new home, a boarding house in Brunswick. When we walked into our room, I was devastated. It is a tiny, dingy, dirty little room. There is a bed with faded sheets in the middle, a chest of drawers at one end and a wardrobe at the other. There are two rickety chairs and a table by the window. The floor is covered with dirty, torn lino. We have to share the kitchen and bathroom with the other boarders. There are lots of men living here. I feel so uncomfortable. Mario could see I was disappointed. He promised that as soon as possible, we would move into our own home. I can't believe he can accept living in these conditions. He was the 'prince' of our village back home. Doesn't he feel like I do? Doesn't everything seem as strange and alien to him as it does to me? I just wish I were at home with my mamma and papa . . .

Winter 1952, Melbourne

I can't go anywhere because I don't understand the language, so I just sit in front of the window, day in and day out, waiting for Mario to come home. If anyone comes to the door, I show them a note Mario has written in English, telling them to come back around 6pm. Silvio dines with us every night and Mario's friends, fellow countrymen, come to visit us sometimes. But I am a woman. I can't sit and talk with them, and none of them have wives . . .

August 1952, Melbourne

I am so ill I can barely walk. Mario took me to a doctor yesterday. I am anaemic. The doctor has put me on a special diet and ordered some vitamin tonic. He also said I am very depressed. I didn't need him to tell me this, but Mario needed to hear it. I miss my family so much I feel my heart is going to burst from the agony. I spend a lot of my time crying. Rosa [a neighbour] says I must be strong, that things will get better. She is the only person who understands me.

30th August 1953, Melbourne

Today I have probably made one of the most important decisions of my life. I have decided to leave Mario. I cannot possibly put up with the humiliation he makes me feel every time he abuses me. He gets angry over nothing. Tonight he didn't like the food I cooked, so he threw it on the floor and demanded I make something else. I said that it was a perfectly good meal and that he shouldn't act so childishly. He retorted by striking me, and said to get moving or he would belt me. So I did as he demanded.

I have tried to understand that life in Australia is difficult for him. He has to work long hours and he doesn't have the social standing he had back home, where he was one of the most wealthy and respected people in our village. But I wasn't exactly a peasant, either. Even though my family was poorer than his, we had our pride and a good reputation. Otherwise he wouldn't have taken me as a wife.

When I first met him, through our courtship until the day we married, I looked up to him and respected him. He was a dashing young man and it was love at first sight. I felt as if my dreams had come true. I thought I would not only have a handsome, kind and gentle husband, but also one who was intelligent and wealthy. What every girl dreams of! . . .

25th September 1953, Melbourne

I went to see Dr G today. He told me I am pregnant. I am very happy to know I can bear children. After nearly four years of marriage, I was beginning to think I couldn't. Mario is extremely excited and has gone out to tell all our friends the wonderful news.

But now I can't leave Mario. No-one will employ a pregnant woman. How would I survive alone with a child? No, it's impossible. I'm trapped. I have to stay.

I love knowing I am going to be a mother, but at the same time, this pregnancy means I have to put up with Mario for the rest of my life. I have to find a way to stop him abusing me, or at least to stop him hitting me. I know everyone says that in Australia, if a man beats his wife, he can be imprisoned. Maybe I'll do that. I'll threaten him by saying I'll call the police if he hits me again. But maybe, now that I'm pregnant and carrying his child, he won't hit me. He will be more careful and gentle. With all my heart, I hope so. *Santa Vergine, dammi la forza*—Blessed Virgin give me strength.

30th September 1953, Melbourne

Mario hit me again today. And I did it—I threatened to call the police and have him locked away forever. He kept on screaming, but he looked scared. Perhaps that's what Mario needs: someone to stand up to him. To show him they're not scared. I think that's the only way I can make him treat me like a human being. I wonder if he realises that by hurting me he could actually damage the child. Sadly, he's not that sensitive.

10th May 1954, Melbourne

Mario has not laid a hand on me since that night I threatened to call the police. He still screams and insults me, but I'm getting used to it.

Sometimes I just block off and let my mind wander onto something else. But if he feels I am not listening to him, it makes him more angry, and he walks out in a huff . . .

18th May 1954, in hospital, Melbourne

Yesterday at 5.25am I gave birth to a beautiful baby girl, Isabella. Mario wanted to name her after his mother. I'm not really happy about it, even though it is our custom . . . Anyway, my little Isabella seems to have taken after Mario's side of the family, blond hair and very fair skin. She is really quite beautiful. The hospital staff aren't very friendly. They sometimes come and mumble something to me but I can't understand what they're saying. I feel very depressed and cry a lot. I'm not normally this sensitive. I asked Dr G about it and he said I'd feel better soon . . .

January 1955, Melbourne

I went to see Dr G today, as I have missed a couple of periods. He says I am pregnant again. He also says I have to stop breastfeeding Isabella. Poor Isabella. It is the only thing that comforts her when she is really grizzly.

June 1955, Melbourne

We have a new business, a grocery. It has living quarters upstairs. It is quite nice.

28th August 1955, Melbourne

I had a beautiful baby boy last night. We called him Roberto after Mario's father. I kept trying to tell the nurse that Roberto was coming, but she insisted there was plenty of time. Just because my English is not perfect, it does not mean I am stupid. Anyway, the pushing feeling started and I began screaming. By the time the nurses came to assist me, Roberto was already halfway out. At least he is all right. The nurses here are the same as the ones in the hospital where I had Isabella. They don't allow the babies to sleep with their mothers. I only see him at feeding times. I can't wait to go home. Isabella is missing me terribly.

10th November 1955, Melbourne

My feeling that something is wrong with Isabella was justified. We took her to the specialist and he said she has an umbilical hernia. She will have to go into hospital next week for an operation. I am so worried about her. Please God, I beg you, let her get well.

19th November 1955, Melbourne

I go to see Isabella three times a day. First I have to feed Roberto, then prepare some food for Isabella and take it to her in hospital. She won't eat or drink anything the nurses give her. They say she just cries all day and cries herself to sleep at night. She is so tiny and helpless. My heart breaks to see her so distressed. When I have to leave she screams 'Mamma no! Mamma no!' I can't stand it. I come home and cry. Mario is also very upset. The hospital won't let me stay with her. At least if they would let me feed Roberto in hospital, I could be with her a little longer. My poor baby. Please God she will be out of hospital soon. Now I understand why my mother used to say, 'Only when you become a mother will you understand a mother's suffering'.

16th January 1956, Melbourne

I told Mario today that I want to help in the shop. I am sick of staying upstairs like a prisoner. I want to meet people. I want to learn something more than just keeping house. Mario agreed, but he said that once I made the commitment I would always have to help out like a partner. I agreed. Tomorrow will be my first day. I am quite excited.

17th January 1956, Melbourne

Today was my first day working in the shop. Mario would only let me serve the Italian-speaking customers. He said when I learn to speak English, then I can serve Australians. Not many Australians come into the shop. It felt strange serving Rosa over the counter. I am so used to her coming upstairs for a cup of coffee. She's offered to help look after Isabella and Roberto.

However, Mario is a bit bossy. He even scolded me in front of a customer. I don't care. At least I'm not upstairs alone. When I heard Mario chatting away, laughing and joking with customers, I used to feel so jealous of his freedom. I think I am going to like working.

Anna-Maria Kahan-Guidi and Elizabeth Weiss (eds), *Forza e Coraggio. Give Me Strength*, Women's Redress Press, 1989

Document 3.11 Legally equal and equally responsible

When the Women's Electoral Lobby surveyed Australian politicians before the 1972 election, it was believed to be the first time such action had been taken by women. In 1951, however, the United Association of Women called upon parliamentary candidates to state their position on several issues that immediately affected the lives of women.

United Associations of Women
Fifth Floor,
61 Market Street,
Sydney NSW
12th April, 1951

Dear [. . .]

The United Associations of Women is an organisation which believes that until the equality of women with men is recognised legally and that until women are welcomed as being equally responsible in the affairs of State, there can be little improvement in the problems which are besetting our Country to-day.

We understand, morever, that the Party to which you belong has expressed agreement with the principle of equality of status and opportunity for men and women.

We, therefore, ask you, as a candidate for Parliament, to give the following matters your serious consideration and let us have your replies to them.

Recognising that women have a special contribution to make in public life as citizens of a democratic community, would you agree:

1   To grant women equal pay, status and opportunity in the Commonwealth Public Service, thereby giving an impetus to outside bodies to follow suit.

2   To rescind section 49 of the Commonwealth Public Service Act and Section 170 of the Commonwealth Bank Act, 1945, both of which forbid the employment of women after marriage regardless of their ability.

3   To appoint a proportion of women to Boards created by the Government, particularly where such Boards affect the welfare of women and children.

4   To appoint a proportion of women on delegations to overseas Conferences, such as the United Nations Organisation in its various departments and the International Labour Organisation.

5   To unify and thus simplify the Divorce Laws of the Commonwealth.

6   To hold a Referendum to provide for a Blanket Bill giving women equal rights, status and opportunity with men and stipulating that any sex discriminations embodied in any laws or regulations be invalid.

Yours faithfully,
(signed) Caroline L. Scrimgeour.
President.

Document 3.12 'The growing interest in boys'

The Catholic Church, responsible for the education of hundreds of thousands of Australian children, had very strict guidelines for parents on how to educate their children in matters of femininity, sex and reproduction. This excerpt from a booklet for mothers outlines the attitudes and behaviours they must encourage in their daughters, and the ways young girls should negotiate the vexed terrain of sexuality.

THE 'BOY' PROBLEM:

The 'teen' age presents another difficulty closely connected with bodily development—the growing interest in boys. This is, of course, as God intended; and while it is to be kept in check, a mother should not regard it as something to stifle. On the contrary, she should provide opportunities where boys and girls can meet under reasonable supervision. But such nonsense as kissing games and frolics with lights extinguished should be completely excluded. Positive training, however, in good manners and genuine courtesy will now be necessary if your girl is to avoid unbecoming behaviour. If her knowledge of how to get along in mixed company has been drawn solely from films and novels, she will certainly have a hard battle to keep decent. So let your advice be positive and helpful, not just a series of 'don'ts.'

We cannot, of course, deal with all this in detail, but we give just some general ideas.

Your girl should know how to *appear lady-like* in manner, when standing having her feet together, when sitting paying due attention to legs and dress. This is quite fundamental modesty, but it is rather neglected at times. Your girl is far more likely to be treated as a lady if she has the appearance of one . . . *In mixing*, she should be friendly and cheerful with all alike, not showing that abominable ill-breeding that pays particular attention to the more attractive and neglects the others . . . She should know the safe old adage, '*Keep with the crowd*,' and should realize that straying away from the others at outings and gatherings in single company is positively rude, besides being dangerous . . .

As a school-girl, she should never be allowed to go to the pictures alone with a boy-friend; and should have one of her parents or a trustworthy adult to bring her home at night from *school dances* or 'mixed' functions. It is not that we distrust our girls; but they are in their formative years at this stage, and should not be regarded as trained, too early in life . . . She should understand that no girl, either with her own sex or with others, can make the mistake of *vulgar conversation* without losing respect thereby . . . She should know the foolishness of *company-keeping* in those all too brief years of girl-hood, when she should be concentrating on acquiring a good knowledge of *all* male nature; so that she will have the ability later in life to make a sound choice of a partner for life. Many mothers have foolish illusions about these early friendships, even encouraging them. They greatly harm a girl's natural development . . . She should be told the danger of *drink*: that it dulls one's sense of modesty, and makes sin easy, especially those drinks women usually indulge in, liqueurs, gin, and cocktails, and the sweeter wines.

In a word, she must, in these years, develop a real Christian friendliness to all; and ever be mindful that she is the guardian not just of her own virtue, but of others' also. Few girls know that even slight immodesty in dress or behaviour on their part can be an overpowering temptation even to a decent boy. How can they guess it if they are not told . . . God has given them a nature that is quite different, a placid, more serious temperament in matters of purity, and a greater reserve against sex temptation. They must be taught to use it to help, not to hinder, the virtue of others.

The main danger in girl–boy relationships concerns a point about which most women seem completely blind. Namely, that close holding, personal touches, and love-making frequently cause thoughts, feelings and desires in a boy's nature; and if such feelings continue for long the seed of life itself may even flow. To him the whole thing is *mortally sinful*. Now the girl who takes part with him in such behaviour may remain comparatively calm and unaffected; but nevertheless she must, in God's sight, share in the guilt of what takes place, for it takes two to commit the sin. And it does not excuse her that the boy himself encouraged her.

Finally, let us remark that it is hard to understand how a mother can allow her girl to grow into womanhood without knowledge that certain concessions to a boy in fondling and petting can constitute not only temptation to him, but danger to herself. Nearly every good-living girl, who has fallen into serious sexual sin, has been led into it because she was ignorant of the effects of certain love-making, that she could easily have checked, had she but known. Prolonged kissing, intimate handling, drink, a hand on the breast . . . How many girls have had to learn the danger of these things by bitter and regretted experience, because the guide and friend whom God gave them was too shy or too short-sighted to make mention of them. Even that exceptional case, the girl passionate by nature, can be brought safely to adult life by a sympathetic parent. She will prove a faithful wife and a loving mother if she receives from her own, understanding and care in her adolescent days.

Once again, Pope Pius XII: 'Your words, if they are wise and discreet, will prove a safeguard and a warning in the midst of the temptations and corruption which surround them, "because fore-seen, an arrow comes more slowly" '.

> *You Are Her Mother*
> Catholic Marriage Guidance Centre
> Melbourne 1953

Document 3.13 The art of marriage

The founding of the Marriage Guidance Council of Australia in 1953 (the amalgamation of separate state bodies) suggests that the marriage relationship and the family were becoming more prominent in public issues, especially nationhood and citizenship. 'Happily married people make the best parents, the best workers and the best citizens' stated one of the Marriage Guidance Council's publications. This excerpt looks at transforming the experience of 'falling in love' to 'lasting happiness'.

THE ART OF HUMAN RELATIONSHIP: HAPPINESS IN MARRIAGE

By a marriage guidance counsellor

Each time I see a young couple planning their wedding I hope and pray for one thing for them—that they may be willing to learn the Art of Marriage, which is one important phase of the Art of Human Relationships. That is the only way I know of whereby, as a long term result, happiness may come to take the place for them of their present transient feelings of pleasure and desire, which they now call 'being in love'.

Not that I minimise the importance of being in love. Just as the original vision of the artist before he has laid his brush to paper can itself be a transcendent experience, blended of joy and excitement, so, falling in love is an experience which comes nearest of all human feelings to the divine.

Why does Jack love Jill? or Jill love Jack? I've asked myself that question a hundred times. Sometimes I've said, She's a pretty lass, and he's a good looking boy. But that doesn't explain it. The plain lass and her unprepossessing boy friend betray just as genuine symptoms of being in love as the others. It certainly isn't purely physical, though physical attraction comes into it. Yet even if the girl were a Venus, and the boy an Adonis, I'd still say their love for one another is fundamentally not physical.

An inseparable blending

I am not writing now of the physical side of marriage. I agree that physical adjustment is a basic importance to real happiness, and that such an adjustment is itself part of the art of marriage, and provides a sound and solid basis for lasting joy in married life. Yet it isn't nearly the whole story. Just as I venture to say that no 'falling in love' is purely physical; so, also, no true and lasting happiness is wholly physical.

Is it, then, spiritual? Of course it is. But I don't like the word 'spiritual'. It is capable of so many misleading meanings. I'd rather use the word 'personal', because to me a person is an inseparable blending of the physical and the spiritual.

Jack is a person. So is Jill. That's what makes them unique. And their work of art is to create a new person, 'Jack and Jill'. This is the personality of two people who have learned to live as one. Lots of people have achieved it—the Smiths, the Browns, the Joneses; you know who I mean.

This new creation doesn't entail the loss of anything important to either partner. It means rather an enrichment of both persons. A man may be made fun of by his friends, who tell him all his freedom will be gone when he marries. A girl may be told that she's sure to be the slave of her home and family. Hardly anyone seems to mention the newborn freedom that makes bachelor independence and carefree girlhood seem by comparison a mere nursery toyland that has lost meaning and interest. Marriage is the real climax to the process of growing-up.

Towards Successful Marriage
Marriage Guidance Council of South Adelaide, 1953

Document 3.14 'At last I've seen a Daimler!'

On Queen Elizabeth's first visit to Australia in 1954 she was greeted with crowds of supporters everywhere she went. It was mainly women who lined the streets, for it was mainly women who could take the time out from domestic work to watch the passing parade. Gwen Badgery shared the excitement with her daughter and son-in-law who were travelling in England.

February 1954

Well, my darlings, you might have seen the Coronation, but I am listening to the welcome of Sydney to the Queen and the Duke and it's absolutely *marvellous.* When I woke this morn to the noise of the welcoming planes overhead, I regretted that I had not made arrangements to go to the city, but now I don't care because the broadcasting is excellent. I can hear and can picture the wonderful scenes on this *perfect* day from the time the Royal yacht Gothic came in the Heads, both on the bridge. I mean the Queen and Duke.

The speech of the Lord Mayor was very good, and then the Queen's reply. It was just as if she was in the kitchen speaking to me, saying 'Australia' just as dear old Dad used to say it, almost 'Orstralia'. So I sat with the tears pouring down my face, smoking madly, with the lid of the polish tin as an ashtray on my knee, having just put the polish on the kitchen floor.

Just here Sylvia and Joe Johnson came in, Joe in white shorts and bare feet heavily trimmed with the biggest bunions it has ever been my misfortune to have to look at, Sylvia in yellow as usual. We listened, still sobbing, to the rest of the broadcast and then Stella phoned to say she had cried into three of Cliff's hankies. Well now it's ended, and I feel such a wreck that I shall go and have a sunbake on the lawn to recover.

Well I've *seen her*, and are my legs aching. Stood in George Street for two hours, in front row, and thought her just beautiful, but she went past so fast that I doubt if I should know her if I met her in an ordinary crowd. A very old girl next me was staying in to see her go to the Town Hall Ball tonight. She said, 'I want to see her in them clothes'. So did I, but I couldn't have stood any longer.

I thought the decorations v. tatty, except inside D.J.'s big store where it's restful, all burgundy pennants with just E.R. on them and huge bowls of real flowers.

Later. Am sitting here in one of your old sunfrocks, very *envious* for one of the few times in my long life, listening to good old Ida Elizabeth Jenkins describe the glorious dresses at the Lord Mayor's Ball. The Queen in heavy white satin, and the fat old Premier's wife, with a face like a black orpington hen, in Royal Blue Shyfon, Heavily Beaded as usual.

Humidity 100% and the Queen's last day tomorrow. Nan and I are going up to Military Road to watch them pass to the Naval Depot at Balmoral. I'm glad she's finished with N.S.W. as I am sick and tired of *crying*. Have two pawpaws with flowers on. One is a lady and the other is a gentleman, pawpaws are like that.

Next day. Well. Nan and I had a very good view of *them* this morning. We set off at 8 am and got a fruit box and sat for three hours on the shady side at Spit Junction. It got hotter and hotter and the crowd was beyond words, all screaming kids and abominable old women who pushed and shoved, but she looked divine in yellow. But never again. *All 21* of the Royal Family can come even to Collaroy if they like, and I would go on the beach and take no notice. We had a terrible time trying to get home, and finally I threw Nan into a bus and fought my way in with umbrella and bag and got into the hottest seat, with kids yelling all round. We *crawled* through the traffic, and it was heaven to get under the shower and have eight cups of tea.

Really Sydney has gone mad over them—a woman in the butcher's saw *her* eight times. I don't feel I've seen her at all, just passing by in a huge car. No wonder some kid said, Why are they sitting in the *boot*? One fond father took his son to see them and when they passed the child turned away and said, 'Well at *last* I've seen a *Daimler*!'

> Toni Mackenzie (ed.) *Mother Stayed At Home: letters to a travelling daughter*, Pan Macmillan, Sydney, 1987

Document 3.15 'By reason of her character and standard of intelligence and development'

Many Aborigines sought exemption from the Aborigines Act in an attempt to reduce the indignities that white Australians imposed upon them. Exemption from the Act granted Aborigines citizenship status, although it did not relieve the trauma of living in a racist culture. Nellie Lester's application for exemption was approved, but her later attempts to obtain a birth certificate revealed the extent of racism perpetrated by a system that did not consider Aboriginal births worth recording. Alternatively, Nellie's mother may not have registered the birth for fear of having her child taken from her.

> South Australia Aborigines Department,
> Kintore Avenue, Adelaide
> 25th May, 1953

To Miss Nellie Lester,
C/- Repatriation Hospital,
Heidelberg. Vict.

Dear Madam,
I forward herewith the final certificate of exemption from the provisions of the Aborigines Act.

You have my best wishes for the future, particularly in view of the fact that you have done so well in the nursing profession.

Yours faithfully

(signed) WR Penhall
Secretary,
Aborigines Protection Board

SOUTH AUSTRALIA, UNCONDITIONAL EXEMPTION FROM THE PROVISIONS
OF THE ABORIGINES ACT, 1934–1939

In pursuance of the powers conferred by Section 11a of the Aborigines
Act, 1934–1939, the Aborigines Protection Board, being of the opinion
that NELLIE LESTER of PORT AUGUSTA, by reason of her standard
of intelligence and development, should be exempted from the provisions
of the Aborigines Act, 1934–1939, does hereby declare that the said
NELLIE LESTER shall cease to be an aborigine for the purpose of the
said act.

The seal of the Aborigines Protection Board was hereunto affixed on
the 6th day of MAY 1953 in the presence of the Secretary, Deputy
Chairman and Member.

South Australia Aborigines Department,
Kintore Avenue, Adelaide
2nd September, 1957

Sister Nellie Lester,
Home No. 2,
R.G.A.
Heidelberg. Vic.

Dear Madam,

Sister McKenzie has passed your letter on to me as she has now retired
from the Department.

I have been in touch with the Registrar General who informs me that
you are not registered in this State and the only way a certificate could
be issued would be for your mother to make a late application which
would cost £1. It would be necessary to produce a witness of the birth.
The Registrar General has informed me however that if you have a
statutory Declaration of your birth that this will be accepted.

Trusting that this information will help you.

Yours faithfully,

(signed)
Welfare Officer
Repatriation General Hospital,
Heidelberg West. Victoria

12th September, 1957

TO WHOM IT MAY CONCERN

Sister Nellie Lester has been a sister with the Repatriation Commission at this address since 13.5.1952. She is now on the staff as a permanent employee with the Commonwealth Government. She was accepted as permanent on the proof of her date of birth on a Statutory Declaration the same as enclosed. Unfortunately, Sister Lester's parents are now deceased and she is desirous of having a birth certificate. On checking with the Government Statist here in Melbourne, they would accept the Statutory Declaration as proof and would register the birth accordingly if it had been in this State.

Trusting that this evidence will be suitable and that Sister Lester's birth can be registered as a late entry and a copy of entry be supplied to her.

Yours sincerely

(signed) A.S. Dunlop
Justice of the Peace

South Australia Aborigines Department,
Kintore Avenue, Adelaide
14th January, 1958

Sister Nellie Lester,
Home No. 2, R.G.A.,
Heidelberg. Vic.

Dear Sister,

Your letter of the 11th August, 1957, was handed to me by Sister McKenzie who has now retired from this Department.

Since that time I have been attempting to arrange for you, in some manner, to receive a birth certificate. Unfortunately the Registrar of Births, Deaths and Marriages cannot supply same, nor can he make a late registration of birth. The statutory Declaration forwarded by you is not sufficient for this purpose. The Registrar states that such a statutory Declaration would have to be completed by some other person that actually knew you and your parent, at the time of your birth. Unfortunately I cannot find anyone who could make such a declaration.

I have, however, obtained a statutory Declaration from Miss R.M. Hyde, and this together with other information in the records of this office permits me to issue the enclosed certificate, which I hope will prove satisfactory to you.

I return herewith £1 as no fee will be charged for this service.

Yours faithfully,

(signed)
Secretary,
Aborigines Protection Board

The Salvation Army
Miss Nellie Lester
Has been known to me before & during her training at Bethesda and I have watched with interest her progress.

She is a Christian & a capable nurse, & for her future I wish the very best.

D. Shaw
(Brigadier)

TO WHOM IT MAY CONCERN.
Re: Mrs. Nellie Nihill.
I have known Mrs. Nellie Nihill (nee Lester) for fifty-one years, both as a young girl at Colebrook Home, Quorn. S.A. through her Nursing Career and into married life.

She was born at Granite Downs Station out from Oodnadatta S.A. in 1924. Her Birth Date has always been known as October 20th. 1924.

Iris C. Wiley

South Australia Aborigines Department
Kintore Avenue,
Adelaide
14th January, 1958

TO WHOM IT MAY CONCERN:
I certify that according to the information available in the records of the Aborigines Department, Nellie Lester was born about the 20th October, 1924, at or near Granite Downs Station, the precise date and place of birth and parentage not being known.

(signed)
Protector of Aborigines and Secretary,
Aborigines Protection Board

Document 3.16 'We kissed and we knew'

Kissing had been advocated as the true test of heterosexual love since the interwar years (see Doc 2.11). Here it proves the test of lesbian love in the 1950s. Although no lesbian subculture was apparent in Australia in the 1950s, as this interview suggests, love between women could flourish under the roof of suburban heterosexual respectability.

When I was about twelve I started to have crushes on other girls, you know. By the time I was seventeen, I was very, very keen . . . started having sexual activity with my girlfriend. Didn't know anything about it, of course, hadn't ever seen anything about it, there was nothing published in books or anything like that. So I didn't know what it was. I just knew I loved her tremendously. Had to keep it secret of course. Kept on being really passionate about her until she decided that she was getting interested in boys. When she was about twenty-two, twenty-three, she became engaged, so, I thought—oh well, I'm never going to love anyone like this so I s'pose I'll get married too. So I got engaged and married. Thought I could make a good wife and mother. I mean, that was all you were expected to do then. I went to work . . . but I didn't know anyone else like I was. Thought I was the only one, of course, so I got married. Had four children. Oh, I think I made a reasonable wife and mother. Did the right things.

When I had three children, twins a couple of months old and the oldest boy, two years old—still going to church regularly, my husband was too—I met a woman from England who'd just come over a few months before and we became quite friendly.

She used to come and help me on a Saturday morning bath the babies and everything, so that I could go to tennis in the afternoon . . . and we got more and more friendly . . . I didn't think much of it. I was about twenty-eight by this time and . . . then we realised that . . . Well, just one night, we were sitting in the car talking and when we were leaving we kissed and we knew . . . We knew there was something there and we knew it . . . shouldn't be like that, and we sort of said 'we must be lesbians'.

We'd sort of heard the word, well I'd heard the word by this time. This was ten years later. Would have been in about '53, '54 somewhere there. I don't know how I knew what the word was or where I'd read it because there certainly still wasn't much around in the papers or anything like that. You didn't read about it.

But going back to when I first became sexually active, about seventeen or eighteen, I was amazed how I knew what to do because there was nothing . . . you didn't have books like you do now, telling you every . . . which way that you've got to do this and that and the other, you know. And yet, it was just so natural—what I had to do and how I did it and . . . I knew far more about it when I was seventeen than what my husband did when he was thirty—when he married me at thirty-one or thirty-two, you know. Strange, isn't it.

I stayed with my husband because there certainly wasn't any Relief for if you left, and I certainly wouldn't leave my three children. So we continued to be secretive and have an affair for three years. We'd have a holiday once or twice a year together and she'd sometimes come and stay and sometimes miss work and have the day together . . .

Then I got pregnant, 'cos I had to keep having sex with my husband because . . . you did. I certainly didn't expect the last pregnancy, but then I had four under the age of four and . . . you know, I think the youngest was about twelve months or so when J from England went back. She couldn't take it any more really. I couldn't blame her I mean I couldn't leave to be with her and she couldn't stand to see me living with a husband so, she went back to England.

And, of course, I swore that I'd be over there in twenty-one years, I'd be with her again but you don't realise when you're young how you can fall out of . . . well, not fall out of love, just . . . it dies, doesn't it. I missed her dreadfully. After about eight or nine years, that's when the first lesbian group started—that I knew of. [It] was written about in the paper. Would've been about 1970 and . . . oh, I couldn't believe my eyes. To see there was a group of women meeting together because . . . I'd searched . . . I'd even gone down Fitzroy Street hoping to find somebody. I don't know what I expected to see . . . lesbian written above their head or something, I don't know . . . I was just searching.

Didn't know where I could find somebody like myself. I knew they must be around but I didn't know anything about where you could find them. I'd heard that . . . in the Hotel in the middle of Collins Street—The Australia—I'd heard that they sort of met underneath there in a coffee shop or something, so I went into town one day and I went down there and expected to find them roaming around but the only thing that happened was that a fellow came and sat at my table, so that was no good . . . you sorta get desperate.

I'd certainly been awakened when I was thirty or so. For eight or nine years I hadn't had it . . . any feminine sex and . . . when you've been used to it and miss it, it's something dreadful. [I] worried that I'd never have it . . . never feel another woman's body for the rest of my life. Oh, it was terrible. Then this group met, so I got in touch with them.

But I was working and couldn't get anything sent home. They said they had a monthly magazine but I couldn't join because I was married— I'd have to get my husband's permission . . . Well, that was the last thing I could do, but they would send me the [little] monthly magazine . . . two or three sheets. So I had to get it sent to work and I made them put it into two envelopes, you know, 'Private', in case it was accidentally opened or something. Petrified in case anyone found out.

Oh, the first time I got one, I couldn't believe reading it, I was so thrilled, to read something that other lesbians had written. You can't believe what it was like.

So after a while . . . I sometimes rang them up . . . I went to see Claudia and she said, 'Oh, you could come to a Sunday afternoon meeting. I have them in my home. They're, sort of, not to do with the Club but I can invite whoever I like,' and so, that was *really* something—I was going to see some other lesbians. Bought a special outfit, 'cos she wanted to interview me at her house up at Fitzroy or somewhere, one of those suburbs—and I was an ordinary housewife, a mother of four and you know, I dressed like one: skirt and jumper and coat. I certainly wasn't dressed in slacks or anything at that stage.

She said, 'Oh, have you got anything else to wear?' and I said, 'Oh, what's wrong with what I'm wearing?' Sort of opened my eyes, that there was something wrong with *me*! So I went and bought a special outfit—a slacksuit, they used to call them. Really wasn't me—it was bright orange . . . it was dreadful! When I look back on it (laughs). Anyway, I turned up at this thing on the Sunday afternoon and there was one woman there who was as desperate as I was, so, I had a bit of a fling with her, and it was terrible! I didn't love her, but . . . anyway, then they said that if you didn't have permission to become a member, you could go to the coffee nights, so we used to go to the occasional coffee night—they had one about once a month.

I met a friend there, and . . . we became mates and we were together for fifteen years. Two and a half years before I separated from my husband and then we lived together for another twelve years.

Document 3.17 'All I wanted to do was to have an abortion or die'

Information about birth control was not accessible to all women, nor always reliable when it was practised. For many women the only solution to an unwanted pregnancy was abortion, an act which was first legalised—with severe restrictions—in South Australia in 1969. In contrast to the interwar years, when discussion of abortion was common, in the 1950s the topic of abortion went 'underground'. There is little written evidence of women's experiences of abortion. Here 'Irma La Douce' remembers her experiences of a 'backyard' abortion in 1956.

We migrated in 1950. Before that we were refugees because of the Second World War, and we migrated to Australia in 1950 and came to South Australia. 1952, I think, my parents bought this block of land in Wingfield and our houses were built out of packing cases in those days and we lived in two packing cases, the three of us, which were fourteen feet by eight feet, and another room eight feet by eight feet. In 1953 I got married and we built another box on which was twelve feet by eight feet. So that was the accommodation we had, for four at first and then five, because my daughter was born in 1954 . . . [In 1956] we were still living in that hut in Wingfield, the five of us, and my daughter was about two, and I was pregnant for the second time . . .

I was feeling terrible because we couldn't possibly have another child in those circumstances. I mean, there wasn't enough room, and there wasn't any washing facilities, for instance. When we had our weekly bath we heated the copper in the backyard and took a tin bath inside the kitchen and had a bath in the tin tub and somebody, you know, took it outside on to the garden afterwards again . . .

I wasn't aware of it being hard at all, but looking back I don't think anybody would live like that nowadays. Everybody's so spoilt. No, that wasn't my problem. My problem was my alcoholic husband. So apart from that everything was fine, but I was very unhappy about being pregnant, and so was my husband, and we tried to bring on an abortion by me sitting in a hot tub and those things, but it wouldn't work. So I was three months, or maybe a little bit more pregnant, before I finally went to this woman who performed—Well, she didn't perform the abortion, she interferred with the pregnancy so that I miscarried . . .

How did you know where to go and find this woman?
I don't really know. She was our friend and neighbour.

Another Estonian woman?
Yes. I think other people had come and enquired, and I had heard the women talk about abortions. Her daughter was my friend at that time too. So we were pretty close with this other woman, and my mother being a dressmaker, we had lots of women call. There were people coming every day, and often women would, when they were [in] desperate need for an abortion, would ask my mother if she knew of somebody who could help them and she would say, 'Well go and talk to'—this other woman—'and she might know of something'. So I had an inkling. I didn't know, but I sort of guessed.

So when I was in desperation after three and a bit months, I went and asked her too, and this was secret from my mother. Only my husband knew and the other woman knew. What she told me was to get a bottle of whisky or Vodka or something strong and then come back next morning. She had this sort of rubber syringe with warm soapy water and she squeezed that into my cervix to interfere with the foetus, and that was fine. She said, 'Well, go home now and go back to bed, and when your husband comes home, drink this botttle of spirits'. The first night was all right. It was OK—nothing happened the first day. The evening I started feeling contractions, but they were slight. It wasn't anything drastic, and then I got drunk anyway.

The next day my husband went to work because we wanted to make out that nothing had happened. We didn't want to tell my mother really anything—we wanted to have the privacy about this thing. But I had to look after my daughter. She was outside and I had to go inside because the contractions got stronger and stronger, and I just had to go inside. So I just left my daughter outside, and my mother was doing gardening and I thought, 'Well, she'll be all right'. But after, you know, a couple of hours and nothing was seen or heard of me, my mother came into my room and started to say, 'What are you doing with his child? Why are you neglecting her?'—you know. 'She wants this and that thing'. Then she found me almost passed out by that time because I was so weak from losing so much blood that I wasn't quite aware of what was going on any more. Everything was sort of floating, but the bed was covered in blood.

Well she went into shock about this and she somehow cleaned me up. She said she buried the foetus and she was sorry that we'd done this thing, and she looked after my child. Well I stopped haemorrhaging after a while. I lost a lot of weight and I was very pale and very weak for a month or so afterwards, but I was still bleeding and this wasn't much good. I think I went back to the woman who performed the abortion and asked her what I should do about the bleeding—that I was still bleeding brown muck after a month, or maybe a little longer. She said, 'Well, go to the hospital and have a curette' and that's exactly what I did. I went to the Royal Adelaide Hospital and told them a bullshit story about, 'I think I might have been pregnant and somehow it must have aborted, and I don't know, I've been bleeding for a month now,' and do they think they should have a look at me, and they did. They asked me questions but I was sticking to my story and that was that. So I had a curette and that was that . . .

[*Do you think the woman who did the abortion for you did a lot of abortions?*]
I think she did really lots and lots and lots and lots—I would say hundreds.

But I'm not sure because I never talked to her before or since about abortions. But I knew that they would come and they would go and see her again and she had lots of people visiting her house too . . . They were mostly European migrants. People came to her crying. Because there was no way out and she was the last resort for everybody. She did it as a humanitarian service . . . This woman was very intelligent and clever. She knew lots and lots of Slavic languages, and Danish and German. I don't know what else but she would have known about ten languages—Polish, Russian, Yugoslav, Czechoslovakian. You name them, she knew all these languages. She could talk to every one of those migrant people . . .

See with all being refugees and with all being through several occupations in Europe from the Russians and the Germans, and I think one learns during the hard times how to look after oneself, because there must have been a lot of rapes going on during wartime, and in desperation women learned how to get rid of foetuses, because they wouldn't have wanted the chidren . . .

I'm very glad I had the abortion because to have had two children within two and a half years would have changed my life from what it became later completely. All I wanted to do was to have an abortion or die . . .

Were you more careful about getting pregnant after that abortion?
Yes, I never would wish that on anybody, because bringing on a late term termination like that was very, very painful. It was really excruciatingly painful. Nothing compared with childbirth at all. It was ten times more painful and I wouldn't wish that on anybody, and I was just not going through it again.

Interview conducted by Barbara Baird, no. OH91/11
'Abortion in South Australia before 1970 Project'
J.D. Somerville Oral History Collection
Mortlock Library, South Australia

Document 3.18 'Every day my hunger for my baby gets worse'

The stigma of being an 'unmarried mother' was considerable during the post-war years, and the mothers of ex-nuptial children were strongly encouraged to have their babies adopted. Without any government assistance there were financial as well as social reasons behind this pressure. The following letter to New Idea's *'agony aunt' tells of one woman's trauma after relinquishing her child. Her story*

prompts an early and sympathetic call for government support of the
'unmarried mother'.

'HELP FOR THE UNMARRIED MOTHER'

The query is: 'Could you please tell me some names of homes where
unmarried mothers could go to have their babies? I am Church of England
religion and want to have the baby adopted. I am 20 years old. How do
I have the baby adopted?'
My correspondent is a Melbourne girl and so I have advised her to seek
the assistance of the Almoner's Department at the Royal Women's Hospital, Carlton. The hospital will confine and care for the mother and
arrange to have the baby adopted.

This seems to be the moment to quote the young married woman who
sent the following poignant letter to me some weeks ago. This reader
writes:

'Six years ago I had an affair with a man whom I did not love and
soon parted from. I found then I was pregnant. When my parents knew
they were horrified and upset and afraid of the scandal. They stood by
me—in a way—but they insisted I have the baby adopted at birth.

'I was sent to stay with a relative in a distant town, duly had the baby
and never ever saw her, although I was told she was a healthy girl. Some
hospitals who help unmarried mothers believe that the mother who wishes
to have the baby adopted is better for never seeing the child.

'Now, the strange part about it is that I never—*then*—regretted my
decision, but simply went home after I had recovered and resumed my
normal life. A little over a year afterwards I fell in love with a wonderful
man and we married. I told him frankly of my story. It made no difference
to his feelings for me.

'But the story hasn't ended happily. Since marriage I have had two
lovely children and I adore both of them and my husband. But the arrival
of these two little ones has wakened, years too late, a yearning for my
first baby. I signed the adoption papers and agreed never to try and find
her. I am forced to stick to this decision by law, but every day my hunger
for my lost baby gets worse and my heart is sad and heavy all the time.
Sometimes I do not know how to bear the burden of just never never
seeing my own child and holding her in my arms.

'Will you please print this letter for the benefit of other girls who
may be similarly placed and just don't know what they are doing when
they sign away their own child? I made a terrible mistake, and it will be
with me for the rest of my life. Please, please tell other girls not to panic,

but to think very carefully before they decide to have their illegitimate babies adopted.'

My own feeling is that we need a branch of social service which will help the unmarried mother. She especially needs help if she wishes to keep her baby, and needs maintenance for herself and the child after the baby is born. It isn't enough to find employment for her. She needs to find a job where she can take her baby with her, or where adequate creche or nursery facilities are provided while she is at work.

Many a girl who is forced to have her illegitimate baby adopted does so because she is economically helpless. And many a girl who has been afraid to face scandal has lived bitterly to regret parting with her child.

New Idea, 12 March 1958

Document 3.19 Save Our Sons

Australia's involvement in the Vietnam War, particularly conscription, provoked opposition from many groups in Australian society. One of the earliest groups to organise against conscription was the Save Our Sons Movement, which consisted mainly of middle-class suburban women who soon opposed the war itself. As this report of their first delegation to Canberra indicates, the Liberal Government sought to portray them as communist stooges and clearly felt threatened enough by their presence to have them barred from King's Hall.

S.O.S. CANBERRA LOBBYING MISSION REPORT

The Save Our Sons Movement delegation to Canberra comprised six representatives from Sydney, one from Newcastle, seven from Victoria and two from Queensland.

The nine delegates who arrived at Canberra station from Sydney at mid-day on Tuesday, September 21, were welcomed by Mr. A. James, Labor M.H.R., Mr. W. Rigby, prominent in the Association for International Cooperation and Disarmament, and several Canberra citizens. The latter offered to make transport available during our stay, and immediately took us to our guest house.

At 1.30 p.m. we went to Parliament House, and joined up with the Victorian delegates. What a happy meeting this was as we introduced ourselves, held a short meeting and were interviewed and photographed by the press with our banners, wearing our S.O.S. sashes, and with Victoria's lovely S.O.S. flag. Next day photos and stories appeared in *The Australian*, *The Canberra Times* and *The Age*.

Barred from King's Hall

At Parliament House we started to enter King's Hall, the traditional place
for interviewing Members. Attendants stopped us, telling us of a new rule
issued at 12 noon that day, barring people from the King's Hall. Labor
Members were astounded at this, and at question time Mr. James asked
about the ban. He was replied to quite rudely by the Speaker, at which
Mr. Calwell protested.

Although this ban was an attempt to hamper our mission it did not
succeed. We were ushered into a small waiting room just inside the
entrance to Parliament House. This became our 'office'. In it we sorted
out our authorisations, wrote out application cards to see Members, held
discussions and even had Members of Parliament coming to speak to us
there. In any case, after the questions were asked in the House, the ban
on King's Hall was relaxed and we conducted our interviews there.

We think the ban harmed the Government more than it did the
delegation. Through it we got extra publicity in newspapers, radio and t.v.
Our presence and mission in Canberra became widely known.

Interviews with members

From the time we arrived in Canberra a number of Labor M.P.s set out
to help make our visit a useful and pleasant one. They entertained us to
afternoon tea on the day of our arrival, and gave us good advice. We acted
on their suggestion that we should concentrate on interviewing Government Members, as Labor Party policy was already against conscription
for overseas.

We particularly want to thank Mr. James, M.H.R., who went out of
his way to be helpful at all times. We also express appreciation to Mr. G.
Bryant, M.H.R. and Dr. Cairns, M.H.R. Dr. Cairns undertook to have our
petitions presented, with over 700 signatures protesting against conscription for overseas. Labor Members advised us to have deputations to visit
Federal Members in their electorates, especially those we were not able
to see in Canberra.

We began lobbying by presenting to each Member interviewed a copy
of a letter, appealing for repeal of the clauses relating to conscripts serving
overseas, and imposing harsh penalties for infringements of the Act. We
asked for more publicity to be given to the right of conscientious objection,
and also that volunteers for constructive community projects in Australia
or in underdeveloped countries be exempted from military service.

However, the reaction of all Government Members was to stand firmly
by Government policy and to defend it. Significantly, they associated
conscription with the Vietnam war. They claimed it was necessary to send

conscripts to stop Communists invading Australia. Although we tried to limit discussion to our policy and aims, we inevitably became involved in a discussion on Vietnam, as a result of Government Members' attitudes.

We pointed out that S.O.S. had no official policy on Vietnam, but that mothers in our organisation, when it was made clear that conscripts would be sent there, had investigated the different viewpoints about this war by attending public meetings, teach-ins, debates etc. At these both Government and opposition views had been presented. As a result we were not convinced that Government policy was correct. A considerable body of Australian opinion, including that of very prominent churchmen, was against the Government's policy.

Some Liberal Members received us with more courtesy than others. Some were rather arrogant and contemptuous, particularly at the beginning of interviews. For instance, one Member called us 'Communist stooges' and referred to boys who did not want to go to Vietnam as 'slobs'. However, their attitude changed when we made it clear that we represent a large group of people, including their own supporters, who are strongly opposed to their legislation and are determined to work for its amendment.

Overall, we feel we achieved something, even if the results may not be immediately obvious. Some delegates suggest that another visit to Canberra at some future time would be in the interests of the S.O.S. Movement.

Excerpts from interviews with members

Mr. Irwin (Lib.)
Said he was in favour of the boys going to Vietnam. Asked S.O.S. delegates 'Why don't you take the first plane to Peking?' He broke off the interview by walking away.

Mr. W.C. Wentworth (Lib.)
Said he was against the proposals in our letter. Gave very little opportunity to the women to talk and claimed that S.O.S. had 'befouled itself by associating with Communists'.

Mr. Turner (Lib.)
A protracted interview with seven or eight delegates. In discussing sending 20-year-olds overseas said it was better for people with no responsibilities to fight. At one stage he said boys who did not want to go were 'slobs', told delegates they were 'Communist stooges' and claimed there were Chinese in Vietnam. He retracted some of those remarks after the women protested, particularly when a delegate told him that she had up till now been a Liberal stooge, but would be one no longer.

Dr Mackay (Lib.)

Gave delegates a courteous hearing in a lengthy interview and said he understood their feelings as mothers. However, he supported Government policy. It was pointed out to him that no opportunity had been given Australians to vote on conscription for overseas in a referendum. He said a referendum would not be carried—that they 'never are'. This was challenged, it being pointed out that some referenda had been carried when people were convinced the policy was correct.

Mr. Turnbull (Country Party Whip)

Agreed with Government policy. However, in the course of the interview he acknowledged that S.O.S. was a genuine movement of women, and should not be branded as 'Communist' merely because it opposed Government policy.

Sir John Cramer (Lib.)

Refused to see the delegation, without explanation, although one of the delegates is in his electorate.

Mr. Jack (Lib.)

Fully supported Government policy. Would see only one delegate. In addition to the above, delegates spoke to other Members, Liberal and Labor, from Queensland, N.S.W., Victoria and Western Australia; also some Senators.

Delegates paid their own guest houses and travelling expenses, except for some assistance given by the Sydney Branch to the Brisbane and Newcastle delegates on account of distance.

S.O.S Newsletter, September 1965

AIMS OF S.O.S.

The Save Our Sons Movement is organised by mothers who oppose the present National Service Act on humanitarian, religious or pacifist grounds, for any one or all of the following reasons:

- They totally oppose conscription of youth into the armed forces.
- They object to conscription for overseas service.
- They object to the undemocratic nature of the present National Service Act.

The objective of the Save Our Sons Movement shall be to seek the repeal of the present National Service Act and to support progressive amendments particularly with regard to objectionable clauses relating to service abroad, long periods of service, penalties for infringements, and inadequate conscientious objection clauses.

S.O.S. Newsletter
June 1968

For Mothers' Day
A baby nestles, close and warm
To Mother;
Confidence and Love—
This is the link
We share with all the human race
Be damned to all who speak
Of brown, or white, or black
As someone set apart—
For therein lies the start of War.
Think of a Vietnam baby
Napalm burned,
Or shot while cradled
To his Mother's breast—
Then stand with her in agony.
O come, and join your voice
To all the rest.
With passion and compassion
In rising volume calling
'End to War.'

Take your Place with others for Peace
Save Our Sons

Authorised by Mrs. F. Garbour

Part 4
Liberation, 1969–1993

In a referendum in 1967 white Australians voted to allow Aborigines citizen rights. The vote came at a time when growing numbers of Aboriginal groups were seeking to free themselves of the thinking and influence of white paternalists. Their activities were wide-ranging—they called for Land Rights, for self-determination, and for Aboriginal health and legal services in inner Sydney. Aboriginal women were prominent among the activists and established their own groups to attend to the needs of their people.

White women activists focused on the demands of Women's Liberation. As the beneficiaries of post-war prosperity, and fresh from their experiences of sexism in New Left groups, young middle-class women had the education and skills to assess their own oppression. They called for the liberation of women from roles that confined them to sexual stereotypes, adopted the phrase 'the personal is political' from the American writer Kate Millet, and began to analyse the myriad ways in which social structures worked to locate power in the hands of men. White women had rediscovered their oppression. The concept of sisterhood encapsulated the belief that all women shared the experience of subordination and thus shared common interests, while consciousness raising groups provided women with small forums where they could explore the effects of sexism in their lives. The practical application of this feminist critique became manifest in women's refuges, health centres and child care centres, and gradually in the bureaucratic process itself.

Criticism of the concept of 'sisterhood' came from two main sources. From within the Women's Liberation Movement lesbians began addressing the heterosexism of other members, while Aboriginal women charged feminists with racism. White women's insistence that the oppression of women was just as prevalent in Aboriginal communities as in theirs, and that Aboriginal women ought to confront it, was considered by many Aboriginal women as just another attempt to divide Aborigines and impose white agendas on them. Aboriginal women sought forms of activism relevant to their own lives. They campaigned about black deaths in custody, Aboriginal health and living conditions and the destructive effects of alcohol on their communities.

Working-class women and women from non-English-speaking backgrounds were also very under-represented in Women's Liberation or the Women's Electoral Lobby. The daily hardships of their lives left little time for political organisation or consciousness-raising. Groups such as the Working Women's Centre and Action for Family Planning (later Women in Industry and Community Health) were formed to support working-class and migrant women. Conscious of how class, racial and sexual oppression dominated the lives of women, these groups sought liaison with unions and state and federal governments, and gradually achieved both funding and representation at union and government level.

Women who had been active in all aspects of the feminist movement sought, during the 1980s, to represent women's needs in government. 'Femocrats' (feminist bureaucrats), initially an Australian phenomenon, began to lobby for legislative change to ensure women's rights. Thus the process of 'naming', already an established aspect of feminist analysis, introduced terminology such as 'sexual harassment', 'domestic violence' and 'equal opportunity' to legal discourse. Attempts to make the law more attuned to women's experiences achieved mixed results and white middle-class women have tended to benefit the most from them. Laws on rape, both within and outside marriage, and judicial attitudes to rape victims have remained some of the most difficult to change.

The impact of feminism is not confined to legislative change nor to women's increasing prominence in public life. As in previous decades, women have struggled with the meanings of love and sexuality. While the prevalence of sexually transmitted diseases has brought changes to sexual activity, sexuality itself has become contested ground. Many women have challenged the clear distinctions made between heterosexual and lesbian love, arguing for a continuum of experience and meaning. Others have challenged the links popularly assumed to exist between sexuality (or race and class) and identity.

In response to the challenges levelled by many groups of women, the feminist analysis of women's subordination espoused in the early days of Women's Liberation has emerged during the 1980s and 1990s as a more sophisticated and powerful critique. The concept of 'difference' rather than 'sisterhood' has gained ground as feminists have tackled the question of which women are represented by feminism. They have had to reassess their own and earlier feminist positions. They have joined the long feminist tradition of critiquing the multiple manifestations of oppression in women's lives and celebrating women's daily forms of negotiation and resistance.

Document 4.1 'Deep down within we have dignity'

Faith Bandler's address to the Annual General Meeting of Kirinari, the Aboriginal Children's Advancement Society, questions the principles that had formed the basis of liberal attitudes to Aborigines for decades, including the Federal Council for the Advancement of Aborigines and Torres Strait Islanders of which she was Vice-President. Her words reflect the changes occurring in Aboriginal politics and the growing urgency of calls for land rights and self-determination. Her calls for action on maternal health—fifty years after white reformers had raised similar concerns in the white community—are being repeated by others in the 1990s, when maternal deaths among Aboriginal women are rising.

Gordon Bryant has spoken, Mr Chairman, about the need for political action to further the advancement of Aborigines, and of course being on the Federal Executive of the Federal Council for so many years I am convinced that political action is absolutely vital. I thought that you might think for a short time this afternoon about what education has to do with Aboriginal advancement.

In the first place, I find it hard to accept the word 'advancement'. I am rather sorry that it has been used in various committees established to assist the Aboriginal people. I am not convinced that it is advancement for the indigenous Australians to become like the European Australians.

When one thinks of the murder, rape, and theft and all the crookery under the sun that has been introduced into this country since the invasion of the white man, I am not sure that this word advancement is used advisedly in connection with a better deal for the indigenous Australians. I don't think there is any doubt at all that there is tremendous emphasis on education and this is one particular field that I have never bought into myself, mainly because I have concerned myself with legislative changes and employment.

No doubt, education has a very real part to play. But when you sit down and talk about the kids who are ready to go into secondary school or the kids who need a scholarship to go on to university I think it is a serious mistake not to think about the mothers of these children.

Now Gordon over there is probably thinking 'There's Faith on her hobby horse again'. When one has a house to run as well as help run *his* Federal Council one thinks of the needs of the people on this earth who give birth to the population—the mothers. It is my belief that tremendous thought should be given to the mothers of Aboriginal children not only in NSW but throughout the whole of Australia today.

I am not necessarily thinking about nursing mothers, once the baby is born. I am thinking about the pre-natal period, because it seems to me that if you are going to have children grow up and have the powers to concentrate, to do the work that is set before them, and at the same time to work in a school with the curriculum set out for middle-class white people, then you have got to have relatively healthy kids to stand up to it.

I have yet to find a family, be they black, white or brindle, where the mother has been undernourished or underfed in the pre-natal period where [subsequently] a child of very high I.Q. has been produced. I would ask you to give some very special thought to this and when you are going to your State or Federal member, you might ask that they consider providing a little extra finance for the mothers of Aboriginal families in order that milk may be bought and that bread and butter and other day-to-day necessities may be there in the house. If you don't give some thought to the mother and the infants, it is silly to start at the top of the tree. To my way of thinking it is merely mowing the lawn without getting to the grass roots. I would like to point out I have come to this conclusion over a period of 8 or 9 years, in consultation with some of our Sydney medical people who have given this tremendous thought, particularly two who spent some considerable time in Walgett and Broken Hill.

I would say 'So much for education', and you must think about this new aspect which I have just briefly mentioned. To me this question of advancement has to do with dignity. How can anyone have any dignity at all if they are permanently living on the receiving end. Now Alan Duncan told me just before this session started, about 'Grants in Aid'. It seems to me that if such a thing as this were introduced we are going back to 1930. Dignity is a very important aspect of Aboriginal advancement. I hope the time is not too far off when you can close up shop.

It is still necessary to seek public money, but I have to confess that on the days of door-knock appeals for the assistance of Aborigines, be it for Hostels or be it for whatever you like, these are the days in the year that I put a sari on, because this appeal has to do with my dignity. You are not going from door to door for the crippled, or the deaf or blind, you are knocking on people's doors asking for financial assistance for a particular group of people whose skin happens to be the wrong colour for a fair chance of education. While I do see the necessity in the next few years for this particular type of work—the building of hostels, and the special assistance being given to children for education—I only hope that you can see the end of it. An end to this help can only occur if something is done about employment. I have said this before and I shall say it again.

I was born in poverty myself. The other day when we were looking at a plan for the re-development of La Perouse, and I made a suggestion about the right of those people out there to own the seven acres, someone said, 'Well that's all right for you Faith, you live up there.' Well I didn't always live up there. I lived in conditions far worse than the people living at La Perouse. Deep down within, we have dignity. It so happened that I was born into a family that understood what trade unions meant. Because of this we didn't work for lower wages than the chap with the white skin. We became very independent people. If I thought that were it not for good well-meaning European people who are prepared to get up and go and do something, my children would have no chance of a higher education, then I would almost despair with deep regret and shame. I would want to know that my kids would be educated out of the money that came into my home each week, and I believe that this is the sincere hope of every dark Australian, right throughout the country. They have got to be independent, they have to have equal pay for equal work to begin with, they must be able to build their own houses wherever they wish, they want to be able to pay for their own houses.

In essence, I am saying that we must work towards the time when this special assistance must surely end, and the Aborigines will be equal in the true sense of the word. I don't want you to feel for one minute that

I don't appreciate and value the magnificent work that you are doing here at Kirinari. But I remember when we set about forming the Aboriginal–Australian Fellowship, that one night on the verge of tears and desperation, and not knowing which way to turn, I hopped in the car and went down to Narrabeen to see Alf Clint, and he said to me 'Don't worry girl, you know if we don't work ourselves out of a job in the end, then we aren't working the proper way'.

I think this should be your goal—to eventually work yourselves out of a job by bringing the Aboriginal people in this country to where they no longer need any special help. They will merely get their ordinary wages and get the concessions in Social Services as all other Australians do. They will also contribute as far as taxes are concerned.

I'm afraid I am a very poor substitute for Kath Walker, and I must confess that I didn't have sufficient time to prepare all the things I wanted to say to you. Forgive me for having rambled, but I want to say first of all that I look on the Federal Council (this is not another commercial by the way) for the Advancement of Aborigines and Torres Strait Islanders, as an organisation that has worked for and given tremendous confidence to Aboriginal people not only in one state but throughout all states. It is true that at first nobody would stand up and have a say, but recently one of the teachers from the Teachers' Federation who was at the last conference said to me, 'You know Faith, I don't know that I'll go to another of your Conferences,' so I said 'Why not?' 'Well I've got to paint myself black if I want a chance to say anything.'

I think this is a fair indication of an organisation that has worked in a very sincere and genuine way, truly providing a platform for the Aboriginal and Islanders' voice.

Kirinari (Aboriginal Children's Advancement Society)
Kirinari, vol. 1, no. 4, March 1969, pp. 23–4

Document 4.2 'It came down to suicide or abortion'

Jeannie Dempsey's experience of abortion, just before it was made legal in South Australia in 1969, conveys the secrecy that still surrounded abortion and sexual activity then. Jeannie grew up in a small country town and had a Catholic upbringing. Her story highlights the dramatic juxtaposition of 'public' and 'private' worlds and the skewed priorities of governments who funded space exploration in preference to research into contraception. Jeannie begins her story with a discussion of contraception alternatives.

Birth control was condoms or, if you were very brave or knew a doctor, you could maybe go on the pill. Though even when I was younger the pill just wasn't an issue. I mean, unless you had gory periods (laughs) it was the only way you could get the pill. But I'd moved away from home when I was sixteen. I'd run out of school in the country town, as it was the way young girls came to the city. I became sexually active at, I suppose, about seventeen or eighteen. I mean there was no way I would go and buy a packet of condoms. I probably wouldn't have even known what one looked like at that stage anyway. The boys didn't either I don't think, way back then.

So it was the rhythm method. You know, the idea that you avoided fucking in the four days each side of the middle of your menstrual cycle. I'm sure I wasn't even particularly careful about that. Say I was seventeen when I first started screwing boys, and I was twenty-one, I think when I had the abortion, so that was four years of a lot of waiting for periods to come at the end of a month and thinking, 'I'll never do that again,' but you did [laughs].

Would you have heard of other women who'd had abortions?
Commonly it was girls leaving town and just going off and having babies and having them adopted . . . Certainly our local girls did that, or got married. They got married incredibly early . . . I was quite exceptional, going to Teachers' College and out teaching. A lot of my friends were pregnant at seventeen, eighteen. I can remember walking home from school, having done my intermediate exam, and bumping into a friend who was racing home to get the nappies off the line—in intermediate. I was fifteen, so was she.

At the time I did get pregnant—I had the abortion in 1969 and I was twenty-one—I was sharing a house with six females, and I found out later that two of them had abortions within the same twelve-month span that I did, but nobody ever discussed it. We didn't even admit to our best friends that we actually went to bed with boys. It's just so ridiculous—we pretended we didn't. It wasn't nice (laughs).

Where were you living?
I was living in a much larger country town, so there was a little anonymity. I was not dating anybody seriously. There were probably a stream of men. The particular man that I got pregnant to at that stage was married, but I wasn't emotionally attached to him in any way and I didn't even tell him. I was teaching. This was the month where I didn't get the period, you know. I remember I was home with my parents on holidays when the period didn't come and I was just terrified . . . I can remember taking

iron pills furiously, thinking that maybe I was just anaemic—it was this horrific two weeks of going to the toilet and checking myself the whole time and nothing happened . . .

But I still wouldn't go to a doctor. I mean, I couldn't—I'd gone out with half the doctors in the town. The father of the child was actually one (laughs) and I still wouldn't go to a doctor and ask—I just couldn't do it. It didn't occur to me to even lie that I was engaged and go to a strange doctor in town to get the pill, or anything at this stage. I was just so nervous of the whole thing. We just didn't talk about it. It had no exposure.

I definitely contemplated suicide. I mean, that seemed like the easiest option. The three options were suicide, getting rid of it or coming clean to everybody and going into a St Joseph's house or whatever and having it. That one I just ruled as impossible . . .

And so it came down to suicide or an abortion. I decided I had to tell somebody and it had to be somebody who was going to be able to help me. I had a friend who was a pharmacist. He was a dear friend and I thought, 'Well I'll tell him and see if he can help me in any way'. . . And around that time I started suffering awful morning sickness . . .

There I was, living in a house with two women and another three right next door. I used to get up in the morning and vomit silently in the toilet so they wouldn't know, and go off to school, and have a bucket in the porch outside my classroom. And I used to have to sneak outside and throw up all the time, and nobody could know. I just used to retch half the day.

That's when I had to think seriously about, well it was abortion or suicide. I used to stand there at road crossings a lot with buses going past and picture just—. All I had to do was take a few steps out there. And I used to ring my chemist friend a lot, and he used to call around a lot. I talked to him about abortion, but not having a clue how to go about it, and he happened to know somebody who had had an abortion and he got the phone number for me and it went from there.

It was a Sydney address. I can remember walking down to this phone box one night . . . They wanted to know instantly how pregnant I was, and I didn't even know how to count how pregnant I was. I didn't understand all that. All they were interested in was the money.

Can you remember how much money they wanted?
I have seventy-five dollars in my mind, but whatever it was, it was a hell of a lot of money. It really did feel like a lot. But that might have been with the plane fare included. I know they were determined that the money was going to be up front before anything (laughs).

And they made a time. It was Monday July 21st. That was it. Nobody was to know. It was so important. And that's what's so amazing . . . There must have been some amazing forces operating against it for me to have been like that. I had to plan how I was going to get to Sydney and back without anybody knowing, and that was probably the hardest thing of the lot. I was so naive . . . I had to plot to get away without anybody knowing where I was going . . . I was also scared because there had been a real lot of publicity just prior to that . . . Within a week before the event [there were] the Wainer busts in Melbourne where abortion clinics [were] raided. It was front page of *The Advertiser*. So all I could see were photographers out front, police cars outside the abortion clinic, and all of a sudden me being on the front page of *The Advertiser* for my parents to see. So there was an extra terror introduced at that stage. . . .

[A friend of the pharmacist] took me down and put me on the plane on the Monday morning. It was an early flight out. She was a teacher, so I suppose she went off to school then. And she was there to meet me when I got back. I can remember that. I can remember what I was wearing—a viyella paisley dress with pin tucking, and a waist, and it was getting terribly tight because I was thickening somewhat around the middle. I sat down on the plane and immediately thought, 'I'm going to throw up . . . I just threw up silently as I'd learnt how (laughs) most of the way to Sydney.

And got to Sydney. Had the address. The address was Maroubra and it was a flat—a flat in a number of blocks in Maroubra. I hopped in a taxi and said the address, and the taxi driver turned around and gave this sneer, and I thought, you know, 'here I go, front page in the paper' again (laughs).

So I got there and it was just built in the thirties, forties. A very ordinary looking block of flats, loud music coming out of the one that I had to knock on. And I remember walking in and the first thing I was asked if I had the money. It was a woman answered the door and she just took the money and then told me to go into this room and take my clothes off and put on . . . just a floral brunch coat and some socks. And they were just, you know, like the bloody socks in the bottom of my washing basket . . . I mean, it really didn't look terribly surgical, and at that stage, with the loud music and this lack of surgical atmosphere, I mean, I freaked. I had no idea what to expect. I thought at that stage I was going to a doctor and that he was skilled in his work. I knew that it was without anaesthetic, but that didn't mean much to me because I had no idea. I had never had an internal examination in my life, let alone anything more drastic. Then I had to go and wait . . .

Then it was my turn. Oh, it was my first view of stirrups and things like that. The doctor was there. He had a mask on and a white coat, and all I could see were these cold steely eyes . . . It felt like something very cold and cruel. I didn't think, 'here's this wonderful humanitarian man saving we women in trauma'. I had this horrible feeling that this man got some perverse joy out of watching young girls scream . . . there was no conversation with him or anything. It was just, you know, 'Open your legs, put your legs in the stirrups'. The woman—I think it was the same woman who let me in—came and held my hand, and she fainted in the middle of it. She got all squeamish and fainted . . . There was, as I said, no anaesthetic, there was no pain killing. It was the most excruciatingly painful thing, and I mean I know I was writhing around and sort of grabbing on to her and probably making some pretty ungodly noises. And the main thing was not knowing how much longer. I can remember that, not knowing how much longer it was going to be and thinking, you know, 'If it's only going to be another minute I can stand it, but if it's not, I'm going to die'. It seemed to go on forever. I suppose it was about a ten-minute operation, I don't know.

He was giving you a D & C—a proper abortion?
Yes, I mean I guess. I didn't have a clue what he was doing, apart from ripping my whole insides out, and I didn't want to think about it . . . And when it finished he gave me a pack of sulphur tablets and some panadol and I was sent out to the waiting room. I was told that the best thing for me to do was to exercise—to keep walking. Nobody wanted to know how I was going to get back to Adelaide or anything. So I had a cup of tea. I was allowed to have my first sulphur tab and Panadol, and as soon as I finished the cup of tea I was shooed out. I don't know how I got back into Sydney. I suppose I walked until I hailed a taxi . . .

I suppose I had five or six hours to kill before my plane left, and I knew nobody in Sydney, or certainly nobody that I would have contacted to let them know I was there. So I just had to walk the streets of Sydney until it was time to go to the airport and get on the plane back. That was the mind-boggling time, walking around with my whole life just being quite shattered there, and not knowing whether I was going to all of a sudden start haemorrhaging. I mean, I must have read Dymphna Cusack by then or something. I'm sure I'd read tales of people dying with backyard abortions and, you know, I thought I had a better chance than many because this person was a doctor, and I believed him to be so. But I had no idea what the next step would be in my healing.

So I walked around and there they were—the men on television screens in every window in Sydney, and crowds of people standing around them—the men bouncing on the moon, their first steps. Neil Armstrong leaping across the moon, and there was I, this pathetic little creature in a blue paisley dress (laughs) waiting to see whether I was going to haemorrhage to death in the streets of Sydney.

Anyway, I made it. I can remember coming back being given a commemorative spoon of the men landing on the moon (laughs) . . .

There've probably been years when I've hardly mentioned it. You know, it just hasn't been an issue. But yes, all of my close friends know the story. You know, if anybody talks about the day the men landed on the moon (laughs) I usually chip in with a bit of a yarn.

> Interview conducted by Barbara Baird, no. OH 91/9
> 'Abortion in South Australia before 1970 Project'
> J.D. Somerville Oral History Collection,
> Mortlock Library, South Australia

Document 4.3 WOMEN'S = HUMAN Liberation

The Australian Women's Liberation Movement followed on the heels of its American counterpart. Other intellectual influences are revealed in this manifesto from the Adelaide Women's Liberation Movement— for example, the early emphasis on socialisation as a force that shaped 'sex roles'; calls for the abolition of the family; and the entrenched feminist demands for child care, for the right to control one's own body and for equality between the sexes. The contradictory tendencies toward individualism and collectivism emerge throughout this document, and its stress on securing the cooperation of men in the struggle for women's liberation marks it as a document from 1971, the very early days of Women's Liberation.

MANIFESTO—WOMEN'S LIBERATION MOVEMENT, ADELAIDE

Women's Liberation is *not* a feminist movement, i.e., it is not narrowly confined to the struggle of women for equality with men in the present society. The aims of Women's Liberation are *total* in the sense that the liberation of women must concur with the liberation of *all individuals* from a situation in which the only social accepted mode of self-expression or development is in terms of pre-defined sexual roles.

A woman is never taken for *herself*: she is always 'Bill's bird', 'the little woman', or just 'mum'. Her greatest humiliation lies in the situation where her decorated body, being the subject of male phallic fantasies and the consequent source of much commercial profit, determines her *value* both in her own ideas and those of the male.

But that the male regards the female in this way indicates that he, too, is imprisoned within a sexual role: potency and/or virility become for him fetishized and, in worshipping them, symbols of his *power* over woman. (The woman, knowing herself to be desired, exploits this male obsession: in this sense, and in others, the power relationship is reciprocal.) This situation, because no male can ever measure up to such absolute potency, leads to male fears, real though false, as to his 'virility', his 'masculinity'. Just as the woman is required to fulfil expectations of her role as sexual object, wife, mother, so is the male required to fulfil expectations of him as actor in the outside world. To *succeed* as bread-winner he must develop qualities required for success in our society: aggressiveness, competitiveness, emotional detachment, and, since he is always involved in authoritarian work structure, authoritarianism. More-over, in a national society that relates to other societies in terms of power (economic and military), he has to be trained, psychologically and phys-ically, for the military role, as instrument of his nation's power-obsession. If he rejects this role on political/moral grounds, society calls him 'coward', 'sissy'; and, since much of self-definition and security is based in the dominant role of 'masculinity', his whole being in relation to the existing world may be called into doubt.

Our society talks of 'love' between male and female; but this 'love' is a mystification, the rationale for the modern marriage/family institu-tion—for how can spontaneous feeling or communication of self take place when individuals relate not to each other as individuals, but to each other as the occupiers of predefined roles? How can the generous free reciprocity that is human occur when the nature of these sexual roles is to make the male dominant over the female?—for reciprocity can only occur in a situation between equals.

Accordingly, the freeing of woman from her subservient role, the assertion of her freedom as an individual, must *simultaneously* involve an attack on the male *role*. Men must have demonstrated to them the destruction of human relations that they perpetuate in clinging to their dominance as males. For males are frustrated in their possible wish for communication of their dreams and despairs to the individual closest to them by the obstacles arising from the predefinition of the other (the female)—a pre-definition usually mutually established and maintained—as illogical, irrational, ignorant of the affairs of the world, gossipy, frivolous, etc, particularly when that other expects him to know how to handle the world and despises him if he admits any failure here.

If we believe that men and women are individuals, each with an experience of the world unique to them, who can relate to this world as active critical subjects rather than passively behaving as the occupants of pre-defined roles, then why does this individuality not express itself, throw off these chains? The answer lies in the nature of the social system in which they exist. As Herbert Marcuse says: '*Domination* is in effect whenever the individual's goals and purposes and the means of striving for and attaining them are prescribed to him and performed by him as something prescribed'. In a society where hierarchical top-down organisation predominates, a minority (of men) will dominate the rest. This domination is based not just in their actual power (control of the economy, of the political and military systems) but in their more or less conscious perpetuation of a culture that induces people to see this system of domination as *natural*. This cultural control successfully whittles down the imagination of most to conceive that society might be organised so as to minimize domination and allow each individual effective participation in the decisions governing his/her life. Domination, in requiring effective control of the many by the few determined to hold on to their power, requires that people be *taught* to *behave* in organised, *predictable* patterns that service the structure of domination. This is why sexuality and human relations have to be *institutionalised* in the marriage-family. Spontaneity is the arch-enemy of this system and spontaneity arises when individuals exercise their right to *act*, to choose, to determine their lives, because it is then that the particular chain of behaviour is broken . . .

We can change this situation, which is historical not natural.
It is significant that Women's Liberation, in being the first expression of political radicalism to be consciously and directly concerned with the individual, in effect, with the intimate relation between two human beings with human relations generally, has erupted in the modern, western societies in this time of affluence and of the struggle for acceptance of the common humanity of other (women constituting the largest group with minority status) minority groups, the negroes and the Vietnamese.

Women's Liberation has to evoke what women already, if only partially, know—that they are denied individual creative potential, denied recognition as individuals in their own right. Every woman who has looked ahead, passively and/or despairingly, to a *closed* future of marriage, children and housework knows this; every woman who has wanted education sufficient to get a job in which she can express herself to some degree, who has sought after good jobs or who has suffered routine jobs knows the brutal, discriminatory practices all along that line. We should be more inclined to believe the myth of the 'happy housewife' if it could be demonstrated that woman ever had any choice to be otherwise. Such 'happiness' may be the symptom of more or less mature, more or less tenuous adaption [sic] to a virtually inescapable situation, rather than *real* happiness. That the situation is inescapable for most middle-class women as for working-class women suggests the obstacles to be not only, or even primarily, material. On the whole, middle-class women only escape the pressures of *Women's Day* ideology and social expectations, made most effectively by the family, if they, by educational attainment or some 'break', have partial refuge in a community (university, bohemian deviant social groups) which goes part or all of the way in accepting her as an individual first, a woman second. As the last phrase indicates, even here she is likely to be fragmented into roles with their respective functions.

Women's Liberation can spearhead the change, but to do this it must show itself as *human* (individual) *liberation*. It must, in this latter sense, always remember there is little point in claiming equality if the nature of the latter is to make us equal to unfree them. Yet while men are unfree, women are materially, socially and psychologically more unfree—hence *Women's* Liberation. *Women's = Human* Liberation since, in freeing ourselves, we must free men (and vice versa).

Programme

The following aims and demands may be classified as two types:
(A) *Structural*—those that would challenge and eventually destroy the existing system of domination.
(B) *Reforms*—i.e., although significant change would be required for their achievement, they do not challenge the basis of the system of domination.

(A) Structural (the general critique made above is already assumed: only specific points are made here)

WE ARE WORKING TOWARDS:
(1) An end to the socialisation of children and adults—by the family, the education system, the mass media, and socio-cultural agencies in general—into their respective sexual roles.
(2) The abolition of institutionalisation of relationships between men and women. This means abolition of the family as an *institution*, an end to the laws bonding together the members of a family.

There is no reason why people may not freely *choose* to live in a familial situation; but they should remain in that situation only by their free will. Equally, people should be free to choose other relational situations—e.g., small communal groupings.

(3) The democratisation of inter-sexual and inter-generational relationships. In the relations between man and woman, between parents and children, there should exist reciprocal recognition of each as an individual in his/her own right, with capacity and right to participate in the decisions governing that relational situation, and with freedom to pursue his/her own life as he/she deems fit. (While small, children may not be able to exercise such rights, nonetheless, they should still be respected as individuals; the age at which they can exercise such rights is problematic and should be left flexible to accommodate the differences in growth of individuals.)

(4) The end of commercial exploitation of women as sex-objects, of human sexuality in general. This would require the ends of the economic system to be human, rather than profit and production as overriding ends in themselves.

(5) The end of a situation in which most individuals, for the bulk of their working lives, are involved in alienated labour. The development of a situation in which, so far as we have to meet material necessity, we do so communally and democratically, in which, therefore, the labour process and product are our own and not another's. A situation in which each and all, having met material necessity, possess the means whereby to develop and express themselves.

(B) Reforms

We demand:

(1) Democratisation of the existing family institution, at least so far as the limits of institutionalisation allow it.

(2) The equal sharing of housework and child-care between husband and wife, with the work situation adjusted accordingly. (e.g., guarantee of women's right to work; the granting by employers of free shopping time during working time to both men and women.)

(3) The rationalisation of housework in the provision of communal facilities, such as local and cheap dining facilities, child-minding centres, and laundries for those who want to use them.

(4) If women are forced by temporary necessity (the care of infants), or *choose* to undertake the bulk of the domestic work, that they be paid a wage by the state for what is essential productive labour.

(5) That women have the right to control their own bodies:
- That the government initiate and finance a widespread education campaign on birth-control, and establish local community birth-control

centres for the dissemination and distribution of birth-control information and devices.

- That such information and centres be extended to cover the various physiological disorders the female body is susceptible to.
- The abolition of sales tax—at present 27.5%—on contraceptives.
- That free abortion on demand be instituted.

(6) The removal of all barriers to equality for women in *work*:

- The full integration of all areas of work, i.e. an end to the labelling of some areas as being fit only for men, or only for women. (Only if this occurs can 'equal pay for equal work' really mean economic equality.)
- Equal pay.
- The payment of maternity allowances to women workers at least three months before births and one to two years after births.
- Guarantee of the same or similar job to a woman returned after absence through pregnancy.
- The establishment of free, small, professionally-staffed child-centres in every work place (factories, offices, stores, universities, schools); these centres could be directed by a committee of elected parents and staff.
- That further training, promotion, etc., be equally open to women as to men.

(7) The abolition of all sexual differentiation in *education*: i.e.

- The establishment of all schools as co-educational in every sense.
- The abolition of any sexual differentiation in subjects and vocational choices.
- If there exists training in schools in health, cooking etc., that boys and girls be required to undertake it. (This demand is important in the present situation so as to legitimize male interest in cooking, etc., to destroy the inbuilt male resistance to such tastes and thereby free girls from their future burden of having been the only ones inducted into these 'arts'—Once this has occurred, compulsion should give way to individual choice.)
- The encouragement of and provision of opportunities for all girls to develop their education as far as possible, to develop interest in the traditional male preserves of politics and technology, and to secure equal training in these fields.

(8) The provision of educational training or retraining schemes and employment for women of an age no longer burdened by the care of children, so that they may regain their self-respect as individuals in developing their capacities and contributing to the community.

(9) The repeal of the law that makes it an offence for male homosexuals to express their homosexuality as they choose; the end of all discrimination in employment, and in social life generally, against homosexuals.

(10) That women be written back into history; that analysis of their historical role, of the source and development of the division of labour between the sexes, be made.

We appeal to women to *combine in solidarity* to make these demands and simultaneously, to secure the understanding and cooperation of *men* in making them.

Liberation, no. 4, June 1971

Document 4.4 'A mixed feeling of sadness and hatred'

While white women were campaigning for health services, child care and educational opportunities, Aboriginal women were living in 'conditions without hope'. The National Council of Aboriginal and Islander Women organised to assist those most in need. This report from Geraldine Briggs, the National President, recounts the extremes of poverty faced by many Aboriginal communities, their vulnerability to disease and malnutrition and the responsibility of the white community for perpetuating such injustice. Aboriginal communities, however, were far from defeated.

YARMUK

At last we have been to Alice Springs and I can't describe the feeling I had when I saw Aborigines living in the Todd River. It was a mixed feeling of sadness and hatred which, when analysed, boiled down to frustration. Sadness because my people have to live in such conditions without hope. And hatred to think anyone would let human beings live in such terrible conditions. Many people we spoke to said 'Aborigines want to live like that' but this is not true, as we spoke to all the people living in the Todd River in their different tribal groups.

Three members of the National Council of Aboriginal and Island Women were with me—Trudi Longbottom, La Perouse, Sydney; Cecilia Smith, Queensland; and Pat Eatock, New South Wales; and Merl Jackomos of Melbourne. The first ones we spoke with were a family group, a grandmother, her daughter, her grand-daughter and great grand-daughter. The grand-daughter's husband had deserted her, and she did not know how to go about getting a pension—all she received was her child endowment for two children. The younger one assured us she wanted to be in a house. Also the older women, but they did not want to be parted from any of their family.

The second was a group of men who were there from the stations. They, too, said they thought that Aborigines should have better homes. There was a white man with an Aboriginal wife. He said they could not get a house. Then there was a couple with three children all under the age of six. The baby was four months old. They had been there twelve months, waiting for a commission home, and they were told they will have to wait for two years. When the river was in flood they moved under the school which is built very high off the ground, and the police told them they had to move. The mother asked them to put the children in a home until they found a place to live or until the rain and flood cleared up, but they were refused. No wonder the children are sick.

The next family had an old lady with TB and it was a pitiful case, she wouldn't stay in hospital because she wanted to go home to South Australia where she originally comes from. They had no food to give her, so two of our members bought the things that she wanted—milk, eggs, soup and nourishing food. She was very grateful. We asked a high government official to send her back to where she comes from, and he has promised to do so, with her permission. There was also a baby there and others, and I can quite easily see how this terrible disease can spread.

Yuendumu settlement

We went to a large settlement which has over a thousand Aboriginal people. We walked around and spoke to a lot of people with an interpreter, because most of them, especially the young women and old women and men can't speak English at all. The young babies were carried in coolamons which was really fascinating to see. The women make beautiful beads out of seeds gathered from the bush and the men make quite a large number of artefacts which they sell themselves on the reserve. The houses they live in I was quite disgusted with. They consist of one room, about ten by twelve. All the family sleep in this room. They have no room for tables or beds. There were toilets and showers, but they were about a hundred yards from each house. The houses have to use one tap and in this group they had no toilet facilities. We were told they had to go into the bush. The pensioners mostly live in humpies made of tin and rags, so low that they would have to crawl into them. They too have no toilet facilities. One of these pensioners was crippled, and got around by crawling on her hands and knees. There was also one blind. In spite of this these women smiled happily when we told them through our interpreter my grand-mother and mother and also the other Aboriginal girl's (Merl's) grandmother came from the tribe.

The area around where these people live was kept very clean. They have a large Church which is as modern as any in the city. I wonder what they think when they go into that Church and know that they have to live in these abject conditions. The Aboriginal girls are the most beautiful girls I've ever seen, and their carriage was perfect, and the men are very handsome. They're all black and beautiful.

Mr Hans Bandler spoke to the people through an interpreter and explained what the conference was held in Alice Springs for, and I spoke to the women after, through a woman interpreter. Some women complained of working for $37 a week in laundry and housework etc. and the nurses get $52 a fortnight. They say they have to work every day and start early in the morning. We asked were they happy with their one room, and they said they wanted more. We were told by one of the men that his people were so grateful to have us go there. They knew that someone cared.

We had tea in the canteen which caters for several hundred Aborigines, then went to the hall where many joined in singing and dancing. The children's dancing was enjoyed by all the visitors. They had their own band there, and the children have the Western style of dancing. They wriggled their bodies and shoulders as if they were doing the hula. They were also doing the twist. It was really good to see it. I'd like to congratulate Mrs Bandler and Mrs Clague for making the conference a success. . . .

Contact

Now we have contact all over Australia with our sisters. So girls, we have a lot of work in front of us. We need your support and help, as no-one gets paid for work in our committees.

Yarmuk (meaning 'my relative') is the voice of the National Council of Aboriginal and Island Women.

Newsletter on Aboriginal Affairs,
no. 2, July–Sept. 1972, pp. 23–4

Document 4.5 'Interview with a lesbian'

As the title of this document suggests, lesbians were considered unusual, even by those in the Women's Movement: a somewhat strange breed in need of explanation. The lesbian interviewed here conveys the political and emotional dimensions of her choice, and signals the 'discovery' of the clitoris in women's sexual pleasure.

Q.   How would you define being a lesbian?
A.   Relating emotionally and sensually to other women.
Q.   What prompted you to sensually relate to other women?
A.   I was fucked off with male dominance and their lack of emo-
         tional understanding.
Q.   So are a lot of other women but they don't become lesbians.
         Why did you?
A.   I associated with other women in preference to men when my
         marriage broke up because I found that men were not interested
         in me as myself but tried to use me purely as a sex symbol. By
         associating almost exclusively with other women I found that
         these were either single women or deserted wives or unhappily
         married women who fundamentally had the same feeling
         towards male dominance that I had.
Q.   Did you sexually relate to any of these women?
A.   To several of them in a guilty, unfulfilled sort of way.
Q.   Why was it guilty and unfulfilled?
A.   Because of the feeling of being socially disapproved of and the
         inbred, brainwashed feeling of not being 'normal'.
Q.   How long did this phase last?
A.   Quite some time. Until I finally realized that my life was mine
         and no person or social system had the right to dictate to me
         how I should feel or think or express myself.
Q.   Do you feel guilty and unfulfilled now in your relationships
         with women?
A.   No. I accept myself as a lesbian and although I don't blazon it
         from the roof-tops, I don't find it necessary to hide this part of
         myself either.
Q.   How did your friends and family react to the fact that you are
         a lesbian?
A.   Usually with shock, embarrassment and disbelief.
Q.   How did you react to this?
A.   At first with indignation, because I knew that I was always the
         same person with them that they had always known and I
         thought it was unfair of them to be upset because they seemed
         to judge me without knowing the facts and really when I tried
         to reason with them and inform them it was something they—
         'Didn't want to talk about.'
Q.   What eventually happened to your relationship with these people
         who disapproved?
A.   Most of them I cut out of my life and rejected, just as they had

rejected me, but some who had found previous relationships with me to be worthwhile still continued to see me and with perseverance and understanding on both sides formed closer (non-lesbian) relationships than ever before.

Q. Do you think that women should admit to being lesbians, especially professional women?

A. I know that a lot of women, especially professional women, feel the necessity to hide the fact that they are lesbians because of the social pressure and disapproval they would have to face under the present male dominated role-playing society in which we live. But ideally, I feel that they should not hide in fear and shame the fact that they may love another woman.

Q. There is still a lot of suspicion in society among heterosexual women particularly against lesbians; what do you think accounts for this?

A. The fact that most of these women are completely misinformed about what a lesbian really is. They imagine a 'butch looking Charlie' with slick-back hairdo and coarse manners lurking around lavatories with a bag of boiled lollies to entice luscious young 'Lolitas' into a life of lesbian lust. (The melodrama is intentional!)

Q. Why do you think that heterosexual women have this view of lesbians, apart from the fact that they are misinformed?

A. Because a certain small percentage of lesbians who have not adjusted to the fact that they are simply women who love other women, try to role-play pretending that they are men. They must be very dissatisfied with themselves as people. They have not been able to identify as women successfully and try to play the role of men as to them this seems to endow them with some sense of power which their own insecure image doesn't give them.

Q. What do you think of the typical 'butch' lesbian image?

A. I don't like it at all and avoid this type of lesbian where possible, because they seem to fall into the 'sick' category of role-playing and insecurity in themselves and seem to be a propped up shambler of a human being.

Q. Do you find lesbian relationships to be more rewarding than heterosexual ones?

A. Yes. Both physically and emotionally. A loving and understanding woman partner is much more sensitive to another woman's sensual, erotic, psychological and emotional needs than most

men know how to be. They have the advantage for a start of
knowing the exact bodily needs of a woman in lovemaking.

Q.   Do lesbians use artificial penises or dildos usually?

A.   No. I know many lesbians and have never known any who use
these things. Why would they? After all the vaginal climax is
a myth dreamed up and propagated by men in a male dominated
society. It is the clitoris which really counts.

Liberation, June 1972, pp. 8–9

Document 4.6 'Why do straight sisters sometimes cry when they are called lesbians?'

This excerpt comes from a paper presented to the Women's Liberation Theory Conference at Mt Beauty in January 1973 by members of the Hobart Women's Action Group, who charge the advocates of Women's Liberation and its principles (e.g. consciousness-raising and sister-hood) with sexism. The paper was not well received and many at the conference failed to see the connection it made between feminism and lesbianism. The writers argue: that 'Women's Liberation is about female sexuality, female autonomy and about freedom from sex role stereotypes: the lesbian issue is not a private one but exists at the core of the women's issue'. The paper begins with a quote from Sappho was a right on woman *by Sidney Abbot and Barbara Love, followed by an exchange between Alic Schwartzer and Simone de Beauvoir.[1]*

It is still very hard . . . for feminists to seriously consider what
is most threatening, the point by point substantive links between
Feminist theory and Lesbianism.[1]

'A.S.: Do you think that female homosexuality as the most radical
form of the exclusion of men—could be a political weapon at
the present stage of the struggle?
Simone de Beauvoir: . . . I haven't thought about it. I think that in
principle it's good that there are some very radical women. The
lesbians can play a useful role. But when they let their judgement
be obscured by their preconceived notions, they run the risk of
scaring off from the movement women who are heterosexual. I find
boring and irritating their mystique of the clitoris and all those sexual
dogmas that they would like to impose on us.'[2]

As with so many anti-lesbian comments, the real nature of this statement
may be revealed by comparing it with similar statements by left-wing men

about women in 'their' political movements. In both, the oppressed groups—women or lesbians—are acceptable as long as they subordinate their demands or individuality to the 'broader' aims of the movement. Just as women in left-wing movements became dissatisfied with waiting in the wings until the socialist revolution solved everyone's problems, lesbians have become increasingly dissatisfied with the women's liberation movement that demands the same of them. There is, however one significant difference in this parallel. Women will become equal with men 'after the revolution', but lesbians (poof) will disappear.[3]

We see the unfortunate position of lesbians in W.L. as a symptom of W.L.'s failure to come to grips with sexism inside the movement itself and therefore in society as a whole.

This paper is an attempt to demonstrate this in two ways:

1   Through our own experience in women's liberation.
2   Through an examination of directions and tendencies which W.L. thinking has been taking. This will take us not into a reinterpretation of W.L. theory in order to include the lesbian, but back to a restatement of what we see as basic W.L. theory which depends for its validity on the inclusion of all women and on an understanding of sexism.

We feel it necessary to clarify what we mean by the sexist society: A sexist society is not necessarily a patriarchal society—it could equally well be a matriarchy or a society in which the sexes have equal power and influence providing that their spheres of action are different and enforced as different. In a radical feminist critique of society, sex is the principle by which society is organized, which precedes all other organizing principles i.e., power, wealth, status, etc. Patriarchy is not a precondition of sexism. Sexism means organizing people according to sex and sexual behaviour, and attributing various behaviour, personality and status traits to people on the basis of sex. Without sexism, patriarchy is deprived of its organizing principle and of its ideology of consent. Sexism then is sufficient basis for patriarchy but does not necessarily lead to it. In other words, sexism is a way of structuring society; patriarchy and matriarchy point out who get the goodies at any particular time. Unlike capitalism, it doesn't tell us both how society is structured and who benefits from it, only how it is structured.

FROM THE PERSONAL . . . a catalogue of experiences.

1   Being called a bull dyke for speaking out at Gay Lib/Women's Lib session on sexism.

2   Having one's consciousness 'raised' by a discussion on how to cope
     with being called 'that horrible name' at our first women's lib meeting.
3   Being told to keep out of the movement because 'some women won't
     come if lesbians are there, and those women shouldn't be put off
     because Women's Liberation is for all women'.
4   Having to change the pronouns at consciousness-raising meetings (or
     just shut up) for the above session.
5   Being told you're simply a media problem. (Remember?)
6   Standing on the edge of the dance floor at a Women's Lib party
     knowing that sisterhood is only for straight sisters.
7   Throwing yourself into the child care/pram, bus, struggle to prove
     you haven't got any interests of your own.
8   Being told to 'come out' and risk your job (if you're honest) and then
     working flat out to help other women to get jobs of their own.
9   Being told lesbianism is a 'passing phase' in women's lib.
10   Finding out that the lady you're in bed with is a 'real woman'
     (liberated variety) and you're only a hardened lesbian (sick variety).

. . . TO THE POLITICAL

Lesbians are discriminated against personally in a variety of ways inside
women's liberation, but more importantly the nature of some of the basic
women's lib institutions are discriminating by their very structure.

(a) Consciousness-raising:

Consciousness-raising is a very heterosexually based institution, insofar
as, as well as translating the personal into the shared into the political, it
assumes two things: that personal relationships can be honestly discussed
because the other person in the relationship is not there—which is often
not true of lesbians; it also assumes that what is personal is also shared,
and this will bring women themselves (normally divided against each other
by class, competitiveness, etc.) closer together. How this works when
lesbians are involved is difficult to say. In lesbian groups, c.r. at the very
personal level seems unnecessary. In mixed groups, not only is the
lesbian's experience likely to be purely personal and not shared, but the
lesbian is being asked to assume a degree of vulnerability before other
women not expected of them. At present, few lesbians feel enough
confidence in their 'sisters' to risk consciousness-raising. More importantly
few feel it particularly relevant to their situation or to the exploration of
patriarchal relationships.

   The necessary hypocrisy that most lesbians get away with makes them
question the 'sincerity' of many straight accounts of personal experience

(sometimes reminiscent of male bar room 'consciousness-raising') or more to the point, the usefulness of this sort of activity.

(b) Sisterhood:

Sisterhood is based on the idea that women have for so long competed against each other for men that they now have to learn to appreciate each other as people. Lesbians do not appear to be so handicapped and, theoretically, should fit perfectly into the sisterhood ethic. In fact, tendencies in W.L. literature have been towards using lesbians in just this way. At one level the literature purports to show women how to love other women by referring to lesbians, but at another level the literature simplifies discussions about women by stressing the shared situation and minimizing differences (e.g. language, colour). The attempt to do this with lesbians has been very clumsy and has hinged on the emphasis on 'natural bisexuality'. (See Altman's discussion of the polymorphous perverse). The jump from discussing homosexuality in the present to discussing the panacea, a bisexual millennia, is conspicuous in writers as normally rational as Firestone and Koedt as well as in Altman. Note the confusion and intolerance in this sentence: 'As a matter of fact, if "Freedom of sexual preference" is the demand, the solution obviously must be a bisexuality where the question becomes irrelevant.' [4]

A variant more common in Australia is to evade discussing homosexuality in the present altogether, by discussing bisexuality *in the present*, a much easier proposition because it takes the conversation back to heterosexuality again. (Bisexuality, whatever its meaning, is used at present to describe extensions to the behaviour of heterosexuals). This seems to be a typically Australian reaction to any problem of minorities—to be only able to envisage a happy society as one in which everyone will eventually behave in the same way.

The use of 'natural bisexuality' as a concept which will help transform lesbians into 'real women' has only succeeded in ignoring lesbians qua lesbians (see experience No. 10). It is as irrelevant as talking about black problems in terms of melting pot theory . . .

Sisterhood basically attempts to invest the old values of the 'female world' with a new status, so rejecting de Beauvoir's denigration of the female world. At the same time, still sharing many of the attitudes of de Beauvoir by the rejection or dismissal of lesbians, not in terms of their sexual preference, but in terms of their lack of relationships with men, and so their irrelevance to women's liberation. This accounts for the emphasis placed on bisexuality. For straight women, this leads to closer relationships with women, but it asks lesbians to move out of the 'feminine' sphere, to 'de-emphasize' the bonds felt with other women and to establish real relationships with males. ('Lesbians are Women'—*Camp Ink* vol. 1, No. 8). This whole way of thinking still assumes a sexist division of society. All it aims to do is alter the balance of power and esteem between the sexes. It continues to assume the differences between the masculine and feminine worlds. The lesbian is still a misfit in this situation . . .

We have attempted to show by an analysis of the literature of Women's Liberation and by personal experiences with Women's Liberation groups that Women's Liberation has so far failed to come to grips with sexism either inside or outside the movement. In fact there are signs that it is moving further away from grappling with this problem towards merely an updating of the stereotypes of masculinity/femininity. They have avoided basic questions and a commitment to basic ideology by simply attempting liberation through attacking some of the symptoms of sexism evident in patriarchal society.

This is illustrated by the situation in which lesbians are seen as having no particular relevance or as something of an embarrassment. The panacea of bisexuality only offers a situation where lesbians will no longer exist as such and this has been used to avoid discussing the real problems of now. It may be that most of the women in the movement have a vested interest in not delving too deeply into the reasons for their oppression, and that we, as lesbians, have no such vested interests because we have no stake in the present sexist set-up.

If neo-Ruskinism triumphs, and W.L. acquiesces in the creation of new stereotypes of masculinity/femininity, it will simply have failed in what should be its major aim, that of turning sexist controlled robots into people.

Hobart Women's Action Group
Refractory Girl,
Summer 1976, pp. 30–3.

NOTES

1   Sidney Abbot and Barbara Love, *Sappho was a right on woman: A liberated view of lesbians*, Stein Day, New York, 1972.

2   Interview between Alic Schwartzer and Simone de Beauvoir in *Le Nouvel Observateur*, March 1972.

3   See *Mejane* No. 9—Lesbians in Women's Liberation in England; see also Love and Abbott's article on the Lavender Menace, 'Is Women's

Liberation a Lesbian Plot?' in Vivian Gormick and Barbara Moran
(eds) *Woman in a Sexist Society*, Basic Books, New York, 1971.
4   Anne Koedt, 'Lesbianism and Feminism', *Notes from the Third Year:
Women's Liberation*, Basic Books New York, 1971.

Document 4.7 'We desperately need not just one but many refuges for women'

*One of the early and highly successful Women's Liberation campaigns
resulted in the establishment of women's refuges. 'Elsie', the first of
these in Australia, opened in Glebe, Sydney, in March 1974 and was
founded and staffed entirely by volunteers. As this document suggests,
it was a somewhat precarious arrangement. The success of Elsie
highlighted the desperate need for more women's shelters. Funds from
a sympathetic Labor Government made it possible to establish more
refuges and to pay the workers involved.*

ELSIE WOMEN'S REFUGE: PARTY TO RAISE FUNDS SATURDAY MAY 4TH 8 P.M.

Admission 50 cents.

Report from Anne Summers:
Elsie Women's Refuge (73–75 Westmoreland St., Glebe) has now been
open for over a month and so far more than 35 women and children have
come for shelter or for advice or at least to talk with other women about
their problems. We have had fantastic support from local residents and
from many other people. We have operated with virtually no money but
with the willingness of the women on roster and the time and gifts of
bedding and other essential things from supporters of the refuge we have
been able to survive. We are slowly getting both houses into good condition and we have painted, replastered, put in hot water, cleaned up the
gardens, built a children's play area and generally improved the houses
from being two derelict vacant houses to a warm and friendly comfortable
shelter. But we feel that for us to avoid becoming an impersonal institution
it is essential that as many women from the movement as possible have
some involvement in the place. We keep Elsie open 24 hours a day with a
volunteer roster of women. Each roster shift lasts four hours. At present the
number working the roster has dwindled from the enthusiastic 40 or so who
were around during the weekend we took over the houses to about 12
people and this is not enough. Our legal situation has now improved as the
federal government has bought the houses occupied by the shelter as part
of the Glebe Housing Scheme. We have approached the Department of

Urban and Regional Development which is administering the Scheme about taking out a legal tenancy and the indications are that this will be approved. So the illegality of our position is becoming increasingly irrelevant and we hope women who were previously deterred from becoming involved in the refuge because of this will now change their minds. Already it is clear that the need for the shelter was urgent and each day, as more and more women contact us, it is obvious that we desperately need not just one but many refuges for women. But they can only exist if they are widely supported and we do need more women to become involved on the roster. The best way to do so is to either ring or to call in to Elsie, see what times need to be filled and put ourself on roster duty. All of the people who have worked there already have found this practical activity very rewarding and a welcome change from abstract theorising about how badly society treats women while not actually doing anything about it. Therefore it is important to support Elsie. She is helping women to help themselves but she needs help too.

Sydney Women's Liberation Newsletter, May 1974

Health care was central to the Women's Liberation demand of a woman's right to control her own body. The Leichhardt Women's Community Health Centre was a pioneering development in women's health care.

LEICHHARDT WOMEN'S COMMUNITY HEALTH CENTRE
164 Flood Street, Leichhardt

The Leichhardt Women's Community Health Centre was set up by a group of women from within the Sydney Women's Liberation movement, to provide an alternative to existing health care for women. The Centre is funded by the Australian Government under its Community Health Services scheme.

Medical and para-medical and social services will be provided by an all-woman staff. Stefanie and Susan are the Doctors, Lorraine and Patricia are the Nurses, Judith is the Administrator, Kathryn is the Education Officer, Jeni is the Research Officer and Margaret keeps the house looking cheerful and clean.

All the staff, as well as using their technical skills in the service of other women, will be sharing what they have learned about themselves as women, both as individuals and as members of society.

From birth, the girl-child is conditioned to see her life in terms of its biological and reproductive function, while the boy-child is conditioned to see his life in terms of its physical and intellectual functions.

Woman   The Body

Man   The Mind

In society's terms, woman expresses our animal nature, man expresses our human nature. So it is that men have set up and administer all the institutions that supposedly cater for our bodily needs, but which in fact, serve only to reinforce man's psychological needs. On the one hand, women are told that their reproductive role is primary, while on the other hand they are told that bodily things are base and shameful.

Male doctors express amazement at the prevalence of frigidity in women and treat it with psychology. What is truly amazing is that any woman manages to reconcile the contradictions and live an integrated life. All our societal institutions present women with a picture of themselves which, while it reflects the cultural patterning, in no way corresponds to what women actually feel about themselves.

Women are beginning to question their role in society and in doing so are realizing that until they reinterpret their biological function and regain control over their own bodies, they cannot gain control over their own lives.

This is what the Leichhardt Women's Community Health Centre is all about.

Women have no frame of reference, relevant to the actuality of their lives, from which to understand the nature of their problems or to initiate action to overcome them, whether they be medical or social. It will be a necessary function of the Centre to define frames of reference from within which to work. To attempt—at this point in time—to state specific areas of activity would be to simply imitate existing institutions. What the Centre does will be determined largely by the use to which it is put by the women who come to it.

Sydney Women's Liberation Newsletter,
March 1974, p. 12

Document 4.8 Is there any relevance in the Women's Movement for Aboriginal women?

As suggested in Document 4.4, the concerns of Women's Liberation were a far cry from the basic needs of many Aboriginal women. Here Pat O'Shane, who later became a magistrate in the NSW Magistrate's court, argues that racism is the greatest problem facing Aboriginal

*women. Calls from white feminists for Aboriginal women to join the
movement not only demonstrated their endemic racism but failed to
acknowledge all the initiatives that Aboriginal women have already
taken. This piece is taken from an article in which O'Shane argues
that racism is the greatest problem facing Aboriginal women. She
discusses different views of the position of Aboriginal women vis-à-vis
Aboriginal men and white women, and suggests that the perception
of Aboriginal women having a higher status than Aboriginal men is
a comparison made possible because of the impact of racism on
Aboriginal communities. Black men pose a greater threat to male
dominance in white society than do black women 'and it is for this
reason that black men have been so enslaved, caught in the "pub-
to-gaol" phenomenon'.*

That Aboriginal women pose no threat to white men is very clearly seen
by the fact that they have so often been, and continue to be, considered
as easy game for the racist rapist. (This particular circumstance has
contributed, I contend, to some of the racist attitudes of white women
towards black women. The black woman's sexuality has been used by
white men as a threat over white women and rather than developing the
total fight against racism and sexism, white women have fallen victim to
this ideology and developed a competitive spirit which operates against
black women. This of course is a superficial element in the whole situation,
but it is nevertheless there, and deserves some serious consideration.)

The problem of racism is one that all women in the women's
movement must start to come to terms with. There is no doubt in my
mind that racism is expressed by women in the movement. Its roots are
many and they go deep. Let me give one very personal example of one
particularly subtle and pernicious expression of racism.

Very shortly before my admission to the NSW Bar, as the first
Aboriginal lawyer (male or female) in Australia, I spoke to a WEL group
about the situation of Aborigines in Australia. At their next meeting, one
of the women put forward the resolution that the branch send me a message
of congratulations on my admission. A number of women spoke against
the resolution on the basis that 'she (i.e. me) is not really an Aboriginal.
Her father is white. And anyway she doesn't look Aboriginal'. That
expresses very precisely, in fact, the extent to which racism pervades
Australian attitudes. Australian society has always classified the children
of inter-racial unions as black. The terms 'half-caste', 'quarter-caste',
'coloured' are terms coined by white Australians and mean only one
thing—rejection of people classified as blacks! In the Northern Territory,

for example, until quite recently it was the practice of white administrators to separate 'half-caste' children from their mothers and send them to institutions for 'half-castes' only.

At the same time as these sorts of attitudes were expressed, and found implementation in the ways outlined above, Aborigines were entreated to become white—become educated, live and work like us and we'll accept you, was how the yarn was given. So we have done, and the result is—rejection as non-blacks!

It has been said before, and I think it worth repeating, that racist attitudes go right through Australian society. It is evident in the education system, the legal system, the economic structure, the political structure. The whole social organisation is based on the premise of white (male) supremacy. It is expressed at both the individual and the institutional level.

So far as the women's movement is concerned it is necessary for women involved to examine carefully whether or not their aims as white women are necessarily those of black women. Necessary because there appears to me at times, to be an attitude amongst some of the 'activists' that black women ought to be involved in the women's liberation movement at the same level and in the same organizations as are white women. Obviously black women in this country do not have the same social status as white women—the racism which is so rampant in this country takes care of that.

But it appears to me that, whereas, for the majority of women involved in the women's movement, sexism is what the great fight is all about, for Aboriginal women—when they look at all the medical, housing, education, employment and legal statistics—it becomes very clear that our major fight is against racism.

Sexist attitudes did not wipe out whole tribes of our people, sexist attitudes are not slowly killing our people today—racism did, and continues to do so!

All of the factors outlined above, and including the sexism emanating from Aboriginal men towards Aboriginal women, mean that all the burdens of ensuring the continued existence of black communities fall squarely on Aboriginal women.

There does not exist, as far as I am aware, any sort of organized black women's movement such as exists amongst white women. We don't have, e.g. annual conferences of black women which discuss the need for more women to play a greater political role or the need for more child-care centres or the desirability of working out our ideology. But there is no doubt a tremendous spirit of sisterhood amongst Aboriginal women. That we have our differences is only an indication that we too are human and subject to the tensions of living in this oppressive society.

In just about every part of the country Aboriginal women have established their own pre-school centres, many of which are learning centres not only for the children but also for the mothers. Aboriginal women, concerned about the continuing health problems of their children, are involved in Aboriginal Medical Services as field officers, with enormous scope for their becoming paramedicals (a situation not yet realized but certainly on the way) and it is Aboriginal women who express the desire to become medical students.

Concerned about the overwhelming involvement of Aborigines in the criminal (so-called) justice system, Aboriginal women are involved in the Aboriginal Legal Services at both the administrative level and at the fieldwork level. In South Australia, Aborigines form only 0.7 per cent of the total population yet in the year ended June 30, 1965, Aboriginal men comprised 13 per cent of the total male prison population whilst Aboriginal women comprised a staggering 31 per cent of the total female prison population! It is worth noting that in that state it was the women who were instrumental in getting the Legal Rights movement off the ground, and it is they who maintain the service, at administrative level.

Aboriginal women are particularly active in the education system, not only at pre-school level as already indicated, but also as teacher aides in the primary schools and there are many who are presently undertaking teacher training courses. The women are also active in initiating on-going cultural activities; they are active in housing associations; they are producing their own newspapers.

Without doubt the biggest issue in terms of identity and self determination is that around land rights. The destruction of Aboriginal society has been wrought largely through dispossession. In the struggle to regain their land, Aboriginal women play a particularly vocal role. In fact in every sphere of human endeavour, Aboriginal women are in the forefront of activising and maintaining programs. And the basic object of these exercises is to demonstrate that Aborigines do have the abilities to resurrect what remains of a once proud and dignified race and do have the ability for self-determination.

Whilst there is no doubt a need for esoteric debate on such questions as the ideology of the women's movement, so far as Black women are concerned it is the nitty-gritty struggle around such issues as health, housing, education and land rights that is of the greatest moment. And when the white women's movement takes head-on the struggle against racism, which is the greatest barrier to our progress, then we've got a chance of achieving sisterhood and, through our combined struggles, liberation of all humankind!

Refractory Girl, no. 12, Sept. 1976, pp. 32–34

Document 4.9 'Swinging'

The widespread availability of the pill and changing attitudes to sex facilitated significant changes in sexual activity. Sex became a frontier, and its boundaries were to be ever extended. In a decade relatively free of sexually transmitted diseases, the possibilities seemed limitless. One activity that received much discussion was the practice of 'swinging', where couples swapped partners for the night, or made love in the presence of others. 'Swinging' parties were much talked about, although how common they really were is more difficult to assess.

SWINGING BRIDGE SET

Four couples

I want to thank you, not only for your wonderful magazine, but also for adding a lot of joy to the lives of eight people. My husband and I are one of four couples who have played bridge together for years. It was really getting a bit boring, when one night the host brought out several copies of *Forum*. We girls were shocked at first, but gradually we became intrigued with the letters. After a bit one of the men suggested that the women undress to the waist. The girls then insisted that the men show their genitals, which they did, and of course we all got excited. (I hadn't seen a naked man aside from my husband since I'd been married!) The boys then stripped us and turned out the lights, at which point things really started to happen. I think we were a particularly ideal group for swapping as none of us drink, so nobody gets rowdy.

The first experience was on a Friday night. When we woke up in the morning we were all pretty much embarrassed, but we soon got over it and decided to stay nude for the entire weekend. We read a lot of sex books, watched porno movies and tried a variety of positions. We then decided that we would meet on a monthly basis, and made only two rules. We would not swap except at the monthly sessions, and man and wife would not have sex with each other at these meetings. It has worked out beautifully. We actually count the days until our next get-together.

The best part of our arrangement is the way it has improved our everyday home lives. While I wasn't frigid before, I was indifferent. Now my husband and I have a wonderful sex life. We bathe together, sleep in the nude and I never wear underwear when he is at home. I exercise my vagina several times a day until I can now squeeze even my little finger. I could go on and on telling you what pleasure I've discovered lying between my legs just waiting to be aroused. I think every couple should be in a group like ours. It has changed my whole life.

(Name withheld by request)
Lincoln, Nebraska

Friendly relations

My husband and I had a terrific experience that I would like to share with *Forum* readers who are considering swinging as an alternative to their marital sex relationship.

One night our friends came over to watch a very stimulating show on television. After it was over, everybody was feeling pretty randy. One thing led to another and we girls found ourselves on the floor with our husbands giving us back massages.

Soon our shirts were off. At first we were both very embarrassed. Both of us were hugging the carpet. But after a few more drinks we relaxed and became natural nudists. Our husbands removed all of our clothes and then proceeded to take off all of their own clothes.

Soon we decided that the bed would be more comfortable so all four of us moved into the bedroom. We didn't trade partners but we still found excitement in caressing our partners in front of each other. Everyone touched everyone else but the actual lovemaking was confined to our mates. We had a fabulous sexual experience which was entirely spontaneous. The next day we talked things over and found out that nobody had any hang-ups about what had gone on the night before.

We've had a few more sessions, not all as rewarding as the first, but at least they have been different. We still get together with this couple for other activities so our relationship is more than sexual. I don't think mate swapping would work for us, but for those who do swing, I can see nothing wrong with it.

Mrs B.B., Brisbane, Qld
Forum, vol. 4, no. 6, 1976, p. 11

Document 4.10 Contraception is an industrial issue

In 1977 AFP (Action for Family Planning) was formed. Aware of the lack of access migrant women had to information on health and contraception, AFP set up factory visiting programs to disseminate such information. Committed to educating migrant educators, AFP also sought to develop a network of contacts with the trade union movement and to foster an awareness of working women's needs and desires. Their stance was overtly political and overtly feminist. The support of government funding in 1981 promised the AFP a more secure future. In 1982 the name changed to Women in Industry— Contraception and Health (WICH) and in 1991 it became Women in Industry and Community Health. WICH has remained an avenue for women from non-English-speaking backgrounds to participate in the broader women's movement. This document is taken from an AFP policy meeting held on 19 June 1982.

Item 2. AFP as an industrial project

There was much discussion around this issue especially in regard to the actual requests made of the educators in the factory visits.

2.1 There are constant requests to go beyond contraceptive issues to other health areas such as hysterectomy and breast cancer. Issues arising at the workplace such as access to safety earmuffs, tenosynovitis, etc. seemed to indicate a necessary area of involvement if AFP is working in an industrial context.

2.2 The educators felt for their work to be credible, the program must be action based rather than only information based. Further, it was felt that this was not only the responsibility of the educators but of AFP as an organization. This could be achieved if information provided by the educators after factory visits was taken up by the coordinators and membership of AFP with the relevant bodies, eg. trade unions, WHAG, government, etc.

2.3 Whilst AFP has a responsibility to look to other issues concerning women, it was agreed that AFP is an industrial project and therefore has the workplace and the issues it throws up as the limit of its involvement.

2.4 Contraception was seen as an industrial issue. This is because contraceptive information is not generally available to migrant working women outside working hours and because it is part of the broad quality of life concerns that unions should be on about. Family planning is included in the ACTU endorsed Working Women's Charter and endorsed at the last ACTU Migrant Workers Conference.

Item 3 Working with trade unions

3.1 The role and content of community visits was discussed at length. Whilst some felt that such community talks should be around family planning issues, many of the forum participants felt that because of limited funding and our industrial base, that such visits should be limited to a discussion on contraception as an industrial issue and as part of a description of AFP and its factory-visiting program as a model which other groups may like to take up. Further discussion was deferred to the afternoon group.

3.2 It was agreed that AFP should be more public on certain issues especially those related to health and safety of women workers in the factories we visit. Information provided by the educators should be taken up with Trade Union officials. In this regard several concrete suggestions were made:

> (i) A TU organizer could accompany the educators and take up issues as they arose. (This had proven very useful with Helen Davis from the AMWSU);
>
> (ii) That relevant information from the discussions after factory visits be taken up with union organizers who could be invited to workshop sessions;
>
> (iii) That we work with several rather than many unions and really work to develop contacts within these unions;
>
> (iv) That we work to establish support groups of women in factories. In reality this was seen to be very difficult as there is always a fear of losing jobs among the women. This could however be done through the women organizers and information could be sent to women in the factories of ongoing contacts [and] could be made to work.

3.3 It was agreed that AFP has a responsibility to change the policy and practice of Trade Unions in regard to migrant women.

3.4 AFP has an important role as a community group outside union structures, as we can work in cooperation but also take on an advocacy role from the outside.

3.5 AFP as an organization needs to establish formal and strong links with the union movement.

3.6 AFP itself cannot take up certain issues, eg. wages. These are the specific concerns of unions but support to unions in this regard could be given.

3.7 It was agreed that where appropriate AFP should attempt to influence management through unions.

3.8 AFP should have independent links with other bodies, especially government bodies.

Item 4 AFP's commitment to women

4.1 First, there was considerable discussion about what a 'feminist' organization is. It was agreed that this meant a focus on issues of concern to women, a concern with equality, women's rights and control over their own lives. This however does not imply the exclusion of men in AFP visits though the emphasis is on women, and in the long term the aim must be cooperation between men and women.

4.2 Women have rights in regard to contraceptive issues, rights to information, to access and to choose. It was noted that men have a responsibility in regard to contraception.

4.3 The issue of feminism with regard to multi-culturalism was much discussed. It was generally agreed that AFP should support women with an awareness of cultural difference.

4.4 It was agreed that AFP support those women's organizations who endorse the aims and objectives of AFP especially those concerned with industrial and right to work matters.

4.5 It was agreed too that AFP should have links with those progressive ethnic organizations who support the same aims and objectives that AFP does. It was suggested that women in factories get more information about these groups from AFP.

4.6 Abortion—It was agreed that AFP has to make its position clear. It was agreed that women have the right to choose, that they have the right to information about abortion and the right to safe contraception and safe abortion.

After a break, these discussions were formulated and ratified.

Item 5 Resolutions

5.1 AFP is an industrial project. While providing information on contraception and health matters to migrant working women, it focuses on these issues as industrial matters within the context of the Labour Movement.

5.2 AFP understands that contraception as one of a range of health issues, is important to women in the workplace; is an industrial matter. This is so inasmuch as Trade Unions have a role to play in the range of political, economic and social issues which affect the quality of life, and insofar as they are concerned with the general health and welfare of their members.

5.3 By virtue of AFP's involvement in the industrial context, AFP seeks not only to disseminate information but to take action on issues of concern as they are raised by women in the factories or brought to the notice of AFP by other means.

The above resolutions were moved by Melissa Afentoulis, seconded by Maria Chimenton and carried unanimously.

5.4 AFP is concerned to develop and maintain links with trade unions both to gain access to factories for its factory visiting programme and to influence the practices of management, unions and Government.

5.5 AFP believes it has an important role to play in lobbying trade unions to better meet the needs and wishes of migrant working women.

5.6 Despite the difficulties associated with encouraging working women to participate in decision-making within the work place and with the development of women's support groups inside factories, it sees these as long term aims and will offer support to working women in such developments.

5.7 AFP will develop links with suitable ethnic organizations particularly women's ethnic groups, which are in agreement with the aims and objectives of AFP.

5.8 While AFP sees itself as an industrial programme, thereby limiting its involvement in the area of community visiting, it supports groups involved in women's health issues which operate outside the industrial context.

The above resolutions were moved by Margaret Kerec, seconded by Rhonda Small and carried unanimously.

5.9 As a feminist organization, AFP is concerned about the inequalities experienced by women. It upholds women's rights to work, to choose and to make decisions about their bodies and their workplace. AFP is primarily concerned with the rights and needs of women but holds to the long term aim of cooperation between women and men.

5.10 While AFP respects cultural differences between ethnic groups, it upholds women's basic rights as women. The aims indicated in policy statements above will be pursued in a way which does not jeopardise migrant working women in their respective cultural setttings nor judges their particular beliefs.

5.11 While recognising abortion as a sensitive issue, AFP upholds a woman's right to choose, to information about abortion and contraception and women's right to safe and accessible abortions.

The above resolutions were moved by Ann Myers, seconded by Maria Chimenton and carried unanimously.

Document 4.11 Affirmative Action (Equal Opportunity for Women) Act

The Affirmative Action Act was hailed by many as a significant development for women, and came with hopes that it would enable women to overcome the barriers preventing their entry into traditional male areas of employment and help them to attain management positions. As the accompanying document 'Landmarks reached in Law and Motherhood' suggests, those who have benefited most from the principles of Equal Opportunity have been white middle-class professional women.

AFFIRMATIVE ACTION (EQUAL EMPLOYMENT OPPORTUNITY FOR WOMEN) ACT 1986

No. 91 of 1986

An Act to require certain employers to promote equal opportunity for women in employment, to establish the office of the Director of Affirmative Action, and for related purposes

[Assented to 3 September 1986]

Be it enacted by the Queen, and the Senate and the House of Representatives of the Commonwealth of Australia, as follows:

Part 1—Preliminary

Short title

1. This Act may be cited as the *Affirmative Action (Equal Employment Opportunity for Women) Act 1986.*

Commencement

2. This Act shall come into operation on a day to be fixed by Proclamation.

Interpretation

3.(1) In this Act, unless the contrary intention appears—

'affirmative action program', in relation to a relevant employer, means a program designed to ensure that—

    (a) appropriate action is taken to eliminate discrimination by the relevant employer against women in relation to employment matters; and

    (b) measures are taken by the relevant employer to promote equal opportunity for women in relation to employment matters;

'authority' means—
- (a) a body (whether incorporated or not) established for a public purpose by or under a law of the Commonwealth or of a State or Territory, other than a higher education institution;
- (b) the holder of an office established for a public purpose by or under a law of the Commonwealth or of a State or Territory; and
- (c) an incorporated company over which the Commonwealth, a State, a Territory or a body referred to in paragraph (a) is in a position to exercise control;

'appoint' includes re-appoint;

'club' means an association (whether incorporated or not) of not less than 30 persons associated together for social, literary, cultural, political, sporting, athletic or other lawful purposes that—
- (a) provides and maintains its facilities, in whole or in part, from the funds of the association; and
- (b) sells or supplies liquor for consumption on its premises;

'confidential report' means a confidential report referred to in section 14;

'discrimination' means discrimination as defined in section 5, 6 or 7 of the *Sex Discrimination Act 1984*;

'Director' means the Director of Affirmative Action;

'employer' means a person who employs a natural person—
- (a) under a contract of service, whether on a full-time, part-time, casual or temporary basis; or
- (b) under a contract for services;

'employment matters' includes—
- (a) the recruitment procedure, and selection criteria, for appointment or engagement of persons as employees;
- (b) the promotion and transfer of employees;
- (c) training and staff development for employees; and
- (d) conditions of service of employees;

'higher education institution' means a university, college of advanced education or other institution of tertiary education (other than a technical and further education institution within the meaning of the *Commonwealth Tertiary Education Commission Act 1977*);

'operative day', in relation to a relevant employer, means the day specified in relation to that employer in section 7;

'public report' means a public report referred to in section 13;

'relevant employer' means—
  (a) a higher education institution that is an employer; or
  (b) a natural person, or a body or association (whether incorporated or not), being the employer of 100 or more employees in Australia, but does not include the Commonwealth, a State, a Territory, an authority or a voluntary body;

'trade union' means—
  (a) an organization of employees registered pursuant to the *Conciliation and Arbitration Act 1904*; or
  (b) a trade union within the meaning of a State Act or law of a Territory;

'voluntary body' means a body or association (whether incorporated or not) the activities of which are not engaged in for the purpose of making a profit, but does not include—
  (a) a club;
  (b) a trade union;
  (c) an association that provides grants, loans, credit or finance to its members;
  (d) a higher education institution; or
  (e) the holder of a licence under the *Broadcasting Act 1942;*

'woman' means a member of the female sex irrespective of age.
(2) For the purpose of paragraph (b) of the definition of 'relevant employer' in sub-section (1)—
  (a) a corporation employs a person where the person is employed by another corporation which is a subsidiary of the first-mentioned corporation; and
  (b) the question whether a corporation is a subsidiary of another corporation shall be determined as it would be determined for the purposes of the *Companies Act 1981.*
(3) Where, in accordance with section 4, this Act extends to Norfolk Island, a reference in this Act to Australia includes a reference to Norfolk Island.
(4) Nothing in this Act shall be taken to require a relevant employer to take any action incompatible with the principle that employment matters should be dealt with on the basis of merit . . .

Part II—affirmative action programs

Employers required to develop, &c., affirmative action programs

6.(1) An employer who, on the commencement of this Act, is a relevant employer shall commence the development and implementation of an affirmative action program on the operative day.

(2) Where, after the commencement of this Act, an employer becomes a relevant employer, the relevant employer shall commence the development and implementation of an affirmative action program on the operative day.

(3) Where, at any time, an employer ceases to be a relevant employer because the number of employees of the employer falls below 100, this Act continues to have effect in relation to the employer as if the employer were a relevant employer unless and until the number of employees falls below 80.

Timing for development, &c., of affirmative action program

7.(1) For the purposes of sub-section 6(1), the operative day for a relevant employer is—

   (a) in the case of a higher education institution—1 August 1986 or such later day as is prescribed; and

   (b) in the case of a relevant employer (other than a higher education institution) who, on the commencement of this Act, employs in Australia—

      (i) 1,000 or more employees—1 February 1987;

      (ii) 500 or more employees but not more than 999 employees—1 February 1988; or

      (iii) 100 or more employees but not more than 499 employees—1 February 1989.

(2) For the purposes of sub-section 6(2), the operative day for an employer that becomes a relevant employer is—

   (a) in the case of a higher education institution—1 August; and

   (b) in any other case—1 February,

in the calendar year following the calendar year during which the employer becomes a relevant employer.

Contents of affirmative action program

8.(1) Without limiting the generality of the definition of 'affirmative action program' in sub-section 3(1), the affirmative action program of a relevant employer shall provide for action to be taken—

   (a) for the issue to the employees, by a senior officer concerned with the management of the relevant employer, of a statement to the effect that the employer, in accordance with this Act, commenced the development and implementation of an affirmative action

program on a specified day, being the operative day in relation
to the employer;

(b) to confer responsibility for the development and implementation
of the program (including a continuous review of the program),
on a person or persons having sufficient authority and status
within the management of the relevant employer to enable the
person or persons properly to develop and implement the program;

(c) to consult with each trade union having members affected by the
proposal for the development and implementation of the program
in accordance with this Act;

(d) to consult with employees of the relevant employer, particularly
employees who are women;

(e) for the collection and recording of statistics and related information concerning employment by the relevant employer, including
the number of employees of either sex and the types of jobs
undertaken by, or job classifications of, employees of either sex;

(f) to consider policies, and examine practices, of the relevant
employer, in relation to employment matters to identify—
   (i) any policies or practices that constitute discrimination against
   women; and
   (ii) any patterns (whether ascertained statistically or otherwise)
   of lack of equality of opportunity in respect of women;

(g) to set objectives and make forward estimates in the program; and

(h) to monitor and evaluate the implementation of the program and
to assess the achievement of those objectives and forward estimates.

(2) An affirmative action program of a relevant employer may contain
any other provision that the relevant employer thinks fit that is not
inconsistent with—

(a) a provision required by this section to be included; and

(b) the purposes of this Act.

(3) In sub-section (1)—

'forward estimate' means a quantitative measure or aim, which may be
expressed in numerical terms, designed to achieve equality of opportunity
for women in employment matters, being a measure or aim that can
reasonably be implemented by the relevant employer within a specified
time;

'objective' means a qualitative measure or aim, expressed as a general
principle, designed to achieve equality of opportunity for women in

employment matters, being a measure or aim that can reasonably be implemented by the relevant employer within a specified time . . .

PART IV—REPORTS BY RELEVANT EMPLOYERS

Public reports

13.(1) A relevant employer shall prepare a public report—

(a) in the case of the employer's first report—on the initial development and implementation of the employer's affirmative action program during the period of 12 months commencing on the operative day in respect of the relevant employer; and

(b) in any other case—on the further development and implementation of the employer's affirmative action program during each period of 12 months commencing on the anniversary of the operative day in respect of the relevant employer.

(2) A relevant employer shall lodge a public report with the Director within 3 months after the end of the period to which the report relates.

(3) A public report under sub-section (1) shall provide—

(a) statistics and related information concerning employment by the relevant employer, including the number of employees of either sex and the types of jobs undertaken by, or job classifications of, employees of either sex; and

(b) an outline of the processes undertaken by the relevant employer—

(i) in the case of the employer's first report—initially to develop and implement the employer's affirmative action program; and

(ii) in any other case—further to develop and implement the program.

LANDMARKS REACHED IN LAW AND MOTHERHOOD

Melbourne lawyer Irene Zeitler, 31, reached a milestone a few years ago when she was made a partner of a big commercial law firm. She reached another last September when she had her first child, Ben.

She left her desk at Freehill, Hollingdale & Page 10 days before her baby was born, not knowing whether she would want to return in one month or 10. She now plans to resume work this month.

She is one of two female partners in the 30-member partnership in Melbourne and, as such, shares in the profits and decision-making. Her specialty is industrial and intellectual property, namely trademarks, copyright, designs and patterns, and trade practices.

One reason why there are so few female partners, she says, is that women in law have not had the confidence to combine careers and motherhood. But their confidence is growing and the attitudes of law firms are changing as a result.

Having children has always been part of Ms Zeitler's plans, but only after she had reached a certain level of expertise. She did not graduate from Melbourne University (with honors degrees in arts and law) until she was 24, so she points out that there has been little time.

She did her articles in 1982, spent the next year with the firm now known as Minter Ellison, and joined Freehills when it was Moules in 1984. She says the partnership has taken her maternity leave in its stride. 'They were very pleased for me. The partnership as a whole realised that I intended having children, I never made a secret of the fact. We discussed what my needs were and what the firm's were and worked it out from there.'

Before she left to have her baby, she contacted all the big companies that make up her client list to explain her situation. 'They are used to contacting me on certain issues, so before I left the firm, I spoke personally with each client and then wrote follow-up letters just advising them that I would be leaving the firm for a short period of time because I was pregnant and gave them an indication of when I would be coming back and who would be doing my work.

'With certain clients, particularly with ongoing matters that I felt difficult to hand over, I indicated to them that they could contact me at home. You can't totally cut yourself off from the office, it doesn't work that way in law.'

She had facsimile and photo-copying machines installed in the study of her East St Kilda home so she could work when required.

Ms Zeitler's mother will care for Ben from this month. Irene and her husband, a senior associate with the law firm Corrs Pavey Whiting & Byrne, plan to have another child in a few years' time. Then, they will probably hire a nanny. Irene knows she is in a fortunate position to be able to afford this.

Wendy Bowler
The Age, 4 April 1989

Document 4.12 A letter from an Aboriginal mother

The Royal Commission into Black Deaths in Custody highlighted the tragedy of Aborigines in the prison system. Ruby Langford's letter tells another side to the story, and a mother's despair at the prospect of her son becoming another statistic of a criminally unjust system.

13 January, 1987

Dear Sir

I am writing on behalf of my people. I'm an Aboriginal and I don't know much about your white system of justice as I've never been in trouble with the law. But I have sons whose fathers are white men and have been involved in prison and police custody since they were children, and in boys' homes. Now I'm not only talking about my sons, but the sons of every mother, be they black or white, who have ever run foul of the law.

I went to court on the eighteenth of December 1986 to hear my son's bail application and I was thoroughly disgusted with the attitude of the Magistrate or Judge that heard his bail application as he was, in my opinion, a very opinionated judge. And after the Crown Prosecutor produced evidence which I thought was not admissible anyhow because it was brought up about him absconding from the boys' home twice when he was a child and here he was, now a thirty-one-year-old man, and the courts were still judging him on his record when he was in boys' homes.

When he was seventeen years old, this son of mine whilst in the company of another youth, aged sixteen and a girl fourteen, and also very drunk, was driven to my home in Green Valley, as he'd had a breakup with his girlfriend and had gotten drunk and asked the sixteen-year-old youth to bring him home to me. What he didn't know was there was a gun under the seat, the sixteen-year-old was driving negligently and the police chased them, then the girl opened up and fired shots at them. I know my son and the only violence in him is against himself. The police had to have a conviction: he being the eldest was the one that ended up in Long Bay Gaol at seventeen years old, when he should have been in juvenile custody, along with the other two. The girl went Crown Witness and blamed him, after the police promised her they'd be lenient with her. She and the other sixteen-year-old youth went into children's homes and my son went to Long Bay where he served six years of a ten year sentence, so where is the justice in that? And here it was in 1986, fourteen years after his childhood evidence was still being used by the system against him, he'd been out of gaol eight years and was a rehabilitated man, worked constantly, as a matter of fact was a workaholic and met a nice lady and lived together with their two children and between them both working applied for and got a $58,000 home loan from St. George Building Society, and they don't give these home loans to bums.

Then came the death of a loved brother at twenty-eight through drugs and his world started to crumble around him. This is what gaol has done to him, he believed he should be the one dead, as he said 'I'm the criminal.

Why didn't God take me? Not David.' He proceeded then to go downhill and have a nervous breakdown, lost his job, was battling to pay the home loan off and he was even ripped off by the solicitor who was handling the home loan for him, to the tune of $1,400. He tried very hard to cope with everyday living, but eventually went down in a screaming heap, he was missing for a couple of days and his wife and I were frantically looking for him and we found him out at David's grave, lying across it, and brought him home.

The next episode of his breakdown was when he was found by police lying in the middle of the road wanting the traffic to run him over and kill him; he wanted to be with his brother and instead of the police taking him to a psychiatric centre for counselling, they took him back to gaol and bashed him. He came out looking like the Elephant Man. These were his own words, so you can see these actions were a cry for help, but no one listened. I encouraged him to go to Brisbane, to my sister's place, to try and get himself together. Coming back he was flagged down by the police, and him with no licence, thought 'Oh God, I"m going back to gaol,' produced a gun that some great mate had given him for his protection, and this mate even supplied the car, and fired at the radiator to stop the police car. How ironic, here he was doing the same thing what he was supposed to have done fourteen years ago, but didn't do, but he still served his time in gaol for it, six wasted years. So can you tell me, where is the justice here?

I'm going to get a petition going, to protest against the bringing of evidence against people who have already done time in custody for things done when they were young and all the courts being able to bring up past evidence up as far back as children's homes, as I don't think it's fair and I guess, so do a lot of mothers like me. And I for one don't want my son to become another statistic of Aboriginal men dying in police custody.

Ruby Langford,
reproduced in Jack Davis et al.
Paperbark: a collection of Black Australian writings
UQP, 1990, pp. 141–3

Document 4.13 'They tell you that they love you'

The increasing demand for women's refuges slowly brought public attention to the prevalence of what feminists came to term 'domestic violence'. During the late 1980s the Victorian Government moved to heighten community awareness of domestic violence, later termed 'family violence', and to dispel myths about it: domestic violence is

*not specific to class or ethnic groups, women do not enjoy being
abused, nor do they ask for it. Survivors of domestic violence began
to tell their stories.*

AN UNASHAMED SURVIVOR

In response to the 'Animals are still out of their cages' letter (June 7), I
would like to say that I, too, am a survivor of domestic violence, and how
true it is that the reality of these situations is just not appreciated within
families; my sister suffered as a victim 10 years ago and it is with shame
I recall my lack of understanding.

I have watched telemovies of the inhumanity towards the Jews under
the Nazis and of extended intimidation in rape situations, and have felt
sick to my stomach and ended up in tears at the unmitigated cruelty of it
all. That same sick feeling arises when I remember the hell I went through
and that many women are still going through.

Mental and emotional torture are part and parcel of the physical
violence. It's not a disagreement, a slap issued as a reflex under stress. It
is a process, long and drawn-out, of intimidation and victimisation. Giving
false hope is part of the process as it was for the Jews under Hitler: 'I'll
never do it again' and 'I love you too much to lose you' are reminiscent
of 'You are only going to work camps' and 'You have been reprieved'.

The details count, their repertoire is infinite. They refuse to let you
move from the one spot for hours, not even to go to your children, refuse
to let you go to the toilet, revelling in the possibility of your humiliation,
they won't let you sleep, won't let you stay up, you must shadow their
every move.

They threaten to harm your children to make you comply. They
disappear to who knows where for who knows how long, then they punish
you when they return for imagined misbehavior on your part, or just to
put you on the defensive.

They don't 'jostle' you or just push you around; they walk some
distance across the room, calculating the angle on the way, to kick you
in the face with the cricket 'dabs' [shoes] you bought for a birthday. They
might even like to sit opposite you on the floor to watch you bleed because
they certainly won't let you get up off the floor to let you clean yourself
up. And while you sit they tell you that they love you but that you made
them do this.

In the morning you'll be allowed to wash out the sheets so that no
one else will see, but only when they tell you that you can get out of bed.
They'll resent the fact that you are cold when they want to make love to
you, but it's highly unlikely that you'll refuse and risk another outburst.

They alienate your family and friends, lose your job for you, show you up so that your standing in the community is lost, they'll lose your house for you, destroy your furniture, your clothes. Then they will cry and plead for understanding, forgiveness, help, they will say they are ill, they need you, can't live without you, will do anything to save your love. But they don't. There will be a pause and then it will all happen again.

If you don't go under completely—for this is hypnosis at its most dangerous, this is mind control—you might see clearly enough just long enough to run and hide with the intention of freeing yourself forever. When you go you will lose whatever is left of what you once had, your belongings and your place in the world.

What will hurt the most is what you were trying to put together for your children: their social network, gone; their treasured possessions, gone. And you will continue to lose. You end up having to start all over again in a strange place, no money, no furniture, no food, no clothes; you soon learn how to beg, and you learn the meaning of dignity when that, too, must go.

The 'pension' comes in and you realise you have entered a social class of its own. You become public property, every move monitored, what your family is allowed to have a foregone conclusion, what you *need* is way down the list of priorities.

Needing public housing doesn't mean you can get it; needing [child care] so that you can work and try to pull yourself out of the quagmire, doesn't mean you can have any. When you are forced to take private accommodation and private childcare there is no subsidy, or nothing realistic.

And when they cut your pension because you have worked a bit to subsidise your own housing or cut down some of the debts he left you with, or replace the kid's winter coats and boots he burned, the $100 childcare you had to pay (whatever the amount, you couldn't actually afford it) will not be taken into consideration.

You'll soon find out that the community and welfare services you were always so sure existed at great expense to the taxpayers are to say the least, inadequate. It will cost society a lot more for you not to work than it would cost society and the taxpayers to help you to work; and oh! wouldn't you like to become one of 'them' (part of society and a taxpayer).

And what becomes of these men (the word is too good for them)? They walk away. They still pocket all their cash, still have a social life, a working life if they choose. They probably still drink and gamble, still have the means to preen themselves, still eat prime cuts of meat, and usually—no, frequently—end up 'bludging off' some other gullible female, mum or girlfriend because they certainly don't want to be alone to have the spur to get their lives in order, and they definitely don't want to have to look after themselves. These are the criminals 'ruining the fibre of society'.

They destroy the families which might have been expected to flourish, or at least survive. They produce offspring which they do not support, and usually deposit them with more than one woman. They are the reason for social security payments to poverty-stricken mothers, they are the reason some women have no hope of providing for their families themselves. But they are not the objects of scorn because they are still invisible.

It's time the tables were turned: make them compensate for the destruction they have caused, let them bear the social stigma. It's time they were hauled out of the public bars and cocktail lounges and made to suffer the consequences of their self-indulgent, totally unacceptable behavior. Why are they allowed such immunity? Why?

Society ought to weigh the cost of its apathy towards the issue of domestic violence. We all 'foot the bill' for these thugs. We all pay socially, economically, morally and we will go on paying far into the future if we don't get things into perspective now. Signs in all the shops attest to the fact that we realise that thieves pass costs on to us and we want them dealt with.

Let's get together and deal with domestic violence which strips us of everything down to our human dignity, without justification, without necessity, without mercy. Society must prosecute. Society must make it quite clear that this bestiality will not be tolerated. If these thugs walked down the streets en masse and did what they do at home in secret, the army would be brought out.

What price the life of a mother and her babies, a wife, a woman? Are only the fortunate women idolised as the ideal, only mothers who live in peace national treasures: are all the rest 'trash' because *he* is crazy? And if we are to have complaints to the papers now because 'too much exposure is being given to this issue', let's have a show of hands. Stand up and be counted, and stop protecting these cowardly tyrants.

If it has happened to you or is happening, speak up, write in, and let somebody know. But whatever you do, get away now, run for your life. That is exactly what you will be doing.

'An Unashamed Survivor'

Letters to the Editor
Malvern–Caulfield Progress, 28 June 1989

Document 4.14 'It is a very male way of thinking to equate love with sex'

Annie and Lyndall met in 1960 and began a friendship that endured for decades. These letters convey the intimacy of their relationship, how their husbands and social attitudes restricted the development of their friendship, their difficulties in finding ways of speaking and writing about their love, and Annie's reflection that their love was not 'sexually based'. Annie begins this first letter by responding to a much earlier letter from Lyndall.

February 1990, Canberra

I read your letter again. Although I had read it many times before a few phrases leapt out at me: 'I had loved it before when you hugged me, held me, kissed me gently. Now I hated it . . . I had been told that friendships between women are okay only so long as they have no sexual overtones'. Although I think you know my thoughts on this, further exploration seems justified in this little review (which may be an epilogue!). My feelings for you were exactly as you described & as I have quoted you. I have never regarded our relationship as 'sexually based', another of your phrases. Never. I loved you. We were in love as your letter so eloquently says, & I longed to be able to express that emotional and yes, psychic love—for it was truly a love of the soul—thro' physical expression of tenderness, consistent with my whole personality. ('In souls there is no sex'—Willliam Penn).

As Elizabeth Jolly says, there are so many different kinds and shades of love & so many different ways of expressing it—a touch, a glance, a smile. You know this. In your letter—which I treasure—you quote me as saying 'What we have for each other is what other people call lesbian love'. It is what I said—'*other* people'. How right that proved to be for someone close to you who could not bear your radiance & the threat I was perceived to be. When asked at the time, Rick [Annie's husband] said he thought we were good for each other. Remember? Overall I think this proved to be so. You were strengthened emotionally & I'm (or was!) a little better in the head (if not the handwriting).

At the time it must have been very, very difficult for you. Really awful. Who could you talk to? Not to me. Not about what you thought of me, called me. Oh the conflict, the fear, the pull . . . [sic] Over the years I often felt it was John [Lyndall's husband] I was grappling with, not you. But surely he too today must have more sense, a less fixed way of perceiving. It is a very male way of thinking, however, to equate love with sex. Such thinking helps to control the way we (i.e. women) relate to each other, thro' fear of labels, of stereotyping.

I can understand John feeling as he did. The sadness is, I believe, his concern was groundless. It was all so harmless & beautiful. Oh how alive we were. And we had such fun. Between us, John & I destroyed something very special. But nothing—not even time can take away the joy & breathlessness of those early weeks & months. Not even 30 years.

You said there are not enough words to describe what we feel for each other Lyndall & turned away from your 'awakening' (as you called it then). I think you were right in what you said then. Thirty years later, words are being found as women explore in writing their world, their feelings as experienced & perceived by them . . .
Love, always,

Annie

20 September 1990, Sydney
And so after many discarded and unsuccessful attempts I sat down this morning and wrote this.

My dear
Answering your letter seems to me to be an enormous task. You have written in such detail with so many references and erudite comments that I am a little at sea. Certainly at Christmas I did miss your not being at Pambula and did not know where you were so was pleased to hear from you on that minor score. Many times John asked me had I been in touch with you so perhaps you are right and he has matured a great deal since the early days.

I think that you are right, that he was very suspicious of our friendship, or perhaps more jealous than suspicious and that I took this on as another guilt inducing factor in my life. I like the comment about marriage in *Shirley Valentine* [a film]. 'Marriage is like the Middle East—no solution. Just keep your head down, observe the curfew and hope the ceasefire holds.'

So it has always been very much easier for me to keep my head down, to deny what is going on, to appear to agree with him and often quite simply to do what he wants or appears to want. As your anonymous article from *The Guardian* says, men have many ways of showing their displeasure, their anger at being thwarted. She was talking about sex, or the lack of it, but I think her comments could be applied over the whole range of the marriage relationship. Especially for me who exchanged my father of whom I had always been frightened and for whom I had unquestioning obedience, for John. I think it was easy to imagine that John had most of the same qualities even when he made considerable moves, often ahead of other educated men of his age to the attitudes and values of the twentieth century. I am not sure how much his attitude about you, suspicion about our doings were really his or whether some of them were my projection of how I imagined he would feel if he knew just how happy I was with you, how much fun we had together, how we loved being together, how much we loved.

Your letter was full of angst: I find this word ghastly and although I keep seeing it in print I do not hear it in conversation very much. I think it sneaked out of the German into English early this century as a jargon word used by literary and philosphical people. To be a little bit erudite I see that Brian Foster in *The Changing English Language* defined it as showing 'a general disgust and dissatisfaction with the state of the world'. E.T. Maleska in *A Pleasure in Words* says it was a 'feeling of anxiety or a gloomy, often neurotic, state of depression or fear'. With anguish, anxiety, neurotic fear, guilt, remorse you would wonder why we really need angst. It must have some special or omnibus quality taking in all five words and their meanings in five letters . . .

Remember when you said when you came to the all white house that it would be a great step forward when I was able to admit some colour into my life. Well the painter is here in the terrace now. The gutters are dark green, the large boards grey, our bedroom blue (is there any other colour except black and white?) and the study dark dark pink. The cornices in the living room are painted in stripes of all these colours. Do you think you will like it? Do you think you will ever come to see it?

With very much love,

Lyndall

11 November 1990

Dear Lyndall,

I too have had trouble writing . . . [sic]

But firstly let me thank you very much for *Stories of Herself When Young*. It is a beautiful book inside & out & I understand your delight in it, which I share. The cover—The Lesson—by Emmanuel Phillips Fox could have been commissioned for the purpose . . .

As you suggest the book is an impressive scholarly achievement. I find I have read very few of the works Joy Hooton refers to but it does whet the appetite. It is affirming too, as a woman isn't it, to have access to such an overview of themes in women's lives, to recognise aspects of oneself in its pages, to have the invisible made visible? The book will I suspect—has already—become a bedside companion for me as I read it, alert for such pleasures as '. . . the women are *clamped* together in a desperate struggle for survival' (my emphasis). What a superb choice of a word.

So thank you *very* much for that thoughtfully chosen gift. I am currently also reading *In a Different Voice*, by Carol Gilligan. I would like to give you a copy for I'm sure you would find much in its pages to engage. It is, in part, a re-examination of Freud's view of women, of taking the moral development of males as normal & regarding that which is not male ie female, as deviant & certainly inferior. Gilligan quotes Virginia Woolf, 'It is obvious that the values of women differ very often from the values which have been made by the other sex. Yet', she adds, 'it is the masculine values that prevail.' The book is engrossing reading, but needs a fresh early morning mind—a habit my protestant conscience connives to prevent me from practising. As yet.

To your letter—still as crisp and pristine as when I first unfolded it on our return from the West, in spite of repeated readings. You have been honest in what you have written I think Lyndall & I do thank you for that, for it is not easy to be & it was a lot to ask.

Angst = anguish, anxiety, neurotic fear, guilt, remorse. I do not see even an omnibus version of these in my letter, but accept that you do & respect your judgment as (nearly) always! Anguish yes, in flashes perhaps. But if I could try & summarise now what I have felt—remembering WB Yeats' comment 'It takes so many years to know what one feels, even to know what the feeling is'. A regret yes, even a grief for what I experienced as the loss of an opportunity to extend & deepen a rare and exceptional friendship, thereby enriching both our lives & all those we touched & loved. That I felt this is I think not news to you, for we talked of it before. Flipping thro' my diary I could perhaps expand on it a little.

> For along with that very satisfying ingredient (a reference to your
> exceptional intelligence) there was a communion of souls. I guess
> it is that which distinguished our relationship beyond all others for
> me & made me prize it so much.

If grief or angst come through my letter to you Lyndall its source has perhaps been a denial or disregard of this as I saw it. For at one level you see—far too complex for words really—I believed that deep down you felt as I did. That one day you might come to accept fully your own feelings & so overcome the anxiety & resistance that society in a sense imposed on you in the way you thought about it all. That you wanted it (ie our relationship) & wanted my friendship.

I believed this in spite of the very clear messages you have given me over the years & the 'incidents' that have arisen between us as a result. Well if I chose to be so fatuous & misguided for 30 years that's my responsibility. Your ambivalence in no way warranted my wrongheadedness, which from your point of view probably appeared as dogged stupidity. No doubt the expectation/hope that I had, was in part a projection of the depth of my feeling for you & an inability & unwillingness to face reality—the reality that you wanted to move on & away long ago, did in fact, & which was your absolute right to do. My tenacity must have wearied you beyond words & been experienced by you simply as demanding.

This letter is not intended to be another demand, nor to discount in any way what we have had intermittently over the years. It is the subterranean currents, not the surface, that I refer to.

'Perhaps', the diary goes on, 'if I could write of anything I could write of this (I still fantasise about writing you see) of how *in part*, the social attitudes of patriarchy as represented by John so influenced, contaminated & undermined our love. For Lyndall, I believe, saw our relationship in his terms. Can I blame her? I do not. I wavered myself & felt guilty.'

Being heavily indocrinated in patriarchal ways of thinking myself I believe I have now reached Ericson's stage of acceptance (versus resignation/despair). No doubt Carol Gilligan will straighten me out—help me to chip away at the chains —& I may gain new insights.

I just do wish I understood it all, what happened to us & why. What in our respective lives led to 'the love that was conceived in the instant of our eyes first meeting'. Do you know Lyndall? You who are a grandmother & so full of wisdom?

Your house sounds full of colour & delight, as I think your life must be these days with your daughter so close and little Samuel flourishing under your very skilful, small brown & loving hands. I can think of nothing more fulfilling or wonderful. You have certainly earned every moment of that joy & privilege.

Love—always

Annie

PS I really do apologise for the messy appearance of this letter, but I couldn't bear to copy it out yet again. I keep altering it, looking for the right or a better emphasis—to remove any suggestion of blame or bitterness neither of which I feel nor wish to convey, nor would be justified. I am mindful however of the so wise comment, 'I do not know what I have said (written) until I hear the response'.

A.

Document 4.15 'Traditional Aboriginal women state very strongly that there is no room for alcohol in traditional Aboriginal culture'

The devastating effect of alcohol in Aboriginal communities became a rallying point for many Aboriginal women. These women from communities in Central Australia sought to have alcohol banned from the Aboriginal Club in Alice Springs and money redirected to resource centres for women who were best placed to service the needs of their communities.

30 May 1990
Liquor Commissioner

Dear Sir,

On behalf of the 380 Traditional Aboriginal Women from 16 remote communities and outstations in Central Australia who took part in the March against grog, and meetings with the Government on 5th May, 1990, we are sending this letter to tell you that we object to a Liquor Licence being granted for the Aboriginal Club in Alice Springs.

1 Aboriginal people in Alice Springs will not return to their communities.

2 Aboriginal people will leave their communities and families to come to Alice Springs to drink at the Club. This will cause even more family and cultural breakdown than we have now.

3 The money will keep being spent on grog in Alice Springs with little money left to buy food for the families, especially the children.

4 Traditional Aboriginal women state very strongly that there is no room for alcohol in Traditional culture. There are already many many liquor outlets in Alice Springs for Aboriginal people to use.

5 Alcohol is already causing destruction of our culture, and in fact, many cases of violence, serious assault and even death to Aboriginal people.

We believe that instead of the Government spending money on clubs for Aboriginal people in Alice Springs, this money could be spent building women's resource centres in communities where we can do the following:

- Provide meals for the very young and old;
- Create employment opportunity for school leavers and women, in their own communities;
- Keep our traditional ways of caring for the aged;
- Teach children about their culture;

- Arts and crafts will become a source of income for Aboriginal communities.

For all of these reasons, we ask you to take into consideration, and therefore ask that you do not grant a liquor licence to the Aboriginal Club in Alice Springs.

Signed on behalf of Traditional Aboriginal Women in Central Australia.

A. Anderson, Esther, Saleen, Sharon, Jeda, C. Raggett, E. Wari, Linda, Mavis, Elsie, Martha, Maudie, Margaret, Lilly, Ester, Molly, Eliza, Coral, Audrey Swift, Elizabeth Raggett, Katie Heffernan, Inky Nampitjinpa

Document 4.16 'The fundamental right of a person not to engage in sexual activity'

The Victorian Rape Act of 1991 represented the culmination of years of work by women's groups. The difficulty in obtaining convictions for rape charges highlighted the injustices of a system that tended to present the rape victim as the one on trial, and the meaning of consent proved very slippery in court. The law seemed designed to offer more protection to the perpetrators of rape than to their victims. This legislation set out to rectify these problems and to expand the understanding of what constituted rape.

Crimes (Rape) Act 1991
No. 81 of 1991
[Assented to 3 December 1991]

The Parliament of Victoria enacts as follows:

1 Purpose

The Purpose of this Act is to reform the law relating to rape and indecent assault in order to—

(a) clarify the concept of consent;

(b) reaffirm the fundamental right of a person not to engage in sexual activity;

(c) give greater protection to complainants in court proceedings.

2 Commencement

(1) This Act (except sections 7 and 8) comes into operation on a day or days to be proclaimed.

(2) Sections 7 and 8 must be taken to have come into operation on 16 April 1991.

3 New Subdivisions (8) and (8A) substituted

For Subdivisions (8) and (8A) of Division 1 of Part 1 of the *Crimes Act 1958* substitute—

(8) Sexual Offences (General Provisions)

35. Definitions

(1) In Subdivisions (8A) to (8G)—

'De facto spouse' means a person who is living with a person of the opposite sex as if they were married although they are not.

'Sexual penetration' means—

(a) the introduction (to any extent) by a person of his penis into the vagina, anus or mouth of another person whether or not there is emission of semen; or

(b) the introduction (to any extent) by a person of an object or a part of his or her body (other than the penis) into the vagina or anus of another person other than in the course of a procedure carried out in good faith for medical or hygienic purposes.

'Vagina' includes—

(a) the external genitalia; and

(b) a surgically constructed vagina.

(2) For the purposes of Subdivisions (8B) to (8E) both the person who sexually penetrates another person and the other person are taking part in an act of sexual penetration.

36. Meaning of consent

For the purposes of Subdivisions (8A) to (8D) 'consent' means free agreement. Circumstances in which a person does not freely agree to an act include the following:

(a) the person submits because of force or the fear of force to that person or someone else;

(b) the person submits because of the fear of harm of any type to that person or someone else;

(c) the person submits because she or he is unlawfully detained;

(d) the person is asleep, unconscious, or so affected by alcohol or another drug as to be incapable of freely agreeing;

(e) the person is incapable of understanding the sexual nature of the act;

(f) the person is mistaken about the sexual nature of the act or the identity of the person;

(g) the person mistakenly believes that the act is for medical or hygienic purposes.

37. Jury directions on consent

In a relevant case the judge must direct the jury that—

(a) the fact that a person did not say or do anything to indicate free agreement to a sexual act is normally enough to show that the act took place without that person's free agreement;

(b) a person is not to be regarded as having freely agreed to a sexual act just because—

(i) she or he did not protest or physically resist; or

(ii) she or he did not sustain physical injury; or

(iii) on that or earlier occasions he freely agreed to engage in another sexual act (whether or not of the same type) with that person, or a sexual act with another person;

(c) in considering the accused's alleged belief that the complainant was consenting to the sexual act, it must take into account whether that belief was reasonable in all the relevant circumstances.

38. Rape

(1) A person must not commit rape. Penalty: Imprisonment for 25 years.

(2) A person commits rape if—

(a) he or she intentionally sexually penetrates another person without that person's consent while being aware that the person is not consenting or might not be consenting; or

(b) after sexual penetration he or she does not withdraw from a person who is not consenting on becoming aware that the person is not consenting or might not be consenting.

39. Indecent assault

(1) A person must not commit indecent assault.
Penalty: Imprisonment for 10 years.

(2) A person commits indecent assault if he or she assaults another person in indecent circumstances while being aware that the person is not consenting or might not be consenting.

Alternative arrangements for giving evidence

In section 37C of the *Evidence Act 1958*, for sub-sections (1) and (2) *substitute*—

'(2) The Court may, of its own motion or on the application of a party to a legal proceeding, direct that alternative arrangements be made for the giving of evidence by a witness if—

(a) the proceeding relates (wholly or partly) to a charge for—

(i) a sexual offence; or

(ii) an indictable offence which involves an assault on, or injury
      or a threat of injury to, a person—
and the court is satisfied that the witness is a person with impaired
mental functioning or under the age of 18; or
(b) the proceeding relates (wholly or partly) to a charge for a sexual
     offence and the court is satisfied that, without alternative arrange-
     ments being made, the witness is likely in giving evidence—
     (i) to suffer severe emotional trauma; or
     (ii) to be so intimidated or stressed as to be severely disadvan-
          taged as a witness.'.

Document 4.17 'Sexual harassment had reduced her life to a "zombie-like existence" '

The Sex Discrimination Act of 1984 provided women and men with legal recourse when they encountered discrimination in employment practices but also, as in the case of this document, for sexual harassment. Women who had suffered sexual harassment in the workplace could now take action against their employer and be assured that their complaints would be taken seriously. For women such as Tina, working in a cheesecake factory, such action could bring some sense of justice after months of humiliating abuse, but the difficulty of obtaining the damages she was entitled to presented other problems.

TROUBLE AT THE CHEESECAKE FACTORY

Three years ago, Tina, a shop assistant at the Charada cheesecake factory in Brunswick, decided to fight back against fellow workers whose sexual harassment had reduced her life to a 'zombie-like existence'. After being forced to represent herself at the hearing, the 26-year-old is now facing another legal battle to receive the $7000 payment the court awarded her.

Last year, light-hearted newspaper stories celebrated the company's all-Australian cheesecake when Charada won a $10,000 award as the country's best new exporter. But today, the manufacturer claims it cannot afford to pay Tina's damages costs until Christmas. Tina's battle with the cheesecake manufacturer raises questions about whether the amounts awarded through the hearing process are adequate and whether claimants receive sufficient support.

Tina started her action against Charada in 1990. As the shop assistant selling cakes to the public, she was one of two full-time women on the 18-member staff. She says the verbal harassment started with a comment about her looks and escalated to a 'sickening, frightening' note pinned to her bike. Written in red ink, it said: 'Tina sux dog's balls all day long.'

Tina says during the harassment, from July to September 1990, she put on 12 kilograms, had severe headaches and eczema, would cry after work, and feared an emotional breakdown. She also changed her name—the note 'really sullied my name for me'—and left Brunswick so she would not have to see anyone she had worked with at the factory. The area 'had so many bad memories that I just had to push it away'.

Tina represented herself at the Human Rights and Equal Opportunity Commission hearing on 17 March. She had been granted legal aid for the case in 1990 but by the time it was heard, funding had run out.

'When I found out I wasn't going to have a lawyer and I would have to be in court with these people, I had no idea what would happen. I was just horrified, I wanted to give in,' Tina says.

Tina, now a full-time student, says she made a pact with herself before the hearing—that 'it didn't matter whether I won or lost, just that I finished it'. She says the media coverage of the factory after the export award made it harder to go on. She says she felt 'what I was doing was just nothing compared to these people who are bringing in millions of dollars to Australia.'

The hearing lasted 11 hours. Tina gave evidence from a diary she had of the harassment and cross-examined witnesses. 'It was a wonderful feeling at the end of the day. I felt so vindicated . . . I felt so happy that day.'

On 7 June, Commissioner Robert Nettlefold said in his judgment that Tina had been subjected to 'serious sexual harassment'. He ordered the factory, as the first respondent, to pay damages of $5000, and a former employee, pastry chef Phillip Quirk, as a second respondent, to pay $2000. Four months after the order, Tina has received no payments. Tina's lawyer, Ms Elizabeth Lee, says letters to the factory have been unanswered and a cheque from Phillip Quirk bounced. And if the damages are paid, at least $1000 may have to go to legal aid.

The managing director of Charada, Mr Diarmuid Hannigan, said the company had been notified by the commission of the finding and was willing to pay. But he said he had not received any letters or phone calls from Tina or her lawyer. 'I don't know where to send the money to and we haven't got it (the money),' he said. The family-run business, which now employs 26 staff, was using all its cash for a Japanese export order.

The decision 'has come as a real shock', he says. Mr Hannigan said although his company did not condone sexual harassment in the workplace, he did not believe companies should be held responsible for the actions of individual workers. (The Sexual Discrimination Act does hold employers responsible under its vicarious liability provision.)

He said staff were told to stop making comments to Tina but it was difficult to 'muzzle' them. Mr Hannigan said the way Australians communicated with each other in a factory was appalling but to re-educate people was 'one hell of an onus' on an employer.

The harassment included:

- A steady diet of comments and insults such as remarks about Tina's 'big tits', obscene gestures with kitchen utensils and an attempt to grab Tina as she walked by.
- Female customers were also unknowing targets of abuse. Tina says all women were marked from one to 10 on their appearance with or without clothes.

Tina says she became frightened of going to work and had her lunch on the pavement outside the shop. She dressed in loose clothes and wore a hat. 'The only part of my body that was uncovered was my face and hands . . . I thought if I was just a big kaftan-looking thing they might leave me alone.'

Although Tina is 'really satisfied with what I have done: it is the thing I am most proud of in my life', she can understand why women would not want to go through the legal system in cases such as hers. She is also angry that the company has ignored requests for payment and seems to 'think it's above the law'. She says the principle of the case extends to the damages payment. 'If they don't have to pay, what have they learnt from it?' Tina says $7000 was more than she expected to be awarded but it could never make up for the stress she suffered. 'You can't take three years out of my life and tell me $7000 is going to make up for it.'

Ms Lee says difficulties in getting legal aid deterred many women from taking action over harassment. Costs of legal action should be included in damages payments, she says. Recent changes to the Sexual Discrimination Act mean the commission's findings are now registered with the Federal Court. In what is believed to be one of the first actions of its kind, Ms Lee will use this registration, which gives the findings the same standing as a court order, to enforce damages payments.

In July, the Tasmanian Supreme Court awarded $120,000 damages to a female council worker for sexual harassment that culminated in forced sexual intercourse. Feminist lawyer, Ms Jocelynne Scutt, questions the small payouts given by the commission compared with payments received for work injuries.

'There is something wrong when a body, whose particular brief is to look at these issues with experience and understanding, is awarding less than a Supreme Court where judges are not appointed with a particular recognition of their expertise in this area.'

On 18 August, a Victorian woman was awarded $50,000 damages by the Equal Opportunity Board for sexual harassment while working at a Melbourne consulting company in 1991 and 1992. It is believed to be the highest award ever made by the board.

The Age, 'Accent', 6 October 1993

Document 4.18 The disorienting mix of femininity and politics

The election of two 'Green' senators from Western Australia in the 1993 Federal Election and the selection of Cheryl Kernot as leader of the Democrats gave three women unprecedented powers in the Senate. The passing of the 1993 Federal Budget gave these women their first chance to exercise their power, much to the chagrin of the two major parties, and the passing of the Mabo legislation gave them another opportunity. As this document suggests, the Green senators were perceived as anarchic and uncontrollable, and were accused of being irrational and of threatening the stability of the elected Government. The language describing them suggests the fear of excessive femininity: slippery, impossible to deal with, liable to throw 'hand-grenades' at any unexpected moment, indecisive. The senators represent the worst fears of the combination of femininity and politics, and their style posed the greatest threat that has ever been made to the two-party system.

ARE THESE TWO WOMEN RUNNING THE COUNTRY?

Round the corridors of Parliament House the two Green senators were beginning to be regarded almost with affection. It's true that their nicknames ranged from the patronising to the sexist, from 'Wendy and Tinkerbell' to 'the Bobbsey twins', or 'just two girls who can't say no'. But their eventual support for the Budget, after having forced through several small changes in last-minute talks with the Prime Minister, prompted a collective sigh of relief in Government ranks. All talk of early elections and changing the Senate voting methods died away.

That was until Christabel Chamarette and Dee Margetts threw a hand-grenade into the works last week by rejecting the compromise Mabo deal and demanding more time for consultation, even threatening to introduce a Mabo bill of their own. The Mabo deal was the lovingly-crafted work of the Prime Minister himself. The compromise was the result of months of wrangling with elected Aboriginal leaders, the most influential body representing farmers, state premiers, bureaucrats from every state, and the Australian Democrats.

Now that fragile consensus on Mabo is perilously close to collapse. The National Farmers' Federation executive director, Mr Rick Farley, is worried that he will not be able to sustain his constituent organisations' support for the deal if the process drags on.

The Aboriginal leaders, who for once appeared to be united, are now splintering into rival groups again. Some, including Tasmanian activist Michael Mansell and Western Australian leader Rob Riley, urged the Greens to seek more concessions. Others, such as Aboriginal and Torres Strait Islander matriarch Ms Lois O'Donoghue and Cape York Land Council official Ms Marcia Langton, are in despair.

They know only too well how so many Aboriginal projects have bitten the dust over recent decades because of splits between the black organisations in different states. In an ideal world, which the Greens seem to believe exists, there would be time for the exhaustive consultation with black elders around the nation on what they want from Mabo.

The political reality, though, is that, if the Government does not act quickly to get this legislation through, a Mabo settlement will be lost altogether. One man still smiling through all this turmoil, albeit through *schadenfreude* rather than pure joy, is Mr Alan Evans, the senior political adviser to the Treasurer. Mr Evans was one of the pioneers in dealing with the Greens after they won the balance of power in the Senate in the middle of this year. A former adviser to the Tasmanian Labor Leader, Mr Michael Field, he is used to dealing with Greens. He says of the WA women: 'I like them, they are delightful people.'

But he says dealing with them is almost impossible. When his boss, Mr John Dawkins, got himself into the headlines recently with his remark that he sometimes wondered whether it was worth the effort getting on the plane each week to come to Canberra, Mr Evans knew that the frustration over the Greens was the main factor.

Government officials were privately scathing about Mr Dawkins' words. Surely, it could not be so difficult dealing with two political newcomers. Now other members of the Government are finding out the truth, and Mr Evans is amused that the grey hairs, the ulcers, the tantrums have moved along the corridor to other ministers' offices.

The Prime Minister was quick to realise the slipperiness of the Green senators. He told his senior officials recently that his talks with the two Greens in trying to persuade them to pass the Budget were among the most 'disorienting' in his parliamentary experience of more than 20 years. This was because there was almost no common ground on which they could negotiate. (For example, they believe all the most commonly accepted Canberra economic theory is bunkum.) Therefore they could not see the point of working towards a lower government deficit.

On Mabo, it matters little to senators Chamarette and Margetts, and their chief adviser, Cathcart Weatherly, that the consensus could come unstitched given further delays. 'We need to know our principles and views are upheld, and we know the public is bewildered and confused,' Senator Chamarette said yesterday. Infuriatingly for the Government, the pair will not make a decision about a Mabo timetable until 9 December. They are threatening to demand a further Senate inquiry to report back as late as 21 February.

While Government officials are gnashing their teeth, there are some faint hopes that the same formula of last-minute talks with the Prime Minister and minor concessions may persuade the Greens to pass the Mabo legislation along with the Democrats, and possibly independent senator Brian Harradine, before then. But this latest panic over the Greens' position is concentrating the Government's mind on a long-term solution to the balance-of-power problem in the Senate. Early next year there will be serious discussions about election dates and tactics in a bid to get rid of the maverick Western Australians' grip on power.

Amanda Buckley
Sunday Age, 28 November 1993

Document 4.19 Racism, women and the law

Racism remains a daily experience in the lives of many people from non-English-speaking backgrounds, especially for those who have cause to use Australia's legal system. The following incidents reveal the extent of the racist stereotypes that migrant women encountered when they sought protection from violent men.

A Greek woman returning to court for a full intervention order was denied a request for an interpreter on the basis that the magistrate believed her sixteen-year-old daughter could interpret for her. He was not prepared to adjourn the matter to another date. The woman spoke of her feelings of humiliation in having to interpret through her daughter, and as a consequence withdrew her application. Undoubtedly, such a situation would have seriously compromised the position of her daughter also.

This situation clearly reveals a perception of the availability of interpreters as a privilege rather than a right. Furthermore, that woman was implicitly being punished for the sheer fact that her accessibility to the English language was limited. The request that her daughter interpret is not one that would need to be made in the case of her Australian counterpart.

A Turkish woman was denied her application for an intervention order on the basis that she should be familiar with the 'extreme patriarchal nature of her culture', and violence was held to be a natural and 'expected' outcome of such cultural values. The magistrate, in expressing paternalistic concern, suggested the woman seek out assistance from within her own community. In this way, she would be ensured of a culturally appropriate remedy.

This case highlights a response that is being increasingly relied upon by some magistrates. It suggests that [certain] cultures [are] causative of violence, and as such, victims of violence need to be addressing their culture and not the economic and political conditions that give rise to male violence. Although couched in terms that suggest acknowledgement of cultural difference, it merely acts as a powerful reinforcement of racist stereotyping.

A magistrate tried to coerce a Muslim woman into swearing on the Bible, insisting that it was the same as the Koran. The woman, through her interpreter, tried to explain the importance of giving a Koranic testimony, as anything else could be suggestive of an untrue testimony. Finally, in exasperation, the magistrate told the woman that unless she was prepared to swear on the Bible, he would throw the case out of court.

A Vietnamese woman had not requested an interpreter as she felt this would be asking for too much. During her testimony, the magistrate made his frustrations known by exclaiming he could not understand her English. Rather than adjourning the case to another date, he proceeded to request that the woman 'act' out the nature of the violent behaviour. Whilst attempting to respond to this totally unreasonable and humiliating request, there was an outburst of laughter in the courtroom. Although the woman was granted the order, she spoke of her feelings of being treated like an 'animal', rather than a human being.

Another Asian woman found herself being lectured by the magistrate about the position of women within Asian cultures, as if they constituted some homogeneous whole. The magistrate made reference to the 'passivity of her type', suggesting that now she was residing in Australia she should learn from the progress made by her Australian counterparts.

man sought an intervention order. The perpetrator was in hearing. His legal representative argued that the perpe-...aware that his actions were of a criminal nature and could ...ue subject of a legal order. He proceeded to indicate that [equivalent] laws were not present in Fiji. After hearing the evidence and testimony of both parties, the magistrate prefaced his determination with a comment about the multicultural nature of Australian society and the corresponding requirement of cultural tolerance. Conveniently pushing aside the longstanding legal principle 'ignorance of the law is no excuse', the magistrate informed the woman that he would not grant the order in this instance due to the perpetrator's lack of awareness of the implications of his violence in an Australian context. However, he warned, should the behaviour continue, then the perpetrator would have no defence. The woman's need for protection from the violence became a secondary, in fact a non-existent issue.

Hana Assafiri and Maria Damopolous, 'NESB women as "deviant": the legal system's "treatment" of NESB women victims of male violence', Paper presented at The Criminal Justice System in a Multicultural Society Conference, May 1993

Index